A Christian Apologetic

A Christian Apologetic

Dr. Lance Waldie

NEWBURGH THEOLOGICAL SEMINARY

A CHRISTIAN APOLOGETIC FOR CHRISTIANS WHO DESIRE

TO CONTEND FOR THE FAITH WHICH WAS

ONCE FOR ALL HANDED DOWN TO THE SAINTS

A DISSERTATION SUBMITTED TO

THE FACULTY OF THE DIVISION OF APOLOGETICS

IN CANDIDACY FOR THE DEGREE OF

DOCTOR OF PHILOSOPHY

DEPARTMENT OF APOLOGETICS

BY

DAVID LANCE WALDIE

CYPRESS, TEXAS

SEPTEMBER 2012

TABLE OF CONTENTS

PREFACE

Having grown up in a Bible-believing Southern Baptist Church in the south, I heard the Gospel of Jesus Christ every single Sunday. I came to know Christ at a very early age, and I gave my life to Him and to His service around the age of 17. As I grew in my faith, however, I longed to know more about *the* faith. I especially wanted to know why atheists existed and whether they had some inside information that Christians were not privy to. All I got when I asked, however, was, "Just believe by faith." So I did. Then in college I would hear things like, "Christians are those who leave their brains in the church parking lot on Sundays." My philosophy professor, though he professed to be a Lutheran, seemed less than impressed with Christianity, and he taught us all the arguments against God's existence from men like David Hume.

When I met the woman who would become my wife, I was introduced by her family to some of the greatest Bible teachers our generation has ever known. I previously knew about Charles Swindoll from a book that a family in our church gave me when I graduated high school, but my wife's family introduced me to men like John MacArthur, Josh McDowell, Charles Ryrie, and Henry Morris—men not well known in the Baptist circles where I had worshiped. Early in my marriage, my wife handed me a book by Josh McDowell titled *Evidence That Demands a Verdict*. I read it three times in one year! I found in that book all the questions I had as a young man growing up that my church had not answered for me. I found in McDowell's research the "scratch for my itch," as it were. After that, my passion for apologetics took off, and I was convinced that philosophical and biblical truths would change the world.

As a pastor and Bible teacher today, I still love apologetics, and I still see a tremendous need for Christians to know why they believe. But I do not think that learning apologetics will change the world. What I do think it will change for the better is the thinking of Christians. For when a Christian knows why he believes what he espouses to believe, he becomes a bold evangelist and teacher. I used to be a soft-spoken and shy person until I learned how powerful the gospel message is and why it should be believed by everyone. Now, I cannot keep my mouth shut about the truth that Jesus Christ of Nazareth is God in the flesh and that by believing in Him, a person is saved for eternity. People do not need to study apologetics to be Christians, but Christians need to study apologetics.

A contribution to the world of apologetic literature is needed in my own church, a basic resource to help equip young Christians who find themselves in a hostile environment away from the safe haven of their homes and church, and also for those who come from shallow churches. Although anyone can benefit from the information in this paper, I have college freshmen who profess to know Christ in mind as I write. I want them to be able to make an argument for their faith in Christ and to make that argument boldly when they are challenged. Ideally, in light of the aggressive nature of today's atheists, I want to see Christians be more aggressive in what they know and how they share their faith. This does not mean shouting at unbelievers that Jesus is the Messiah or that they need to "turn or burn." I am simply saying that because Christians tend to be seen as intellectually inferior to atheists, we need to turn the tables on them.

After all, *we know the God of the universe*, and we have a personal relationship with Him insofar as we are truly saved by the blood of Christ through faith. We have His Holy Spirit dwelling within us, and He fills us with His presence. With that in mind, why should we not have a valid argument for our faith? Why should we not be like Stephen, the first Christian martyr, whose defense of the faith was so overpowering to the authorities of his day that "they were unable to cope with the wisdom and the Spirit with which he was speaking" (Acts 6:10)?

Many excellent apologetic resources are available for Christians—in various forms such as DVDs, books, web pages, and MP3 files—which can equip them to make an argument for why they believe what they believe about Jesus and the existence of God. My work in this paper will by no means surpass the value of those resources. In fact, my goal is to say *less* than those resources say in that I want their esoteric arguments to be more readable in this resource. My goal is to introduce readers to some valid arguments for God's existence and why any Christian can confidently assert that he believes in God with all his heart, soul, *and* mind.

Whereas most apologetic resources will make the same arguments I give in this paper and attempt to conclude that God exists, this paper only introduces the arguments themselves. This is because no argument can actually *prove* God's existence. As McGrath said, "…there are good reasons for believing in God—or, to put it another way, that belief in God can be *justified*, even if it cannot be absolutely proven."[1] Many works that attempt to actually *prove* God's existence spur counter-arguments that are so boring and confusing to read that many people just give up and read the sports page or an internet article like *Iconic Brands That Fizzled*. This paper, therefore, is written to justify the *Christian's* belief not only in God, but in His Son, Jesus Christ, and to believe in the words He spoke.

This project will say nothing new about apologetics. I offer no new ideas, and in fact, I offer mostly old arguments for the existence of God and for Jesus being God. But whether the research is old or new, the more it is written about, the more widespread the research becomes, the more likely Christians will read it. My primary purpose in writing this, therefore, is that every graduating senior and their families in the church where I preach would read this material. The fact that I am their pastor means that at least *they* will read it (or so I hope!). I have quoted extensively from my apologetics heroes—William Lane Craig, R. C. Sproul, Josh McDowell, and my all-time favorite, Norman L. Geisler. I know that after writing this paper I am far more adept at sharing the arguments for God's existence, and I am so deeply grateful that men like them, and those who preceded them, were moved by God as I have been to study the truth and expose it for what it is: *that which sets us free!* (John 8:32).

---

[1] A. McGrath, *Mere Apologetics: How to Help Seekers & Skeptics Find Faith.* (Grand Rapids, MI: Baker Books, 2012), 132.

Unless noted otherwise, all quotations from the Bible are from the New American Standard Bible, 1995 Update (NASB95).

ACKNOWLEDGMENTS

I want to thank, first of all, the authors of the books and articles I have quoted throughout this paper. Aside from the atheists and naturalists I have quoted, these men and women are my heroes, and their intellect and research have motivated me to want to be just like them. Second, I want to thank Paula Perry who painstakingly went through this project page by page to edit, make suggestions for improvement, and let me know that in spite of what my professors might think about it, she was challenged by it. Third, I want to thank Randy and Sharon Walker who allowed me to utilize their vacation home where I could study and research without interruption. The time in that peaceful place was ever-so helpful. Fourth, I want to thank my fellow elders at Harvest Bible Church in Cypress, Texas—the greatest friends I have ever known. They encouraged me to tackle this degree and gave me plenty of time to complete it. There may be men who are equal to them in character, but there are none who surpass them. Fifth, I want to thank my wife who has always been the perfect helpmate to me, who encouraged me throughout this project. Her worth is far above jewels! Finally, I want to thank my Lord Jesus Christ for saving me, for loving me, for giving me one of the finest educations money can buy, and for assuring me of my salvation in spite of the fact that I continue to be a wretched sinner. I long for the day I can see Him face to face, and I pray that day comes very soon.

ABSTRACT

It is common for people to believe in Jesus Christ and call themselves Christians, but it is quite uncommon for those who profess faith in Jesus Christ to be able to defend why they believe what they believe. In this project, I've offered a handful of arguments for Christians to learn in order to argue for the existence of God. The paper progresses from the logical belief that there is a God to the logical conclusion that there can be only one God. From there, the research shows that among the many religions and faiths that exist, only Christianity can be true, and the Holy Bible is in fact accurate in its teachings about Jesus of Nazareth being God and being the only Creator, Lord, and Savior of mankind. There are many different versions of Christianity, but only biblical Christianity has stood the tests of logic and time. Therefore, a person must not only believe in God, they must believe that God is Jesus Christ of Nazareth and that His words are accurately written in the Scriptures—from Genesis 1:1 to Revelation 22:21.

Chapter 1

Introduction

Imagine the scene: *nothing*. That was what there was before there was anything. Yet just saying "before there was anything" implies time, for when there is truly nothing, there is no "before" because there is no time, and there is no space. Since time and space are both something, they could not have existed when there was nothing. By definition, nothing—no-thing—cannot allow for something. Yet before there was anything, nothing existed, nothing was happening, and no one was present to observe the nothing because when there is nothing, there is no one, no thing, no time, no space, no materials—there is simply *nothing*.

No human can fully understand nothing, but we might be able to imagine what rocks dream about, for nothing is what they are thinking about and doing because they have no mind to think and hence nothing is happening within them. Yet before the beginning, while there was nothing, according to the philosophy of naturalism,[2] all of a sudden, by chance nothing was ignited, it exploded into everything, and everything that it became came together naturally in its present form.

Later, as the tale goes, the "everything" that was caused by nothing spread out and became orderly after it cooled down from the powerful explosion. Complex life did not immediately occur, but all the elements for the abundance of life all over the planet were there. Deoxyribonucleic Acid (DNA), the information for life

---

[2] Naturalism is the belief that there is no supernatural and that nothing exists outside the material world. Hence, naturalists believe that life originated and evolved by random natural processes of time and chance independent of a supernatural creator.

2 A Christian Apologetic

itself, was somehow embedded either in the nothing that caused the great explosion or in the nothingness of matter that resulted from the explosion of nothing coming together with nothing. Then, over time (also created by the explosion, along with space and chance), out of all the chaos, the laws of physics came together. And once complex life evolved from the nothingness into the chaos and finally into orderliness, humans recognized moral laws and principles common to all of them.

Once humans evolved, they learned to fight for their existence, and because only the strong could survive, they had to allow for the murder and oppression of their own kind for thousands of years since it benefitted their own survival. But after all that settled, they all, inexplicably, evolved a moral will that was common to all of them. Amazingly, they were able to reason with a mind that transcended their physical brains! From all the chaos of the nothingness that became everything by chance, over the course of billions of years, the human mind evolved in all its brilliance and mystery. And it was able to use logic and reason, judge right from wrong, and observe uniformity from chaos.

Finally, in the modern day, man has evolved into such a fine-tuned specimen that he can now understand that he was formed out of nothing, by chance, as an accident, and has absolutely no purpose for his life. He can now understand that when he dies, there is nothing that is going to happen except that he will become food for worms and once again become just like the matter from which he was accidentally formed. After being turned back to dust, it is likely that his nothingness mind will wonder backward and try to figure out why he did anything. Why did he love, get rich, do good, or write scientific books about nothing becoming everything? It certainly did not benefit him given that he is nothing more than decayed matter inside the digestive tract of a worm. There was no point to his life, so why did he do anything or promote anything? In truth (and of course there is no real truth in naturalism), there was just no point to doing anything. After all, he was a chance life-form that came together by accident.

The Unscientific Nature of Naturalism

Now anyone with an inkling of common sense must wonder where the original "it" came from that ignited and became everything when there was nothing. They must also wonder where all the elements originated that are needed to cause such an explosion. Furthermore, since this event is truly unscientific, it is odd that a naturalist would hold so firmly to their faith in light of the supernatural miracle of nothing becoming everything. Why would this be? Note the words of Harvard paleontologist Richard Lewontin, an academic who holds strongly to the belief that the material world (i.e., materialism, naturalism, atheism) is all there is:

> We take the side of science in spite of the patent absurdity of some of its constructs… in spite of the tolerance of the scientific community for unsubstantiated just-so stories, because we have a prior commitment to materialism. It is not that the methods and institutions of science somehow compel us to accept a material explanation of the phenomenal world, but, on the contrary, that we are forced by our a priori adherence to the material causes to create an apparatus of investigation and a set of concepts that produce material explanations, no matter how counterintuitive, no matter how mystifying to be uninitiated. Moreover, that materialism is absolute, for we cannot allow a Divine Foot in the door.[3]

What can be clearly seen from Lewontin's statement is that naturalists do not possess information Christians do not have; rather, they have simply decided beforehand to favor the nonsupernatural in favor of the natural—no matter how preposterous their conclusions are, even to themselves. Therefore, by faith, naturalists believe that before nothing exploded into everything, there was nothing. And it does not matter that science

---

[3] Richard Lewontin, "Billions and Billions of Demons," *The New York Review of Books*, January 9, 1997, 28-32. Quoted in, J. Budziszewski, *How to Stay Christian in College* (Colorado Springs, CO: NavPress, 2004), 53.

has never observed nothing becoming anything. Their conclusions are based upon their worldview which does not allow them to believe anything supernatural. Per his own admission, it is the naturalist's *a priori* conclusion that God does not exist, and all evidence to the contrary is thrown out based simply on his *a priori* ideas.

After all, before nothing exploded into everything, there was nothing, and science has never observed nothing becoming anything, although if a scientist wanted to engage in observing nothing in order to form a theory, he would do well to begin by staring at rocks and waiting for the content of their minds to explode into other universes just like the one we live in today.

Obviously, nothing has never been observed to become anything, and this is why naturalistic philosophers have redefined "nothing" and called it "something." For instance, if a friend asks you what you did last night and you say "nothing," that would not be entirely accurate. You could at the very least say you were sitting, staring, sleeping, or just existing, because those things are something! Naturalists have foisted this scenario on the moment before the beginning of the universe and posited that although we say there was nothing, there was indeed something. Yet no matter how hard they try to defer their argument, they cannot account for why there is something and not nothing or how something appeared when there was once nothing.

The irony of naturalism is that because it cannot account for its supernatural origins through scientific study, it is a *faith* that, while denying supernaturalism, stands on supernaturalism in order to explain the origins of the universe! How else can it explain how nothing became everything? Indeed naturalism is a faith, and this naturalistic faith stands diametrically opposed to the faith of the Christian theist—one who professes faith in the eternal, supernatural God, Jesus Christ, who has always existed and who brought forth all things that do exist.

Like Christianity, naturalism is a worldview, a lens through which everything is interpreted. Ronald H. Nash said that a worldview is "the total of answers people give to the most important questions in life." [4] Our worldview is the basis for how we answer life's most important questions—questions about God, reality, morality, knowledge, and the essential nature of man. Whereas the worldview of Bible-believing Christians is that God exists, the virgin birth and resurrection of Jesus Christ are true, and the second coming of Jesus Christ will occur, the worldview of a naturalist prevents him from accepting the validity of God's existence and miracles. Nash said, "When faced with a choice among competing worldviews, we should choose the one that, when applied to the whole of reality, gives us the most coherent picture of the world. And that most coherent worldview is the Christian worldview." [5]

Naturalism is the worldview of those who reject the existence of God. They are not bad people in the sense that they murder, rape, and pillage (although some might); rather, they are just helpless people who cannot account for why they believe anything. Many of them strive to be good, but they cannot account for why they do good. Many strive to get rich, believing it is a "better" life, but why? In the world of naturalism, there is no "better"; there is just natural. Many contend for their favorite politician, but why? Some even contend all over the world to convince people that there is no hope, but why? Why would anyone with the naturalistic worldview purposely care about anything or anybody? After all, their worldview has no purpose, no hope, and it cannot account for the fact that most of its adherents strive for purpose, love, and contentment. It is certainly okay to do all these things, but the naturalistic worldview has no foundation for *why* they do any of these things.

Christian theists, those who believe in the divinity of Jesus Christ and who bow to Him as their Lord, also strive for purpose. They too have favorite political candidates, they love, they strive to be successful, and they train their children to be good citizens. But the difference between them and those who reject God's existence

---

[4] Ronald H. Nash, "What Is a Worldview?" *The Apologetics Study Bible: Real Questions, Straight Answers, Stronger Faith*, ed. Ted Cabal, Chad Owen Brand, E. Ray Clendenen, et al. (Nashville, TN: Holman Bible Publishers, 2007), 923.

[5] Nash, 923.

is that the Christian worldview *can* account for why it strives for the things it strives for. Christians want to do the right thing in order to please and worship God. They believe that the world was created by God for a purpose, so they strive to be a part of what God is doing in the world in which they live. They can at least account for why they do what they do.

The naturalist (i.e., the atheist) cannot. He strives for purpose, but in his worldview there is no purpose. Therefore, he has to borrow from the Christian worldview to have a purpose and to justify why he wants the things he believes will make his life better. This is the absurdity of naturalism. Oddly enough, some of the most educated people in the world are naturalists. Worse, Christians are often led to believe that these people know something they do not, as if these naturalists and atheists actually have knowledge beyond that of the Christians and hence know for certain that there is no God. The truth is, Christians have God's Holy Spirit, they have a reason to believe in the resurrected Jesus Christ from the grave, and they have a reason to live for their Lord and Savior. It is the Christian theist, therefore, who knows something the atheists do not. In short, they know God.

The Modern Day Conundrum

In the modern day, the Church seems to be devolving into an anti-intellectual and biblically illiterate culture—a society whose tradition is to take the easy road, play games on a smart phone, download movies incessantly, and drink coffee at Starbucks while conversing about the latest updates on Facebook. What tends to qualify as "Christian" today is how something dubbed "Christianity" makes us *feel*. In other words, if we attend a church that is modern in its architecture, where the music is upbeat and to our liking, where the preaching is not too long-winded or boring, where a Bible is not required, and where coffee and doughnuts are plentiful (to occupy our Bible-less hands!), it is probably a church worth attending. Plus, if it is a mega-church with amenities like video games for the youth, a hipster youth minister, and a preacher who wears jeans and a casual shirt not tucked into his pants, it is probably a church that people will affirm God is blessing.

Church historian David Wells called the present generation of pastors the "new disablers" because:

> They have abandoned the traditional role of the pastor as a broker of truth to his congregation and replaced it with a new managerial model drawn from the professional world which emphasizes leadership abilities, marketing, and administration. As a result, the church has produced a generation of Christians for whom theology is irrelevant and whose lives outside the church do not differ practically from those of atheists.[6]

Yet inherent within churches like these, within this culture of music and biblical illiteracy, a malignant tumor is metastasizing at a rapid pace. The consequences are numerous and can be seen throughout the culture, right up to the people who are voted into public office. Of great concern to me are today's high school graduates who go into the secular colleges and even the so-called Christian colleges to be trained by atheists and even professed Christians. Far too often, these young people, having attended the kinds of churches previously described up to the age of 18, have little to no defense for their professed Christian faith against the professors who await them in the universities—including the Christian universities that deny the authority and inerrancy of the Bible itself.

The belief these young people tend to espouse after growing up in church, namely faith in Jesus Christ, is too often easily shattered by the academics in the universities who challenge the shallow way of thinking these "Christians" are taught in their churches before they go to college. The shallow ways modeled to them through shallow music and entertainment-driven philosophies of ministry are often the root cause of the problem for these college students who represent the next generation of teachers, politicians, doctors, lawyers, and even preachers.

---

[6] David F. Wells, *No Place for Truth* (Grand Rapids, MI: Eerdmans, 1993), 253. Quoted in William Lane Craig, "In Intellectual Neutral," *Passionate Conviction: Contemporary Discourses on Christian Apologetics,* ed. Paul Copan and William Lane Craig (Nashville, TN: B&H Publishers, 2007), 12-13.

All Christians should be prepared to defend their faith when confronted as to why they believe, yet so few are prepared for the lion's den of the universities where trained and experienced atheistic academics prey on them. Since these atheists are not nearly as bold when debating one of their peers who holds to Christian theism, cogent arguments about God's existence must be taught to all those who will encounter atheists and naturalists. As William Lane Craig said:

> Apologetics training is a tremendous boost to evangelism, for nothing inspires confidence and boldness more than knowing that one has good reasons for what one believes and good answers to the typical questions and objections that the unbeliever may raise. Sound training in apologetics is one of the keys to fearless evangelism.[7]

God does not *need* us to argue on His behalf, for God, being all-knowing and absolutely perfect, has no needs. But since God has ordained the preaching of Christ and teaching all that He has commanded (Matt. 28:19–20) as the medium through which He will save those He has chosen for salvation (Rom. 10:13-15; cf. John 6:44), it follows that *we* need to engage in arguing for the truth for our own benefit and the benefit of others. May our arguments not be red-faced screaming matches, but cogent presentations of the truth. As the Apostle Paul wrote, "The goal of our instruction is love from a pure heart and a good conscience and a sincere faith" (1 Tim. 1:5). May that be our goal as well.

A Postmodern Culture?

Contrary to what the so-called church growth experts espouse, the Church of Jesus Christ certainly does not need to reinvent itself. They claim that since we live in a postmodern culture, the Church must adapt to it in order to share Christ effectively. Yet postmodernism, the belief that all things are relative, is not only self-defeating, it is impossible to live by it. For even the staunchest

---

[7] William Lane Craig, *Reasonable Faith* (Wheaton, IL: Crossway, 2008), 21.

relativist will read a label on a medicine bottle to avoid the danger of taking the medicine improperly. Likewise, no relativist will step in front of a bus believing that pain is relative or that the bus will not necessarily run them over. Yes, these people are relativistic in matters of religion and ethics, but that is the textbook definition of *modernism*, not postmodernism.[8] If we did truly live in a postmodern world, and if the Christian Church had to adapt to it in order to reach it, no Gospel of Jesus Christ could be shared with the world. Why? Because in a world where truth is relative, how could the truth of Jesus Christ be preached?

Postmodern, or modern, thinking must be countered with the truth of Jesus Christ. And the truth is that Jesus is the divine Son of God, sent by God the Father, so that believers might be saved from their sins and have eternal life with Him. The bad news is that all are sinners who have fallen short of God's glory (Rom. 3:23), and the wage that we owe for our sin is death (Rom. 6:23). But the good news is that Christ died for our sins while we were yet sinners (Rom. 5:8), and if we will trust in Him, we will have eternal life with Him (Rom. 10:9–10). Jesus is the way, the truth, and the life, and no one comes to God the Father except through Christ the Son (John 14:6). In fact, there is no other name under heaven that has been given among men by which a man can be saved except Jesus Christ (Acts 4:12).

Those who believe in Jesus Christ as Lord and Savior have had their spiritual blinders removed (2 Cor. 4:4), and they are new creations in Christ (2 Cor. 5:17). They have been made spiritually alive by Christ through God's grace (Eph. 2:1–10), and they will never be condemned by Christ, for there is no condemnation for those who are in Christ (Rom. 8:1). Because believers trust in Christ, they possess God's Holy Spirit. As a result, they are able to understand who God is, what He has done, what He is doing, and what He will do. Furthermore, per Christ's commission to believers to make Him known to the whole world (Matt. 28:19–20), they have the responsibility and task of preaching Christ and making a defense for the hope that is in them (1 Peter 3:15). It is this final point that this paper addresses primarily.

---

[8] Craig, 18.

Biblical Examples of Apologetics

Scripture contains a plethora of examples of various people making arguments for the truth of Jesus Christ. Notice in Acts 9:22 that the recently converted Saul, at one time an opponent of Christianity and later known as the Apostle Paul, was "increasing in strength and confounding the Jews who lived at Damascus by *proving* that this Jesus is the Christ" (emphasis mine). Everywhere Paul went, he reasoned with his audiences about Jesus being the Christ (cf. Acts 17:2; 18:4, 19; 19:8–9). Paul made it clear that the elders of the churches of Christ must be able to teach Christian doctrine and refute those who contradict it (1 Tim. 3:2; Titus 1:9). Likewise, Jude exhorts Christians to "contend earnestly for the faith which was once for all handed down to the saints" (v. 3).

Of the numerous examples in Scripture, time and space allow for two pertinent examples. First, let us observe the Apostle Paul on his second missionary journey in Thessalonica (ca. AD 50): "Now when they had passed through Amphipolis and Apollonia, they came to Thessalonica, where there was a synagogue of the Jews. And Paul went in, as was his custom, and on three Sabbath days he reasoned with them from the Scriptures, explaining and proving that it was necessary for the Christ to suffer and to rise from the dead, and saying, "This Jesus, whom I proclaim to you, is the Christ." And some of them were persuaded and joined Paul and Silas, as did a great many of the worshipping Greeks and not a few of the leading women" (Acts 17:1–4, ESV).

Paul's routine was the same in every town. He went first to the local synagogue and reasoned with the Jews, for "the gospel…is the power of God for salvation to everyone who believes, to the Jew first and also to the Greek" (Rom. 1:16). The Jews possessed the Old Testament, so it was an easy thing for Paul to meet first with them. This is what he did when he came to Thessalonica.

For three Sabbaths, Paul "reasoned" in the synagogue from the Scriptures. This word means to "dialogue," which would entail talking about Scripture and answering questions. Paul wrote in Romans 15:4 that Old Testament Scripture was given for instruction and hope. This was what he reasoned about with the

Jews that day. The way he did it was through "explaining and proving" that the Messiah had to suffer and rise from the dead. Jews did not accept that their Christ would suffer and die, but that is exactly what Paul set out to prove from the Old Testament. Many passages prophesied this. The sacrificial system in Israel, as recorded in Leviticus, required that a lamb be offered for sins, and Christ is the Lamb of God. Isaac's near death on Mt. Moriah and the ram that was offered in his place (Gen. 22) is a clear illustration that Paul likely used in proving his case (cf. Psalm 16; 22; 110:1; 118). Isaiah 53 clearly speaks of the Lamb as a man going to the slaughter and being sacrificed for the sins of mankind. These references were supposed to be obvious to the Jews, and Jesus Himself berated the two Jews in Luke 24:25 for not knowing that the Old Testament prophets had predicted His death and resurrection.

As Paul "explained" the Scriptures, he literally "opened" them in the sense of bringing out their meaning. In the New Testament, "opening" usually has God as the active agent. Jesus opened the eyes of a blind man (Mark 7:34); God opened the heavens to reveal the living Christ (Acts 7:56); Jesus opened the meaning of the Scriptures to the men on the road to Emmaus (Luke 24:31ff.). The same word is used in Acts 16:14 when God opened Lydia's heart for salvation.

Paul's explanation of the birth, life, death, and resurrection of Jesus was accompanied by the fact that he "proved" these things. The word for "prove" means "to set before; to entrust." Paul argued like a lawyer before a jury presenting his case that demanded a verdict. Some were not persuaded by Paul's argument. But some Jews, Greeks, and prominent women believed that day, for the message of Christ is for all—regardless of race or class. The noteworthy thing here is how the prominent women are said to have believed. Modern feminist theology rejects Paul as a sexist, yet in his own day, high-standing women not only listened to Paul's message but also believed (cf. Acts 16:14; 17:12; Rom. 16).

The second example comes from an exhortation of the Apostle Peter. In his first epistle, Peter wrote, "But sanctify Christ as Lord as in your hearts, always being ready to make a defense to everyone who asks you to give an account for the hope that is in you; yet with gentleness and reverence; and keep a good conscience so that in the thing in which you are slandered, those who revile your good behavior in Christ will be put to shame" (1 Peter 3:15–16).

Since the Greek word for "defense" is *apologia*—"a reasoned statement; a verbal defense"—*Christian* apologetics involves providing a rational defense for the truth claims of biblical Christianity. The idea of apologetics is not simply about being *defensive* but *offensive* as well. This can and should be accomplished by showing the truths of the Christian faith and the logic of why they are believed. Apologetics must espouse the biblical worldview while deposing all contrary ideas. Faith and reason go hand in hand, so defending the truths of Christianity can and must be done in a convincing and intellectual way. After all, God does not expect anyone to believe that which cannot be believed or that which is absurd. The great reformer John Calvin engaged in apologetics against the enemies of Christ "to stop their obstreperous mouths."[9]

R. C. Sproul noted three various levels of faith within the Christian faith. Quoting the thinkers of the sixteenth century, he calls the first *notitia*—a faith acted upon by the believer through specific content preached to them. This initial faith was the result of the sinner realizing that he is a sinner in need of salvation in Christ alone. The second level of salvation, called *assensus*, concerns a greater understanding of what Christ did on the cross for the sinner. And the third level, called *fiducia*, entails personal trust and reliance with genuine affection for Christ that flows out of a heart of complete understanding and love for Christ.[10] Apologetics addresses all three levels, but the audience sought in this paper specifically is the *fiducia* audience—those who have embraced the faith of Jesus Christ and who desire a deeper knowledge of Him in order to feel more secure in their faith and be more effective in evangelism and teaching.

Since salvation belongs to the Lord who grants it to those He has chosen to draw to Christ, our arguments about God's existence

---

[9] John Calvin, *Institutes of the Christian Religion,* Volume 7 (Bellingham, WA: Logos Research Systems, Inc., 1997), 4.

[10] R. C. Sproul, *Defending Your Faith: An Introduction to Apologetics* (Wheaton, IL: Crossway, 2003), 22.

should only be a medium through which God works. Our job is like that of a car salesman. We are to show the beauty of the product (i.e., our God and His Christ), and then let the product (i.e., the Holy Spirit) do what He does—save souls from God's wrath and equip them for effective ministry.

The Apostle Paul's reasoning with unbelievers serves as an example for all Christians. First and foremost, he believed in Christ, so he set out to preach Christ. On many occasions, he met hostile audiences and had to argue his case repeatedly. Paul was "always ready to make a defense to everyone" who asked him to "give an account for the hope" that was in him (1 Peter 3:15). Second, Paul had no fear of the enemies of Christ, for he held Christ to be holy and working through him. This is how exhorted Christians to be, namely, to "sanctify Christ" in their hearts, to affirm their submission to Christ's lordship, His teachings, and His leadership in their lives. This means that slaves of Christ are those who willfully place Christ first in all things—in their worship, love, devotion, and obedience—as evidence that Christ is foremost in their lives.

There is no day off in the life of a Christian, and Peter wants them to be "always ready." Paul said as much when he commanded Timothy to be prepared "in season and out of season" (2 Tim. 4:2). The term "always" obviously means that believers are to be continually prepared at a moment's notice to respond to scoffers and persecutors if they should slander Jesus or His followers, those who sanctify Him as Lord in their hearts. And what are they to be always ready to do? *Share and defend their faith.*

All Christians, as part of being involved in the Great Commission (Matt. 28:19–20), have the task of both knowing and showing the Gospel of Jesus Christ. In 1 Peter 3:15, Peter exhorts his audience to be able to make a "defense" of the Gospel when asked. This is simply the ability to answer anyone who might question the teachings of the Bible (cf. Phil. 1:16). The Greek term for "defense" is *apologia* (Eng. apology; apologetics). Apologetics is the science of giving a rational defense of the Gospel and the truth claims of the Christian faith. Peter wanted all Christians to be ready and prepared to do this in the face of those who would slander them.

Sadly, many Christians have been taught they need no *reason* to believe in Christ other than that they believe it and that settles it.

Because churches fail to equip Christians with reasons for their faith, people continue to believe that faith is only faith when they believe in something for which they have no reason to believe. Peter, however, commanded Christians to "give an account"—to know the "reason" (ESV; Greek *logos*) for the *hope* they possess. The term "reason" is also "word, message" (*logos*), and it calls for all believers to possess the *logical* truth conveyed in *rational* speech whenever they are confronted in order to be able to defend the Gospel truth.

Sharing the gospel truth concerns a cogent apologetic of "the hope that is in [us]." Peter uses the term "hope" as a synonym for faith; thus, the Christian faith is obviously defensible against those who would scoff at it. This "hope" becomes the epicenter of any conversation about Christ, for it is the life-changing story of all converts to Christ. This conversation must be had with "gentleness and reverence," or respect (1 Peter 3:16; cf. 2:15). As Paul wrote to Timothy, "The goal of our instruction is love from a pure heart and a good conscience and a sincere faith" (1 Tim. 1:5). Thus, making a defense of the faith is not an angry debate or an attack upon another, but a sharing of the truth in love and with a good "conscience." That is, Christians are supposed to actually believe what they say and live what they teach; otherwise, they would be violating their conscience if they taught something they did not believe. Our conscience is clear when we understand the truth and strive to convince others about the truth. The truth speaks without harsh words, silencing the mouths of fools when the apologist's life is in keeping with his words.

This apologetic of the Gospel is meant "so that" when Christians are "slandered," their behavior and logical defense of the Gospel will put their persecutors to shame. The word "slandered" implies that the primary form of persecution Christians faced was verbal abuse and not physical, although the latter became widespread later in the history of the Church.

In the early Church, Christianity was highly scrutinized by the society of the Roman Empire. Judaism was tolerated to an extent, but Christianity eventually came under attack in AD 64 under the Roman Emperor Nero. Christians were charged with sedition because they were perceived to be undermining the authority of the Roman Empire by refusing to worship the emperor, in spite of the fact that Christians were known to submit to the laws of the land and the payment of taxes. Some Christians were even charged with being atheists because they worshiped one God instead of the Roman pantheon of gods. Still others had to fight against the misconception that the Lord's Supper was some kind of orgy (called the "love feast") or that it was cannibalistic in that Christ's body was being eaten. A less serious charge was leveled against them regarding the doctrine of the Trinity, which the Roman authorities did not like because it broke with the beliefs of the Greek philosophers and introduced "myths."

Christians rose up against attacks after the death of the apostles in order to defend themselves and their beliefs, and they were known as "apologists" because they defended the faith. These intellectuals did more than simply defend the faith, however; they also went on the offense by showing the logic and truth of Christianity. They used this logic to propagate the true worldview while deposing the many false ones. What these teachers did was show how faith and reason go hand in hand and how God does not expect anyone to believe that which cannot be believed or is absurd.

All Christians are to be about the objective task of preaching the truth of Jesus Christ, proving the claims of the faith, and persuading all who hear them to believe in the truth and to place their faith in Christ. All this is done with the goal of bringing glory to God and calling all the elect to salvation in Christ. After all, that is the commission given by Christ (Matt. 28:19–20), and since unbelievers can never hear the truth without a preacher (Rom. 10:14), Christians are to reason with them by sharing the truth with them. So let the diligent and true Christian set out to know and defend the faith of the Lord Jesus Christ.

Nothing can exist unless an eternal being exists, and since something exists, then an eternal being must exist! Jesus was a historical figure spoken about even by nonbiblical writers, and He claimed to be God, the eternal and necessary Being. His life, death, and resurrection are all historical facts attested to even by His enemies. Either Jesus was a liar in what He said, a lunatic who thought He was God, a legend invented by His followers, or He is the Lord God Almighty. The truth about Jesus is absolutely defensible, and the Bible He gave us has never been proven to have an error. So go out and defend it!

Chapter 2

IS IT FOOLISH TO BELIEVE IN GOD?

One young woman I know who attends a local college near Houston, Texas, told me that her professor entered the room early in the semester and breathed out the atheistic montage, which went something like this: "Now in order to have an intelligent conversation, you will need to rid your mind of religious ideas, personal preferences, and any personal biases you have, and then put them in a box."

Where did he get this idea? Does empirical scientific evidence teach us to conclude this? Has he, in all of his research and the "alphabet soup" behind his name, found conclusive evidence that religious people, those with preferences, and those with biases are wrong? Hardly. Consider this: If all knowledge was based on observation, how could we know that all knowledge is based on observation since this in itself has not been observed scientifically? Jason Lisle, PhD in astrophysics from the University of Colorado, said, "The empiricist can't really know anything at all since his standard (by which he tests other things) is uncertain."[11]

The professor's words are not only common to the faith of atheists and agnostics but ironic as well, for the statement itself represents a religious belief since it reflects the faith that there is no God. It reflects a personal preference since the professor prefers that no preferences be brought into the discussion. And it reflects bias because it favors intelligent conversation apart from religious

---

[11] Jason Lisle, *The Ultimate Proof of Creation* (Green Forest, AR: Master Books, 2009), 72.

belief, preferences, and bias. In short, the professor began his class with a self-defeating statement since it begs the question by telling the class to put aside their faith, preferences, and biases while adhering to his own faith, preferences, and biases. What is amazing is that he wanted to have an intelligent conversation!

The question is, why did the professor begin at this point? After all, he did not begin without his own preference and bias, for in his mind, his preference and bias was that the only way to have an intelligent conversation was to put aside all religious beliefs, preferences, and biases. Thus, by his own definition of an intelligent conversation, he failed to offer the recipe for an intelligent conversation since he brought his own religious beliefs (that religious beliefs are apparently worthless), his own preferences (that belief in God or the Bible or Jesus is not intelligent), and his own biases (that anyone who believes in God, Jesus, or the Bible is unintelligent). So we must search for another introductory argument if we want to have an intelligent conversation.

Consider Proverbs 26:4–5, which says, "Do not answer a fool according to his folly, Or you will also be like him. Answer a fool as his folly deserves, that he not be wise in his own eyes." At first glance, it looks like verse 5 contradicts verse 4. Verse 4 forbids answering a fool according to his folly, yet verse 5 promotes the practice. So, unless the Bible is speaking illogically or in a circular way, or unless this proverb is simply a truism either way, we need to take a closer look. What we will see is that this passage answers the question of our attitude when we encounter illogical arguments like the one the aforementioned professor presented to his class.

According to the Bible, a "fool" is someone who rejects God's existence (Psalm 14:1; 53:1). The word itself means "stupid; impious; insolent." There is no context in which the word can be used in a positive sense, but since atheists are often academics and hence regarded as intelligent, it seems ridiculous to call a smart person a fool. But would it not be foolish to argue against the existence of air since it cannot be seen when you need to breathe air in order to argue against its existence? That would be foolish indeed! The same is true with God, for you must assume God exists in order to deny He exists.

So before we examine the meaning of Proverbs 26:4–5, let us consider Romans 1:18–23: "For the wrath of God is revealed from heaven against all ungodliness and unrighteousness of men who suppress the truth in unrighteousness, because that which is known about God is evident within them; for God made it evident to them. For since the creation of the world His invisible attributes, His eternal power and divine nature, have been clearly seen, being understood through what has been made, so that they are without excuse. For even though they knew God, they did not honor Him as God or give thanks, but they became futile in their speculations, and their foolish heart was darkened. Professing to be wise, they became fools, and exchanged the glory of the incorruptible God for an image in the form of corruptible man and of birds and four-footed animals and crawling creatures."

The passage speaks of God's wrath literally "being revealed." It does not speak of past wrath per se (e.g., the Flood, Sodom and Gomorrah, etc.) or a future day of wrath (Day of the Lord, the removal of the Restrainer, or eternal hell). It speaks of current and ongoing wrath like God's consequential abandonment of those who have abandoned Him for worldly philosophies and perversions.

It is significant that God's wrath is revealed "from heaven," which is the throne of God, where He dwells in unapproachable light (1 Tim. 6:16). Satan's present domain is the earth, as "prince of the air and of this world" (Eph. 2:2), but as seen in the book of Job, Satan's power is limited by God's command, which comes "from heaven." So God's wrath, which is *being* revealed, is ordered from heaven and carried out as natural law on the earth. While God controls it all, it is man's rebellion against Him that fuels God's wrath.

What fuels God's wrath is "all ungodliness and unrighteousness of men" (Rom. 1:18). The term "ungodliness" speaks of wicked people without a moral compass, their lives without God filled with selfish indulgence depriving God of the worship due Him. The term "unrighteousness," though synonymous to ungodliness, refers to the *result* of an ungodly life. And God's wrath is revealed from heaven against "all" of those who do not respond by faith to the revealed righteousness of God, which is for all who believe (Rom. 1:16–17). No amount of service to the poor or giving to the Church will exonerate them; only faith in Christ can do that.

God's wrath is directed at those who "suppress the truth in unrighteousness"—literally, those "who are continually suppressing the truth." God has targeted "all," for they are the "children of wrath" (Eph. 2:3). Though all have sinned and fallen short of God's glory (Rom. 3:23), believing in Christ saves those who do so through faith alone. Those who refuse to believe actually "suppress the truth" in their unrighteousness.

To suppress the truth, you must first know the truth, and Romans 1:19 clearly states that *all* men know some truth about God, for God has made Himself known to all. He has "shown" (*to reveal*) Himself in the human conscience, through His creation, and in nature (Rom. 1:20). Therefore, no one can observe the created order of the universe and the wonder of the human body and then deny a Creator unless they are a fool, for it is the fool who says there is no God.

In the days of Jesus Christ, who performed miracles and spoke the truth in the presence of thousands of people, many rejected Him. Why? It is because "men loved the darkness rather than the Light, for their deeds were evil" (John 3:19). In other words, people tend to reject those who tell them they are wrong and offer a right way when they long for the wrong way. But aside from Christ's miracles, Romans 1:20 says of God, "For since the creation of the world His invisible attributes, His eternal power and divine nature, have been clearly seen, being understood through what has been made, so that they are without excuse." It is not necessary to see the risen Lord Jesus Christ or witness His miracles in order to believe. God is revealed in Jesus Christ (John 1:18), but His invisible attributes are clearly seen elsewhere, namely in the creation itself.

The passage clearly teaches that there is not a person on the earth who has an excuse, for God has made Himself known to all. It is the creation itself, God's handiwork, that pours forth speech and loudly proclaims there is indeed a God (cf. Psalm 19). Thus, those who fail to acknowledge the Creator God do so *willingly*, and because of this, God's wrath is upon them.

When the Apostle Paul visited Lystra, he told the predominately Gentile audience about the God who "made the heaven and the earth and the sea, and all that is in them. In the generations gone by He permitted all the nations to go their own ways; and yet He did not leave Himself without witness, in that He did good and gave you rains from heaven and fruitful seasons, satisfying your hearts with food and gladness" (Acts 14:15–17). Paul told the same type of thing to the pagan philosophers in Athens, showing them not from the Jewish Scriptures, but from the *creation* that there is one God "who made the world and all things in it" (Acts 17:22ff.).

It is God's unseen attributes, namely His "eternal power" that all humans are made aware of. As such, they are without excuse for their failure to believe. God's eternal power refers to His *omnipotence*—His supreme control reflected in His creation of all things. It is His power that brought forth the creation, and only those who "suppress" this truth choose to believe that some other power brought it forth (e.g., chance, evolution, etc.). Further, God's "divine nature" accompanied His power, and this refers to His gracious provisions He gave to His creation. Paul referred to this when he told the people of Lystra, "He did good and gave you rains from heaven and fruitful seasons, satisfying your hearts with food and gladness" (Acts 14:17).

A look at the creation with just a simple glance out the window should astound the average person. The wonder of the created universe is absolutely awesome. Plant a seed, and a tree grows, sometimes way up into the sky. Look closely at an insect, and see the intricacies that make it what it is. John MacArthur uses the example of the bombardier beetle:

> This remarkable insect is found mainly in the deserts of New Mexico. It was created with a unique defense mechanism that is impossible to explain by the evolutionary theory. The beetle produces two chemicals in separate reservoirs in its abdomen. The two chemicals, hydraquinone and hydrogen peroxide, are harmless by themselves but potentially explosive when combined. When attacked, the beetle releases the chemicals through a movable jet at the rear tip of its abdomen. Catalytic enzymes in a tiny reaction chamber just inside the expulsion valve set the chemical reaction in motion, and at precisely the right moment, the beetle aims his abdominal turret and releases the explosive mixture in the

face of his predator. The combined chemicals instantly reach the temperature of boiling water, creating a surprise and a deterrent that is powerful enough to discourage most predators. The beetle can fire up to five shots in rapid succession, and he instinctively knows how to time the explosion so that it occurs a moment after the chemicals are expelled, never in the reaction chamber where it would destroy the beetle. How does the beetle know how to do this? Could such a complex system possibly have developed through some natural evolutionary process? Consider what all the bombardier beetle's defense system entails: The beetle must be able to produce just the right chemicals, keep them in separate reservoirs, and bring them together at the right time with the necessary catalytic enzymes. He must also possess all the equipment and ability necessary to combine the explosives, aim the mixture accurately, and fire precisely before the moment of explosion. Is it reasonable to think an evolving creature could develop such a system, with so many interdependent parts, through a process of individual, random genetic changes? The answer is clear: The bombardier beetle is the product of intelligent design.[12]

Note also the human eye, ear, and nose and how astonishing each one is in their individual makeup. The human hand is capable of building almost anything, for it is a multifaceted machine more complex than anything it builds. Consider the growth of a baby in its mother's womb or the sexual reproductive system in the human body. Note with awe human language itself! It simply cannot be explained. Look up at the stars and consider the orbit of the planets in the solar system, the rising and setting of the sun, the changing of the seasons, the flight of birds, and the powerful hurricanes, tsunamis, and earthquakes all over the planet. Certainly "the heavens are telling of the glory of God; and their expanse is declaring the work of His hands" (Psalm 19:1). Only a fool would deny this.

---

[12] John MacArthur, *The Battle for the Beginning: The Bible on Creation and the Fall of Adam* (Nashville, TN: W Pub. Group, 2001), 147.

The problem with fools is not that they are uninformed, but that they have rejected truth and opted instead for a lie—on purpose! That is the biblical definition of a fool. Romans 1:21–23 says, "For although they knew God, they did not honor Him as God or give thanks to Him, but they became futile in their thinking, and their foolish hearts were darkened. Claiming to be wise, they became fools, and exchanged the glory of the immortal God for images resembling mortal man and birds and four-footed animals and reptiles" (ESV). So when the Bible calls someone a fool, it is not immature name-calling—it is a title for one who rejects that which he inherently knows to be true.

When people suppress the truth of God, they become "futile in their thinking," literally "foolish in their dialogues" or "reasonings." Of course if something is false, it is foolish to ramble on about the truth of it. Those who exchange the truth for lies tend to perpetuate their ideas, yet their foolish hearts have been darkened. The Greek verb "darkened" in Romans 1:21 means "unable to understand," which is the result of a heart turned "foolish." The "heart" here is used as the rational part of the inner self, and it is clear that man's fallen state includes his heart, or mind—the place where his intellectual reasoning is processed. So the darkening of the fallen heart of man who has rejected the truth of God means that at best, in spite of his education, his thoughts and rationale are foolish.

To reject the truth is to create a vacuum in the heart, a void often filled with idolatry of self or something else. Note the observable history Paul recounted for those who rejected truth for lies. First, they filled the void they created by rejecting God with "images resembling mortal man." Frank Wedekind made the pertinent observation about this passage when he said, "God made man in His own image, and man returned the favor."[13] Man has always worshiped himself in various ways. In fact, Paul warned Timothy that in the last days men would become lovers of self, money, etc. (2 Tim. 3:1ff.). All idolatry is the worship of self, and when someone rejects God as his object of worship, his darkened

---

[13] Frank Wedekind, Quotes Archive. http://www.quotesarchive.com/authors/w/frank-wedekind/quotes (accessed August 6, 2012).

mind has nothing left to choose except unrighteousness, and man's unrighteousness is the basis for God's wrath.

Second, Paul referenced the practice of worshiping "birds, animals, and reptiles" as idols. In the ancient Near East people worshiped such animals as bulls, jackals, hawks, and serpents.[14] Even the Israelites were guilty of worshiping a golden calf they fashioned with their hands (cf. Exod. 32:1–10). Then there were the "reptiles," which included all "crawling creatures" (NASB). The Egyptians were also known to worship the dung beetle, which lives in manure piles. Likewise, the Assyrians and Greeks worshiped snakes, and the Canaanite god (Baal-zebub, 2 Kings 1:2; Matt. 10:25) was "Lord of the flies."[15]

As bad as that was, modern society seems worse than in Paul's day. The worldwide rejection of God has resulted in darkened minds, the very minds that have been granted great authority in universities and governments all over the world. People worship the human body, sports, science, money, and self. After rejecting God, what else is there? Then there are those who worship God *and* idols, those who read their Bibles then check their horoscopes. Considering this, it is not difficult to understand why our world has become so corrupt, so bankrupt, and so selfish. God has been rejected, even by those who believe they are Christians.

It is pride that keeps man from honoring God, and even worse, man's pride deprives God of the worship due Him. David exhorts all believers: "Ascribe to the Lord glory and strength. Ascribe to the Lord the glory due to His name" (Psalm 29:1–2). Likewise, the Apostle Paul wrote, "Whether, then, you eat or drink or whatever you do, do all to the glory of God" (1 Cor. 10:31). So once a person rejects God, they are not left with much to work with in terms of explaining how all things exist. A certain evolutionist said, "I refuse to believe in God, so what other alternative do I have but evolution?"[16] He's right! Since evolution is all that is left

---

[14] Robert H. Mounce, "Romans," in *The New American Commentary*, Volume 27 (Nashville: Broadman & Holman Publishers, 1995), 80.

[15] MacArthur, *Romans*, 94.

[16] John MacArthur, "Romans," in *The MacArthur New Testament Commentary*, Volume 1 (Chicago, IL: Moody Press, 1996), 82.

for fools to believe after they reject God, it is only natural that their foolish belief reflects their foolish mind. Once they abandon the plain words of Scripture and the witness of creation, they show that they once knew God but have decided not to honor or give thanks to Him as God.

The Method for Answering a Fool

Now let us look again at Proverbs 26:4–5: "Do not answer a fool according to his folly, or you will also be like him. Answer a fool as his folly deserves, that he not be wise in his own eyes." It is not that a Christian cannot answer a fool—defined in Scripture as one who rejects God—rather, the Christian cannot answer a fool *according to his folly*. This means we cannot accept the professor's instruction to put away all of our religious beliefs, preferences, and biases before we get started trying to be intellectual. We cannot begin to be intellectual by assuming there is no God, for in doing so, we answer the fool according to his folly and thereby become fools ourselves.

We might rather answer the professor by saying, "I cannot assume there is no God in order to be intellectual, for to do so would make me a fool. And a fool, by definition, is unable to be intellectual." But rather than decline any conversation that demands we first become a fool by denying God's existence, our mandate is found in Proverbs 24:5. We can answer a fool according to his folly, not by adhering to his belief system, but by assuming hypothetically there is no God for the purpose of exposing the absurdity of his premise.

So, instead of falling into the fool's trap of denying God's existence by answering him according to his worldview where religion is to be put away in a box, we answer him in lieu of his folly. We respectfully show the professor how absurd his request is and how he, while telling us to rid ourselves of biases, brought his own bias into the discussion. In a word, we show him his *hypocrisy*! After all, who says that an intellectual discussion begins by putting aside religious beliefs, preferences, and biases? And since that kind of logic begs the question, given that it bases its idea on a *preference*, it is absurd. And absurdity is certainly not intellectual.

Therefore, we see from Proverbs 26:4 that we should not embrace the foolishness of unbelievers, for in doing so we become like them. Rather, we see from Proverbs 26:5 that we should accept their arguments hypothetically *so as to show them the absurdity of their faith*. This will keep the fool from being wise in his own eyes.

What becomes evident in every argument or discussion is that everyone, without exception, enters the argument or discussion *with a worldview*—an *a priori* idea that fuels their entire thought and reasoning process. Theists believe in God, agnostics are uncertain and wonder if anyone can know if there is a God or gods, and atheists outright reject the existence of God or gods. When someone like the professor attempts to rid a discussion of the bias of theistic beliefs, he shows that his worldview is that he does not believe in God. So why entertain his ideas of foolishness when we as Christians know full well that he is the one who is so sadly mistaken?

Where Do We Begin?

Epistemology is the branch of philosophy that investigates the nature and origin of knowledge.[17] It is the discipline that deals with the theory of knowledge, endeavoring to investigate from where knowledge derives. The word itself comes from the Greek *episteme,* "to know," and the Greek *logos*, "study." When we engage in anything with our mind and ask how we know what we know, where our knowledge comes from, and *why* we are able to know anything, we are engaged in epistemology.

Our beliefs are typically formed in our early years by our parents, by our friends and acquaintances, through our culture, and through our churches, to name only a few. We are also shaped by our emotions and feelings. For instance, if a loved one dies when

---

[17] Norman L. Geisler, Paul D. Feinberg, and Paul D. Feinberg, *Introduction to Philosophy: A Christian Perspective* (Grand Rapids, MI: Baker Book House, 1980), 19.

we are young, we are molded and shaped by the pain of our loss. Or if we are physically or sexually abused as children, we are shaped by those traumatic events. All these things teach us and shape our thinking, but none are reliable teachers of truth per se, though all of them can be.

The only way to really know truth is to investigate it and test it, for the Christian faith is based on historical evidence of Christ's life, teachings, death, and resurrection. It is not a feeling but a reality. We can investigate all the claims of Christ, for His life, along with the doctrine of Scripture, are wide open to investigation in order to determine their trustworthiness. Believing in Christ is not blind faith—it is faith based on evidence.

As for science and Christianity living together side by side, science is not the enemy of Christianity. It never has been. Although good science cannot answer all questions about the Bible and its teachings, science will always be in harmony with the truths of Scripture. Whereas some have claimed that science has disproved the first words of the Bible in favor of evolutionary theory, science is actually unable to prove or disprove either evolution or creation. The beginning of the universe is not something that can be tested and retested. If evolution were true, where randomness and chance came together to form everything out of nothing, then there could be no science because science relies on uniformity[18] and predictability. Yet uniformity and predictability are not possible in a universe that was created by chance. Science does not observe detailed order resulting from chaos, the very theory that evolutionists espouse. As Lisle said,

> Ironically, evolution is actually contrary to the principles of science. That is, if evolution were true, the concept of science would not make sense. Science actually requires a biblical creation framework in order to be possible. Therefore, evolution turns out to be more of an anti-science than a science.[19]

---

[18] Uniformity insists that the laws of nature are consistent, behave in a predictable manner, and do not arbitrarily change with time or space, though certain conditions and processes may change.

[19] Lisle, 57.

Lisle also spoke of the preconditions of science:

> In order to do science we take for granted that the universe is understandable—that it can be quantified in a way the mind can comprehend. We assume the universe is logical and orderly and that it obeys mathematical laws that are consistent over time and space. Even though conditions in different regions of space and years of time are quite diverse, there is nonetheless an underlying uniformity. Because there is such regularity in the universe, there are many instances where scientists are able to make successful predictions about the future. For example, astronomers can successfully compute the positions of the planets, moons, and asteroids far into the future. Without uniformity in nature, such predictions would be impossible, and science could not exist. The problem for evolutionism is that such regularity only makes sense in a biblical creation worldview.[20]

Therefore, scientific observation is possible only *because* God exists. This will be seen further in the teleological argument for God's existence in chapter 6. Philosophical principles like rationalism, reason, and empirical evidence are essential for discovering truth, but they only exist because, God, the Intelligent Creator, exists. None of them, scientifically speaking, could exist with such uniformity out of a world that exploded from nothing into chaos. And since science is thought to be the answer to everything in the mind of the naturalist, they must wonder how science is so uniform given that the beginning of the world came together from an accidental explosion of nothing. Scientific evidence has proven that order and uniformity do not stem from chaos, yet if the naturalistic explanation of the universe wins the argument, how can we explain our knowledge of the universe? How can we explain anything for that matter since a cogent explanation demands the existence of the laws of logic (cf. chapter 3)?

Therefore, before a reasonable defense can be made for God and for the Christian faith, we must grapple with *how* anyone can

---

[20] Lisle, 57.

actually know anything. In other words, how can we verify or falsify a rational defense of the Christian faith or anything else for that matter? Enter the field of epistemology. Since apologetics concerns a rational defense of truth, *how* can we ever understand or know truth, or know if truth even exists, is essential. How does anyone know anything? Answer: *God exists and allows for knowledge.*

The Christian's Defense of Knowledge

"In the beginning was the Word, and the Word was with God, and the Word was God... And the Word became flesh" (John 1:1, 14). "In the beginning" is reminiscent of Genesis 1:1 when "God created the heavens and the earth." In this verse, the Hebrew word for God is *Elohim*, a plural word although the verb is singular, which points to a singular God. In His essence, God is one (Deut. 6:4), but He exists eternally as three separate persons: *Father, Son, and Holy Spirit.* This is no contradiction, for that would be illogical. It is, however, a paradox, for although God is one in His *essence*, He is triune in His *person*. So, there is no contradiction in the doctrine of the Trinity. It must be stressed, however, that Genesis 1:1 does not teach the Trinity; it merely allows for it. The doctrine of the Trinity, though introduced in Genesis 1:1 is a doctrine developed and explained throughout the whole of Scripture, especially in passages like John 1:1 where "the Word" (the *Logos*), Jesus, was existing from all eternity before He took on human flesh. What is important to note here is that Jesus is no created being. He has existed from eternity alongside God the Father and God the Spirit as God the Son, the *Logos*.

In John 1:1, the writer takes the reader back *prior* to the creation of the universe into the realm of eternity where the "Word" was existing. This term was widely used in ancient Greek literature. The Greek Heraclitus saw in the common term *logos* a basic defining principle related to the ordering and control of the cosmos.[21] The Stoics employed it for the soul of the world, and

---

[21] Gerald L. Borchert, "John 1-11," Volume 25A, in *The New American Commentary* (Nashville: Broadman & Holman Publishers, 2001), 104.

Marcus Aurelius (d. 180) used the phrase *spermatikos logos* for the generative principle in nature. The Jews used the Hebrew *memra* in the Targums for the manifestation of God like the Angel of the LORD and the Wisdom of God in Proverbs 8:23. John's usage is in keeping with the Old Testament and not of the Stoics or even of Philo, who, unlike John, did not see the *Logos* as a person who existed before His incarnation.[22] In fact, Philo denied the incarnation of the Word, whereas John specifically maintained that the Word became flesh (John 1:14).[23]

In sum, the polytheistic Greeks viewed the *Logos* as a rational principle that governed all things. The Jews used *Logos* in reference to God who created all things (cf. Gen. 1–2), the God who is surrounded by His *powers* like a king is surrounded by his servants. Whereas the Greeks saw these powers surrounding the *Logos* as *ideas,* the Jews saw these powers as *angels* surrounding God.

Whereas the Greeks confined the *Logos* to the creation and the preservation of the universe without connecting it with the Creator God, John describes the *Logos* as *a person*—a person whom John and his cohorts had seen, heard, and touched (cf. 1 John 1:1–3). John described this person as One who had united Himself with humanity by taking on human flesh (1:14) in order to save humanity through a bloody and violent death on a cross. This can be seen in John's progression from the *Logos* as an entity to a *Him*, one who became flesh. John's purpose for writing was to expose Jesus for who He truly is—the Eternal Son of God who became flesh.

Throughout the New Testament, *logos* is used for thoughts, sayings, discourse, doctrine, and reasoning. But John speaks of the *Logos* who "was" *in the beginning.* The Greek imperfect tense of "was" describes a continuous past action, as in "the Word was being." Had the Logos *come* into being, John would have used another Greek term, one that specifically means "to come into being." John uses that particular term in 1:3 in reference to the

---

[22] A.T. Robertson, *Word Pictures in the New Testament* (Oak Harbor: Logos Research Systems, 1997), John 1:1.

[23] D. A. Carson, *New Bible Commentary: 21st Century Edition*, 4th ed. (Leicester, England; Downers Grove, IL: Inter-Varsity Press, 1994), John 1:1-5.

"things" God brought into being and again in verse 14 in reference to the incarnation of the *Logos* (Jesus' flesh had a beginning, but Jesus Himself is eternal). Thus, John is using his verbs to teach that Jesus is not a created being *but has existed from all eternity*, the very truth the Apostle Paul and other New Testament writers attest to (cf. 2 Cor. 8:9; Phil. 2:6f.; Col. 1:17; Heb. 1:2ff.).

Therefore, the New Testament introduces new revelation in reference to the *Logos*, and part of that revelation is that the *Logos* is God, and it encompasses everything that emanates from God and that which He distributes into His created world. It follows that God's *outspoken word,* His created order, proceeds from His eternal reasoning and is manifest in the world He created. This is the *Logos* John the Apostle speaks of in John 1:1 and throughout his writings in the New Testament.

Regarding Jesus Christ as the preexistent "Word of God," New Testament commentator Gerald Borchert concludes three things: First, "the Word was with God" means that the *Logos* existed before creation began…that the *Logos* has an origin that supersedes the created order of time and space. Second, this *Logos* has an identity distinct from the previously understood designations for God. Third, the *Logos* must also be understood as part of the unity of God. Here then are the beginnings of Christian reflection on the mind-stretching concept that became known as the doctrine of the Trinity.[24] It also sets the entire framework for knowledge since an eternal Being has always existed and created the world out of His own eternal reasonings.

Clearly, the Scriptures teach that God is eternal and hence has no origin. So, there can be no creation of God (cf. Psalm 90:2; Jer. 10:10; John 17:5). It is absurd to even wonder how that which is eternal was created, for the eternal by definition has no beginning and hence no creation. This is not only logical, given that all effects demand an ultimate cause, it is also necessary to explain how anything that exists began to exist.

The ramifications for the eternality of God cannot be stressed enough, for the eternal God is the only explanation for why there is something and not nothing, for why there are laws of logic, of physics, uniformity, and the ability to observe rational principles.

---

[24] Borchert, 106.

And God's eternal existence explains why anything that is known can be known. All these *demand* a Creator, for none of these laws and principles could arise out of the hypothetical chaotic explosion of the big bang that supposedly caused an accidental universe by chance. Both Christians and atheists understand these principles, but the worldview for the atheist cannot account for them. The Christian, however, knows exactly where these laws originated, namely with the Creator God, the Eternal Almighty.

Some call Jesus a moral teacher or even a model businessman. But John depicts Him as the Christ, the holy one of God who was in the beginning with God and who *is* God. This is evident not only in the words used to describe Jesus, but also in the way Jesus was opposed by his enemies. John the Baptist said, "I have seen and have testified that this is the Son of God" (John 1:34). Nathanael said, "Rabbi, You are the Son of God" (John 1:49). Jesus said, "My Father is working until now, and I Myself am working" (John 5:17), and because of this "the Jews were seeking all the more to kill Him, because He…was calling God His own Father, making Himself equal with God" (5:18).

When Jesus said, "I and the Father are one" (John 10:30), "the Jews picked up stones again to stone Him" (10:31) saying, "For a good work we do not stone You, but for blasphemy; and because You, being a man, make Yourself out to be God" (10:33). When Philip asked Jesus to show him the Father, Jesus told him, "He who has seen Me has seen the Father" (John 14:9). The Jews hated Jesus, saying, "He ought to die because He made Himself out to be the Son of God" (John 19:7). And Thomas, upon seeing his resurrected Lord, said, "My Lord and my God!" (John 20:28).

Furthermore, John says, "All things came into being through Him, and apart from Him nothing came into being that has come into being. In Him was life, and the life was the Light of men. The Light shines in the darkness, and the darkness did not comprehend it" (John 1:3–5). In verse 3, John says that "all things came into being through Him." Note that the Logos is specifically a "Him," and it is through Him, namely Jesus, that all things were made. Of course, this is consistent with the rest of the New Testament. Hebrews 1:2 says that God created the world *through His Son*. And Colossians 1:16 says that all things were created by Jesus—things both in heaven and on earth, and all things were created *for* Him.

Clearly, Jesus was existing at the outset of the universe in the beginning because He is the Eternal Supreme Being. The New Testament therefore clarifies what the Old Testament merely hinted at—that Jesus the Son was God the Father's Agent in creating all things that exist.

John 1:3b is literally, "Apart from Him not even one thing exists which exists" or "which has been made." The perfect tense of this last phrase conveys the idea of a continuing existence of all created things. So in verse 3a, John gives a snapshot of the created order, and in verse 3b, he gives a picture of the created order as it continues to exist—an existence that is continually upheld and sustained by the *Logos*, namely Jesus.

Among those things that exist are certain laws that are part of God's character. Thus, as He is eternal, so are they. One of those laws is the law of *cause and effect*, which demands that every *effect* has a *cause*. And the cause for all effects in the created universe (itself an effect with a cause) is clearly the *Logos*—Jesus Christ. Everything made was made by Him. So who created Him? No one; nothing! That which is eternal is by definition everlasting and without beginning or end. God is the necessary Being needed for anything to exist that exists—including knowledge.

Understanding the person of Jesus Christ is of utmost importance. He is not just a cute little baby born in a manger who grew up with long flowing hair telling everyone to love one another. He is God incarnate who has existed from all eternity. He is as much the source of knowledge as He is the source of salvation. Knowledge can be attained simply because Jesus has always existed. This explains both how and why we can have knowledge and why there is uniformity in nature. The naturalist believes we can know things too, but he cannot explain how. In fact, his worldview demands that he assume God exists in order to have knowledge, while at the same time making arguments that God does not exist. This is absurdity at the highest level. No wonder the Bible calls fools those who reject God (Psalm 14:1). Only a fool would reject that which he inherently knows to be true.

How Can We Know Anything at All?

In discussions as lofty as the existence of God, Christians should never be heard talking about feelings, for what truly matters is knowledge. Sincere faith is vital, but our argument for our faith must transcend feelings and hunches. The Christian faith is defensible, but our sword in battle should never be our feelings about our faith. Let us always stand on truth, evidence for truth, and philosophical principles of determining truth as we discuss our Christian faith.

Of course, knowledge means "to know," but there are various kinds of knowledge to be aware of. Garrett DeWeese suggests three kinds of knowledge.[25] First, there is *propositional knowledge*, which concerns knowing facts. We know certain facts from experience, things like whether it is raining outside, if we are loved by another person, and if we feel sick. This is empirical knowledge, coming from our senses. Yet all knowledge is not empirical because we believe many things without using our senses. Whether we believe in God is an example of nonempirical knowledge, and everyone has a belief about God. Ironically, to claim that all knowledge is empirical is to make a nonempirical statement. After all, how could that knowledge be had through our senses? It cannot, so it is a self-defeating statement. DeWeese said:

> There are good reasons to think that at least some knowledge of the world is non-empirical (a doctrine called *moderate rationalism*). Beliefs that certain things exist that cannot be directly observed may be inferred from empirical observations. This is how we justify belief in such things as electrons, gravitational fields, beauty, or love. And similarly for belief in God. Further, the analogy between sensory experience and religious experience provides good reasons for the justification of religious beliefs based on religious experience…we can know

---

[25] Garrett DeWeese, "How Can We Know Anything At All?" *The Apologetics Study Bible: Real Questions, Straight Answers, Stronger Faith*, ed. Ted Cabal, Chad Owen Brand, E. Ray Clendenen, et al. (Nashville, TN: Holman Bible Publishers, 2007), 1766-67.

some things without using our senses at all. For example, we can know much about ourselves through introspection (a non-empirical process). We can know that we have minds that think, believe, hope, fear, and so on, and that we are not identical to our bodies. Many ethicists claim that moral knowledge is accessible through intuition or conscience or pure reason. Following St. Anselm, many scholars have thought that the ontological proof—a non-empirical argument—establishes God's necessary existence. Moreover, we have non-empirical as well as empirical evidence of God's existence (Rom 1:19-20), what has been called the *sensus divinitatis*. And since our belief in God's existence is justified, we also are justified in believing what He has revealed to us. For all these examples, we can point to the right kinds of reasons that justify non-empirical beliefs.[26]

Second, there is *knowledge by acquaintance*, which concerns knowing something or someone directly. Third, there is *skill knowledge*, which concerns knowing how to do something, like playing a guitar, building a house, etc. Putting them all together, however, is somewhat confusing. For example, a person can have propositional knowledge from the Bible about Moses, but they do not have the knowledge of acquaintance, having never actually met Moses. Likewise, a person might be an expert golfer but completely bereft of propositional knowledge about force, inertia, or rotational momentum.

All three types of knowledge encompass the Christian faith. First, we must have knowledge of God and of His Son, Jesus Christ (cf. John 17:3). This involves having both the facts and a first-hand acquaintance with Jesus. Skill knowledge, however, given that salvation is by faith and not by works, is a nonfactor in the Christian faith, for we need no skills to know God. But we do need to acquire the skill of reading and studying Scripture, the discipline of prayer, and the joy of evangelism. Thus, all three forms of knowledge comprise the Christian faith.

---

[26] DeWeese, 1767.

Self-Defeating Arguments

According to J. P. Moreland, a self-defeating statement has three characteristics. First, it establishes some requirement of acceptability for any statement, assertion, proposition, or theory. Second, it places itself in subjection to this requirement. Third, it fails to satisfy the requirement of acceptability that the assertion itself stipulates.[27]

Since a statement is about a subject matter, if a statement is included in its own subject matter and fails to satisfy its own standards of acceptability, it is self-defeating. For example, if someone said, "There is no such thing as truth," their statement is self-defeating because they made a truth statement. Likewise, if someone said, "I do not exist" or "I cannot speak a word of English" (spoken in English), their statements are self-defeating. They must exist in order to deny their existence, and they used English words to declare that they cannot speak a word of English.

As we attempt to identify self-defeating statements, Moreland suggests that we be very careful in making sure that the statement actually refers to itself, that it is a part of its own subject matter. For example, if someone claimed in Spanish to be unable to speak a word of English, then the claim would not be self-defeating. With this in mind, we should note that the statement "there are no *moral* absolutes" is not self-defeating. It is false, to be sure, but the statement is a philosophical assertion *about* morality and not a claim *of* morality.

> To be a claim of morality, an assertion must be a moral rule such as "Do not kill," "Abortion is wrong," or "One ought to be tolerant of others." "There are no moral absolutes" is not itself a moral rule. Like a statement made in English about all French statements (for example, "No French statement is longer than three words"), "There are no moral absolutes" is false. But since it is not included in

---

[27]J.P. Moreland, "What Are Self-Defeating Statements?" *The Apologetics Study Bible: Real Questions, Straight Answers, Stronger Faith*, ed. Ted Cabal, Chad Owen Brand, E. Ray Clendenen, et al., (Nashville, TN: Holman Bible Publishers, 2007), 1741-42.

its own subject matter, it does not refer to itself and therefore is not *self*-refuting.[28]

Before Christians can engage in discussions about God, especially heated discussions, they must learn to detect self-defeating arguments about God. Because there are many inadequate tests for truth, Christians must be able to identify them, or they will be duped by them. For instance, skepticism is the belief that nothing can be known for certain. The skeptic claims that since scholars and debaters are divided in so many different areas of thought and philosophy, the only conclusion you can draw is that truth is unknowable. But that statement is self-defeating, for in saying that all truth is unknowable, you make a truth statement! Therefore, a true skeptic would have to be skeptical about skepticism and hence reject skepticism.

David Hume (1711–1776) was a skeptic, but he was a hypocrite because he was not skeptical about skepticism. Likewise, Immanuel Kant (1724–1804) was a skeptic, for he endeavored to show that agnosticism was logical. Yet Kant was not agnostic about agnosticism! Astonishingly, most of the skeptical philosophers of yesteryear, though brilliant, espoused self-defeating views that were adhered to by the world of their day and even into the modern day. They basically laughed at the idea of knowing God or concluding with finality that God actually exists (though Kant believed He did). Good science, however, and an alert apologist who can detect bad arguments and faulty logic, can at least engage in a discussion about God with confidence.

Four Essential Laws and Principles for Discerning Truth

Sproul, in introducing epistemology, noted four principles and laws that are absolutely essential to any discussion about truth and how we can know it.[29] First, because the *Logos* has always existed—the transcendental embodiment of logic—there is the law

---

[28] Moreland, 1741.
[29] Sproul, 30-69.

of *noncontradiction*. This law essentially says that *A* cannot be both *A* and non-*A* at the same time (cf. 1 John 1:22). In other words, it would be completely illogical to say that my son sitting in front of me is both here and not here at the same time, or that he is both my son and my daughter at the same time. Of course, the law itself contains no content since it tells us nothing about *what* to think, only *how* to think. Aristotle said of the law of noncontradiction that it is "impossible that contrary attributes should belong at the same time to the same subject."[30] This is simple logic, and by providing this definition, Aristotle said logic is a necessary tool for human thinking and communication as well as a means for man to grasp the rational structure of the universe. This is a first principle, for without logic, truly no intelligent conversation can be had.

Anyone can comprehend the basic noncontradiction principle, for it is simple logic. This is actually one of God's gifts to mankind, for without logic, nothing would or could make sense. It is noteworthy that the world we live in *does* make sense, so it is logical that the Creator of the world is logical. This is the first inconsistency of naturalism, for it rejects both God's existence and miracles, yet it can neither account for the origin of the universe without a miraculous cause (nothing times nothing becoming everything), nor can it account for how uniformity arose out of the chaos of the supposed big bang explosion from nothing.

Logic in itself allows science to work, for since science is the study of the physical world through observation and empirical evidence, the truths that are observed say something about the One who created all things. In this sense, science reveals many things about God, for when people engage in inductive reasoning, they not only use the gift of reason God has given them, they place themselves on the road whereby they are able to deduce logical conclusions about God's existence, His essence, and His nature.

The logic of the law of noncontradiction is simple, but it is distinguished from other terms often used synonymously with it, such as *paradox, antinomy* ("against law"), and *mystery*.[31] The Trinity, for instance, asserts that God is one in His essence but

---

[30] Quoted in R.C. Sproul, 30.
[31] Sproul, 44.

three in His person. How God can be one and three at the same time might sound a bit like a contradiction, or antinomy. But knowing that the law of noncontradiction means that *A* cannot be both *A* and *non-A* at the same time, the Trinity is explained by saying that God is one in His *essence* (A) but three in His *person* (B). A contradiction would arise if we said, "God is one in His essence (A) and three in His essence (non-A)." Thus, the Trinity is not contradiction but a *paradox*—a statement that, although true, has the *appearance* of contradiction. Once explained, it is clearly not a contradiction. Although the term *antinomy* in classical philosophy was used synonymously with *contradiction*, in the present day *antinomy* is unfortunately used synonymously with *paradox*. Sproul noted that whereas "contradiction" is a Latin word that is fluid and changes with time, "antinomy" is a Greek word that does the same thing.[32] Regrettably, they have undergone different levels of evolution and have arrived at two different though similar meanings. The Trinity is certainly not a contradiction but a paradox.

Finally, "mystery," is used to describe the inability to probe the depths of a given doctrine or truth.[33] The Trinity, for instance, is a paradox, but even the paradox of the Trinity cannot be fully understood by the finite mind of man. Thus, the Trinity is also a *mystery*. And though man may not fully understand certain mysteries, God understands all of them. As Moses taught, "The secret things belong to the LORD our God, but the things revealed belong to us and to our sons forever, that we may observe all the words of this law" (Deut. 29:29).

Emil Brunner (1889–1966), contrary to all sound logic, suggested that contradictions must be embraced and even glorified because in them lie the very hallmarks of truth.[34] This is of course absurd, for if true, then God's entire account in the Bible of man's sin and eventual redemption mean nothing. If Brunner is correct, then Adam and Eve's sin was justified, for they listened to the serpent and contradicted God's command not to eat from the tree of the Knowledge of Good and Evil (Gen. 3). And if what they did

---

[32] Sproul, 44.
[33] Sproul, 45.
[34] Sproul, 38.

was good and to be glorified, then there would be no need for a Savior like Jesus to save man from his sins. After all, if contradiction is to be glorified, then what need would there be for redemption from contradiction? Yet if Brunner's assessment is true, then it is also false, for all you need to do is contradict that which is glorified, and contradicting that which is glorified is defamation. In short, by using Brunner's logic, the way to fulfill God's truth would be to disobey God. The absurdity of such a belief confounds all sound logic and renders logic illogical while logically attempting to render it illogical.

The truth is, God has endowed His rational creatures, made in His image, with logical reasoning so that we can recognize the coherence of His creation and revelation over against the inherent chaos of any worldview that denies Him. We are hence able to reason with those who do not know Him and explain who God is, what He has done, and how they can have a personal relationship with Him through His Son, Jesus Christ.

The second law Sproul identifies in epistemology is law of *causality*. In the law of causality, every effect has a cause (cf. John 3:2). Hence, the earth, being an effect, had a cause. This is an extension of the law of noncontradiction, and it is absolutely necessary for the acquisition of knowledge. It is a "cosmological proof" used as far back as Aristotle who argued that the existence of a supreme being was necessary simply because all events require a cause, and there needs to be an uncaused cause in order to make sense of the world.[35] This law, however, does not promote that *everything* has a cause. It simply states that every *effect* must have a cause. So, when man seeks to know where God originates, he must be reminded that *God is not an effect*; hence God has no cause. He is eternal.

The law of causality does not communicate information about truth, and it does not prove that causes and effects exist in the world. It shows that if many objects exist in the world and if any of these can be seen as an effect, there is most certainly a cause. Philosopher and skeptic David Hume, however, argued that man's real problem with causal relationships was his inability to determine the precise cause of a particular effect. Hume never

---

[35] Sproul, 39.

denied the law of causality, but he denied that man could actually *know* precise causal relationships. Hence, he rejected the idea that man could conclude with finality that God caused all things or that He existed at all. If Hume had been right, however, then science and the entire outside world itself would no longer be useful since both rely on sense perception to understand causes and effects. Besides, if Hume's ideas were correct, then nothing the biblical authors wrote means anything since they wrote of what they saw, heard, and touched (cf. 1 John 1:1–3).

The third law for understanding anything is the law of *sense perception*. This law concerns the things observable by the five senses (John 1:14; 1 Cor. 15:5–6; 2 Pet. 1:16; 1 John 1:1–3). Although this is merely one avenue for knowledge, some have espoused the twentieth century philosophical idea of *logical positivism*, which says that if something cannot be seen, touched, smelled, heard, or tasted, then it cannot exist or be true. As a result of this self-defeating idea, many have become skeptical about God's existence. But this is unnecessary. Just because something cannot be verified does not mean that it does not exist. Someone would have to be omniscient to conclude with certainty that God does not exist (and that would make them God!). The self-defeating nature of logical positivism is that if the only true statements are those that can be verified empirically, then the principle of verification itself would fail the test because its own premise of "only those statements that can be empirically verified have any meaning" cannot be verified empirically. In other words, logical positivism cannot be verified by its own definition since it is a statement about truth without any merit of truth.

The fourth principle for discovering knowledge is the *analogical use of language*, which points out similarities in two or more things so as to provide an analogy. Since man is made in God's image (Gen. 1:26–27), he is enabled to speak of God in a meaningful way even though God is infinite and man is finite. Man being made in God's image means that man has the ability to reason and communicate.[36] God gave this ability so that man can have fellowship with Him, explain Him, and use His creation to illustrate God and His goodness.

---

[36] Sproul, 30.

With these indisputable laws in mind, given to all by the eternal *Logos*—Jesus Christ—we can actually set out to know something, and if we can know something, then we can delve into whether God exists. Those who attempt to deny whether we can know anything about God are essentially attempting to escape His demands if in fact He does exist. What apologists must understand from all this is that every attack on God tends to involve a rejection of one or more of the four basic necessary principles for human knowledge. Thus, communicating properly with the precise meaning of words is vital when we engage in a discussion about God and a defense of His existence.

In part one of his book *Christian Apologetics*, Norman Geisler lists seven inadequate tests for truth, all of which reveal the self-defeating nature of these tests.[37] First, he deals with *agnosticism*—the belief that God is either unknown or unknowable. The Agnostic does not deny God's existence; he denies the possibility of the knowledge of God.[38] Whereas saying that God is unknown might be characteristic of a well-meaning soul who simply does not know God, to claim that God is *unknowable* is self-defeating. This is because the assertion affirms both to not know and to know at the same time. If a person knows *something* about reality, then he surely cannot affirm in the same breath that *all* reality is unknowable. It is impossible to affirm *that* something is without simultaneously declaring something about *what* it is. Only an omniscient mind could be totally agnostic, and finite men clearly do not possess omniscience.

A second inadequate test for truth is *rationalism*—the practice or principle of basing opinions and actions on reason and knowledge rather than on religious belief or emotional response.[39] A rationalist is one who holds that only what is knowable or demonstrable by human reason is true. Rationalism stresses the inescapability of logic, and it affirms that there must be an *a priori* dimension to knowledge. In other words, the human mind must

---

[37] Norman L. Geisler, *Christian Apologetics* (Grand Rapids: Baker Book House, 1976), 13-127.

[38] Guy P. Duffield and Nathaniel M. Van Cleave, *Foundations of Pentecostal Theology* (Los Angeles, CA: L.I.F.E. Bible College, 1983), 59.

[39] Catherine Soanes and Angus Stevenson, *Concise Oxford English Dictionary*, 11th ed. (Oxford: Oxford University Press, 2004).

possess some innate ability of its own to engage in the pursuit of truth. Rationalists believe that that which is inescapable is real, and those rationalists who hold to the existence of God attempt to prove His existence rationally. But this is wrong for at least three reasons. First, logic cannot prove God's existence, for although it can eliminate what is false, it cannot, in and of itself, establish what must be true. Logic can indeed prove what is *possibly* real, but it cannot prove what is *actually* real.

Second, there are no rationally inescapable arguments for God's existence since it is always logically possible that nothing ever existed, including God. Yes, it is actually undeniable that something exists (like my own existence, which is undeniable), but it is not logically necessary that I exist. A person's nonexistence is logically possible, as well as anything in the world, including God. Thus, if it is not logically necessary that anything exists, then it is not logically necessary to conceive the existence of anything, including God. Third, there is no rationally inescapable way of establishing the first principles of reasoning. They are innate but not given demonstrably. Rationalism is without a necessary rational basis to establish itself. Thus, God's existence cannot be proven with logical necessity. So if Christian theism is to be believed on the basis of proven fact, then another test must confirm it. Rationalism cannot do it.

A third inadequate test for truth is *fideism*—a term applied to a variety of doctrines which hold in common belief in the incapacity of the intellect to attain to knowledge of divine matters and correspondingly put an excessive emphasis on faith.[40] Religious fideism argues that matters of religious faith are not supported by reason, for religion requires faith and not reasonable arguments (cf. Heb. 11:6). Yet in testing truth, we cannot claim truth by simply saying, "This is true because I believe it to be true." A fideist might believe in Christianity rather than Hinduism based on its consistency and way of life. But in doing so, the fideist has imported a rational or pragmatic test for truth to support his belief. He might be fideistic in his *claim,* but he is rational or

---

[40] F. L. Cross and Elizabeth A. Livingstone, *The Oxford Dictionary of the Christian Church*, 3rd ed. rev. (Oxford, New York: Oxford University Press, 2005), 613.

pragmatic in his *test* for truth. As a test for truth, fideism fails since it simply *assumes* God's existence and promotes simple faith in Him without ever attempting to prove His existence. Fideism must make a truth claim for it to be a truth test. But, if a fideist offers a justification for his belief—as indeed the whole argument for fideism would seem to be—then he is no longer a fideist, since he has an argument or justification for holding his belief in fideism.

A fourth failure as a test for truth is *experientialism*—the practice of defending the Christian faith by appealing to Christian experience as evidence for the truth of Christianity.[41] Rather than appeal to external evidences, experientialists appeal to internal feelings to justify their belief in God. An experientialist might say, "I felt a burning in my bosom after I prayed, so I know God exists." Though the burning sensation may be true, though not verifiable, as a test for truth experientialism does not eliminate the possibility of other views also being true. Experience is not self-justifying; it is not even self-interpreting. Experience is what people have, while truth is what is affirmed about these experiences. If the experience is truly unique to one view and unavailable to another, then there is no way to use it as a support for truth for one view over others because it is private to that view.

Furthermore, using an experience to prove something true is circular, for the *basis* of truth rests in the experience but not the *support* of that truth. Even the Bible demonstrates that no experience is self-interpreting. The same phenomenon was interpreted three different ways in John 12:28–29. Some took it as the voice of God, others as an angel speaking, and some as thunder. *That* there was some common phenomenon need not be questioned, but *what* it meant differed in accordance with the overall perspective taken by the perceivers.

A fifth inadequate test for truth is *evidentialism*—the practice of using external evidence to prove that something is true.[42] But for testing a worldview, it is deficient since evidential facts are not self-interpreting. All facts are interpreted by the context in which they appear and ultimately by the worldview in which they appear.

---

[41] Norman L. Geisler, *Baker Encyclopedia of Christian Apologetics*, Baker Reference Library (Grand Rapids, MI: Baker Books, 1999), 235.

[42] Geisler, *Christian Apologetics,* 83.

For example, the resurrection of Jesus from the dead cannot be used to *prove* that God exists, for a person would have to already believe that God exists to interpret the evidence of Christ's resurrection in that manner. In other words, it presupposes that which it attempts to prove; hence, it begs the question. A naturalist, on the other hand, might interpret the resurrection of Jesus as an unusual natural event with no *known* cause. Also, pantheism can explain it as a concentrated manifestation of God who is manifest in everything.

A sixth inadequate test for truth is *pragmatism*—a system of belief based on the principle that every truth has practical consequences, and that these are a test of its truthfulness.[43] In other words, something is believed to be true if it works or if it brings desired results. Yet because it is incapable of eliminating opposing worldviews, it cannot be an adequate test for truth. What works for one individual might not work for another. Pragmatically, theism might work for one person, yet atheism works for another. Yet both cannot be true because they are mutually exclusive ways of viewing ultimate reality. Further, how can someone know which system works best for most people in the long run? Some things work very well but are not right. For example, if a student cheats on a test and does not get caught, then their plan seemingly worked! That student might go on to write articles and books on how cheating is the way to succeed. But cheating is only a short-term solution for a passing grade that will not work over the long term. In contrast to cheating, honesty may not work so well in the short term, but it is a good bet in the long term (especially if you believe that God exists!).

A final inadequate test for truth is *combinationalism*—the practice of combining two or more philosophies, like the previous inadequate tests, in order to discern truth. It is simply a combination of all inadequate tests for truth in an effort to plug the holes found in each inadequate test. But if rationalism alone or pragmatism alone or experientialism alone will not suffice, how is combining their inadequacies going to suffice? Unless there is some way to correct the inadequacy of one test for truth by another, adding tests will not provide an ample test for truth. At

---

[43] Cross and Livingstone, 1323.

best, combining inadequate tests to determine truth can only test whether something is false. Thus, combinationalism is inadequate for testing the truth of a worldview.

Can Truth Be Known?

Geisler concluded part one of his book by saying that although finding an adequate test for truth is difficult, *it is possible*. First, a worldview can be proven false if it is unverifiable. Some statements are directly unverifiable while others are indirectly so. An example of a directly unverifiable statement would be something like, "I am unable to express myself with words." Note that it is self-defeating because it uses words to express itself. An example of the indirect kind would be something like, "I have concluded that I know everything unthinkingly." Although the *act* of thinking this conclusion is not self-defeating, the *process* of "drawing" that conclusion was a thinking process, which is at odds with the statement that all knowledge is possessed unthinkingly without inference or conjecture.

The second test for being able to know truth is undeniability. Geisler notes two kinds of undeniable truths: *existential* (relating to existence or reality) and *theoretical* or *definitional* (relating to possible realities). *Definitional undeniability* is when something is true by definition, like a triangle, for by definition, a triangle must have three sides. The affirmation "triangles must have three sides" is undeniably true. But this does not mean that there is in fact any such thing as a triangle. It means only that *if* there were a triangle, it would have three sides. Likewise, someone might claim that *if* there is a God, He must be a necessary Being. This would not necessarily mean that God exists, but that if He does exist, then He could not have come into being or cease to be but must necessarily always be.[44] *Existential undeniability* speaks of existence, for if I truly exist, then it is actually undeniable, for I must exist in order to make the denial. Things that do not exist do not attempt to fight for or against their existence. So when I attempt to deny my existence, it becomes a certainty that I exist by simply questioning

---

[44] Geisler, *Christian Apologetics*, 144.

it. Therefore, something is actually undeniable, namely, my own existence.

The rationalist uses this argument to support rationalism, but since *rationalism does not show logical necessity* but only actual undeniability, the rationalist has left purely rational ground for existential ground when he does this.[45] My nonexistence is logically possible; it is not inconceivable that I do not exist. No logical necessity is grounding my existence. Even if I cannot affirm that I do not exist, I can nonetheless meaningfully think that I might not exist. Of course, I must exist in order to conceive of my nonexistence. But the "must exist" does not mean "*logically* must," only "*actually* must." Unless I actually exist, I cannot conceive of anything, for there is no "I" or "me" there at all. But this does not mean that my existence is based on logical necessity.

We can conclude at this stage that if one view is undeniable, then conversely, the opposing views must be at least untrue, if not unverifiable. And if any view can be found to be unverifiable, then it is by default untrue. Supposing this to be the case when judging *between* worldviews, it must now be determined what is true *within* a given worldview. It is here that combinationalism seems to be the most adequate test for truth for several reasons, not the least of which is that it is difficult to find undeniability in historical and experiential matters.[46]

Once an overall framework has been determined, it follows that whatever most consistently and comprehensively fits into that system is true. If that system of truth is not only a worldview but a world and *life* view, then the applicability of that truth to life also becomes a crucial aspect of that truth. Furthermore, once a consistent worldview of truth can be ascertained, then any and all tests, such as rationalism, evidentialism, etc., can and must be used as tests for truth within that system. For instance, if the world we live in is in fact a theistic universe, and a person refuses to accept the possibility of an empirical event indicating a miracle, they are inconsistent.

Further, if this is a theistic universe and they fail to consider *all the facts,* then they might be led to accept Judaism rather than

---

[45] Geisler, 144.
[46] Geisler, *Christian Apologetics*, 145.

Christianity since Christianity considers Jesus' resurrection as a historical fact pointing to Him being the Messiah. Judaism does not do this. In sum, no facts can be left out of any system when attempting to show that the system is consistent with itself and comprehensive.

In looking for systematic consistency in a test for truth, therefore, we discover that the finite mind of man can neither know all facts nor comprehend all the relationships between all facts. What guides us is probability, that is, whichever view best fits and is most consistent and comprehensive. Good science, which is what filtering bad tests of truth is, and an alert apologist can prove that it is indeed possible to know vital truths about all things, including God. It begins with the God-given gift of logic whereby man reasons with his mind in a logical way. And this is what every rational person brings to the table when they begin to argue for what they believe.

Chapter 3

THE TRANSCENDENTAL ARGUMENT FOR GOD'S EXISTENCE

Everyone has presupposed, *a priori*, ideas that shape their thinking and their argumentation. These grow out of our worldview. We inherit them from our parents, our church, our friends, and our society. Every person has them, but not all agree which of these presupposed ideas are actually true; hence, there is seemingly no end to the various worldviews we espouse. Even if someone were to claim not to have a worldview, *that* would be their worldview!

A worldview works like a pair of glasses, for it interprets the world we see like a pair of glasses brings words into focus. Essentially, however, basic worldviews can be narrowed down to a minimum based on our ideas of God. Some do not believe in God or gods (atheists), others think that God's existence cannot be proven outright (agnostics), some believe in a multiplicity of gods (pantheists), and others believe with full certainty that there is one true God, Jesus Christ. Each of us will view the world in which we live through the lenses of our faith, for how we view the world along with the things in it depends entirely on our worldview. This worldview is what we *presuppose* to be true when we attempt to discuss or argue about anything.

The *transcendental argument* for the existence of God is the designation for an argument about a worldview, which essentially lies at the outset of all arguments. It guides our arguments since it assumes certain truths to be true without having experienced those truths. Everyone assumes some truth without having experienced it. Many of these assumptions are questionable, but there are some assumptions that no one questions. Among these are the basic laws of logic and mathematics, for who would ever agree to a debate or discussion by first throwing out the laws of logic? No one would agree to disallow the law of noncontradiction. Equally, who would ever try to persuade someone that two plus two does not equal four? These presuppositions are common to all those who seek to reason in a logical manner.

Is Logic Arbitrary?

Logic has three basic laws: identity, noncontradiction, and the excluded middle. Identity means that if a statement is true, then it is true. Noncontradiction means that if a statement is true, then it cannot at the same time be false. And the excluded middle means that a statement is either true or false.

Of the many laws known to man—moral, natural, mathematical, legal, and logical—some laws declare how things *should* be. For instance, while moral and legal laws concern "shoulds," natural laws describe *what actually is*. They assert actuality under certain natural conditions. Logic has a "should" element to it, for it would be illogical to charge $25 for a steak dinner and accept $3 for payment. A person would not act immorally in doing so, but they would act illogically. As David Clark said:

> Human logic is patterned after reality. The Creator built logic into the structures of the physical and spiritual worlds. The principles of logic reflect a deep reasonableness that characterizes both God and God's creation. Because the logic of human thought and speech is grounded in God and God's work, logic is not arbitrary.[47]

---

[47] David K. Clark, "Is Logic Arbitrary?" *The Apologetics Study Bible: Real Questions, Straight Answers, Stronger Faith,* ed. Ted Cabal, Chad Owen Brand, E. Ray Clendenen, et al. (Nashville, TN: Holman Bible Publishers, 2007), 930-31.

God and Logic

It is my presupposition that we must begin with logic. We cannot say that we believe in bachelors who are married or circles that have four sides, and we cannot speak in such a way that we say "have circles married eating study argument." That would be absurd gibberish. Thus, my presupposition in this paper is that our playing field is the field of logic, for this seems logical. But since I believe that any and all other worldviews will agree that this is where we start, this is the presupposition from where we begin.

Since I am a Christian, I do not believe that logic is God, but I do believe that God is the embodiment of logic (cf. John 1:1–5, 14). God does not bow to logic, but all statements about Him are obedient to logic whether the discipline involves theology, science, morality, or anything else except gibberish. Although logic is subject to God, God Himself is in one way subject to logic. This is not because God is less than logic, but because the laws of logic are part of God's essence, representing the principles of rational thought, and since God is a rational Being, God must be subject to His own laws. For Him to act contrary to them would be for God to be less than God; hence, He would not be God. One example highlighted in Scripture is that "it is impossible for God to lie" (Heb. 6:18). Therefore, God cannot contradict Himself. If He could, He would expose Himself as not God.

For a Christian, it would be impossible to begin a thought or conversation about God without presupposing the law of noncontradiction, although we may not always realize this is what we are doing. But in doing so, we conceive of logic as being prior to God in that we must use it to think about God in a rational way. It is here that the transcendental argument begins to take shape, for in the very presupposition of logic, God is already assumed to be a reality. As Geisler said, "Logic is prior to God in the *order of knowing,* but God is prior to logic in the *order of being.* Logic is prior to God *epistemologically,* but God is prior to logic *ontologically.*[48]

---

[48] Geisler, *Baker Encyclopedia of Christian Apologetics,* 428.

Bible-believing Christians know that our logic is based on God's logic simply because we are made in His image (Gen. 1:26–27). This is the avenue through which man can think about God, converse with God, understand God, and be saved by God. All of God's communication to man, the pinnacle of His creation in the Bible, is done through logical means and in ways that man can understand God. Hence, man is able to express himself. Theologians can logically express God's thoughts to their listeners from God's creation and from the Scriptures—both of which are logically put together.

Likewise, apologists can make logical claims about God cosmologically, telelogically, ontologically, etc. while other worldviews can do the same. What the transcendental argument attempts to show is that only Christians can account for their ability to reason and use the laws of logic. All other worldviews, though they too adhere to the laws of logic, have no basis for explaining them. For instance, whereas a rationalist attempts to *determine* all truth by human reason, a Christian uses reason to *discover* eternal truths that God has revealed both in His creation and through His words. J. Budziszewski points out, "The motto 'Reason Alone!' is nonsense anyway. Reason itself presupposes faith. Why? Because a defense of reason *by* reason is circular, therefore worthless. Our only guarantee that human reason works is God who made it."[49]

Some have denied that the laws of logic are uniform, that they pertain to each society equally. Yet this is preposterous. Certainly there are many cultural differences, for instance, between the east and the west. But the fact that no philosopher at either end of the spectrum could speak without assuming the law of noncontradiction points to the laws of logic being uniform. Furthermore, the mere denial of the laws of logic with an attempt to explain them away proves that the laws are universal, for you would have to use logic to attempt to explain it away logically!

---

[49] J. Budziszewski, *Written on the Heart: The Case for Natural Law* (Downers Grove: InterVarsity Press, 1997), 54. Quoted in Norman L. Geisler and Frank Turek, *I Don't Have Enough Faith to Be an Atheist* (Wheaton, IL: Crossway Books, 2004), 130.

Some have attempted to trap God in His own attributes, claiming that although the Bible claims God is omnipotent, in reality there are many things He cannot do. They therefore see a contradiction in God's character. For instance, the Bible does say that "nothing is impossible for God" (Matt. 19:26), and an omnipotent being by definition can do all things. With this in mind, one might wonder whether God could create a rock so heavy that even He cannot lift it. But though this may seem like a clever question, it is based on the skeptic's misunderstanding of God's nature. For when the Bible says that nothing is impossible with God, it means that what is impossible for man is not impossible for God.

However, there are indeed things that God cannot do. God cannot violate the laws of logic; He cannot contradict Himself. If He did, He would not be God. For instance, it is impossible for God, who is eternal, to die or cease to be, for that which is eternal can never cease to be. Likewise, God cannot create a square circle or create a bachelor who is married. These ideas are absurd, and if God could do them, He would violate His rational nature. Morally speaking, God cannot lie (Heb. 6:18; cf. 2 Tim. 2:13), for that would violate His character. Thus, God can neither violate His moral character nor His rational nature. As the omnipotent Being, God is capable of doing only that which is noncontradictory to His nature.

Naturalists have posed the question that if God cannot violate the laws of logic, then why does He violate natural laws through miracles? After all, God raised Jesus from the dead, granted sight to the blind, healed the sick, and parted the sea. All these miracles violate natural laws. So why does God not violate the laws of logic when He has a reputation for violating the laws of physics? The problem is that this is an invalid analogy. Geisler said:

> Laws of nature are *descriptive,* whereas logical laws, like ethical laws, are *prescriptive.* That is, laws of logic tell us how we ought to reason in order to conform our thought to how things really are. Like moral laws, they are universal prescriptions. Everyone should reason that if all triangles have three sides and this figure is a triangle, then it has three sides. There are no exceptions; everyone

should come to this conclusion. Laws of physics are descriptive generalizations. They merely inform us about the way things are; they do not exhort us about how something ought to be. As descriptions of the way things usually occur, they admit of exceptions. A miracle is an exception. As such it does not contradict the general law. The comparison between physical laws and laws of thought is invalid. Further, God did not create laws of logic. They simply manifest His uncreated nature. God is rational, and there are certain basic principles of rationality that cannot change any more than God can change his own essential nature. The laws of physics are not so. Presumably, God could have created other kinds of worlds, with other kinds of laws. The law of gravity, for example, applies in a material universe. It does not apply to angels with no physical bodies.[50]

It seems impossible that logical absolutes do not exist, for to argue against their existence is to use logic against itself and form a logical conclusion, and that would be absurd. Logical absolutes are abstract by nature and are independent of time, space, and physical realities since they were not made from the physical properties of the universe. In fact, if the universe itself were to disappear, the laws of logic would still exist. And two plus two would still equal four. These laws exist regardless of whether the human mind exists, for the mind merely *recognizes* that they exist. This means that logical absolutes exist on their own and are not sustained by any other reality.

This being the case, is it not logical that an absolute transcendent Mind is authoring logical absolutes? After all, how could logical absolutes exist in a world created by chance or accident? Is it logical to believe that the uniform nature of the universe, our ability to study it given its uniformity, and the order of the universe has a Designer who is Himself/itself logical? Certainly Christians believe this is so, and they believe this Designer is God, for no other explanation trumps the God explanation.

---

[50] Geisler, *Baker Encyclopedia of Christian Apologetics,* 429.

The laws of logic are laws, and logically speaking, all laws require a lawgiver. In essence, there are only two options: God exists, or no God exists. Yet for the theist, the Bible is clear that God is the embodiment of logic. This means that the atheistic naturalist, who also believes in the laws of logic, is *borrowing* from the Christian's worldview to make his logical argument against God. After all, the naturalist cannot account for the laws of logic with his worldview. His worldview of nothing creating everything and of an explosion that transformed itself from chaos into order cannot account for the laws of logic, physics, and morality.

The Transcendental Argument

Transcendentalism is the philosophical idea that divinity pervades all nature and humanity, and according to Immanuel Kant, it is based on the idea that in order to understand the nature of reality, you must first analyze the reasoning process that governs the nature of experience.[51] The transcendental nature of the argument for Christian theism is that it argues for God's existence without having experienced that which it seeks to argue for or against, because it assumes that the reasoning process, given by God, governs all reasoning processes. In other words, the transcendental argument assumes at the outset of the argument that God exists. The apologists who have espoused this (e.g., Cornelius Van Til, Greg Bahnsen, John Frame, and Jason Lisle) contend that without God, no argument could be made for or against Him. Therefore, we must begin with the assumption that God exists. This may seem like circular logic, for if the conclusion is that God exists, then the premise that He exists begs the question.

The transcendental argument can be illustrated with the issue of air. If I argue that air does not exist, then I would have to breathe in air to be able to make that argument. Furthermore, in order to be heard, my voice would have to travel through the very substance I claim does not exist, namely air. Cornelius Van Til

---

[51] Catherine Soanes and Angus Stevenson, *Concise Oxford English Dictionary*, 11th ed. (Oxford: Oxford University Press, 2004).

used a different illustration of this principle by telling of a time when he witnessed a young girl sitting on her father's lap slap her father in the face. His observation of that event was that the girl had to be sitting in her father's lap to have the capability to slap him. In the same way, the atheist must exist in God's world and assume His existence in order to attempt to disprove His existence.

Van Til called the transcendental argument "reasoning by presupposition."[52] He said that the argument attempts to show the conditions that make anything what it is, particularly the conditions or presuppositions necessary for rational thought. Van Til was convinced that the Christian God is not merely another fact to be discovered in the midst of other facts, but that God is the fact from whom all other facts derive their meaning and intelligibility. He sought to be "indirect rather than direct,"[53] as a *reductio ad absurdum* of the non-Christian's position. In this, he sought to show that the alternatives to Christian theism destroy all meaning and intelligibility.

Van Til believed that "...all reasoning is, in the nature of the case, *circular reasoning*. The starting point, the method, and the conclusion are always involved in one another."[54] So, no matter how harshly the atheist treats the Christian for using circular logic, the depravity of all unbelievers causes them to suppress the truth about God (cf. Rom. 1:18–32; 2 Cor. 4:4), for they themselves are governed by their own presupposition of unbelief, which governs their conclusions. Because of this conundrum, Van Til recommended that "The Christian apologist must place himself upon the position of his opponent, assuming the correctness of his method merely for argument's sake, in order to show him that on such a position the 'facts' are not facts and the 'laws' are not laws. He must also ask the non-Christian to place himself upon the Christian position for argument's sake in order that he may be shown that only upon such a basis do 'facts' and 'laws' appear intelligible."[55]

---

[52] C. Van Til, *The Defense of the Faith* (Philadelphia, PA, 1955, third edition, 1967), 99.

[53] Van Til, 100.

[54] Van Til, 101.

[55] Van Til, 100-101.

The Bible teaches that those who know Christ as Lord and Savior come to know Him only by the grace of God, who not only foreknew them before the foundation of the world (Rom. 8:29; Eph. 1:4; Rev. 13:8; 17:8), but who also predestined them to eternal life (Rom. 8:29; Eph. 1:5) after effectually calling them to salvation (Rom. 8:30). God the Father draws all of His elect children to His Son, Jesus Christ (John 6:44, 65), for all whom He appointed to salvation will believe (Acts 13:48). Salvation is a supernatural phenomenon given by God to those whom He chooses. Jesus Himself reveals the Father to those whom the Father draws to Him (John 6:44; cf. Matt. 11:25–27; John 1:18). And those who have been transformed by the saving power of Christ are enabled to know God's mysteries through the Holy Spirit, who gives God's children "the mind of Christ" (1 Cor. 2:9–16; cf. 2 Tim. 3:16).

When someone comes to faith in Christ, they can know for a fact that they are saved and have assurance of eternal life (1 John 5:7), recognizing that Christ holds all things together (Col. 1:17) and in Him "are hid all the treasures of wisdom and knowledge" (Col. 2:3). They know this because "the fear of the Lord is the beginning of knowledge" (Prov. 1:7) and "the beginning of wisdom" (Psalm 111:10; Prov. 9:10). Therefore, a true Christian cannot begin any argument, discussion, or debate except with the existence of God. To begin elsewhere is to become a fool (cf. Prov. 26:4–5), for to suppose the contrary is to willfully suppress the truth. Only by trusting God's Word can we come to a saving knowledge of Christ (John 5:24; 8:31; 15:3, Rom. 10:17). And since God's Word is the foundation of all human knowledge (cf. Deut. 18:18–19; 1 Cor. 14:37; Col. 2:2–4; 2 Tim. 3:16–17; 2 Pet. 1:19–21), our apologetics must presuppose the truths of God's Word.

The way out of this conundrum, so as to not appear circular in logic, is to trust in God while using everything God has provided to persuade the non-Christian that the biblical presuppositions are true. We must not announce that we are quoting Scripture in order to prove Scripture, for that is blatantly circular. In other words, we cannot come out and say, "The Bible is God's Word because it says so, and I believe it." What is far more convincing is, "The Bible is God's Word because the prophecies were fulfilled hundreds of years after they were given, because the miracles were witnessed by numerous people at one time, because archaeology supports the Bible's claims through archaeological digs, and because nothing in Scripture has ever been proven wrong." This broad way of asserting the Bible's truth presents more data to unbelievers and challenges them to consider it seriously.

By measuring the worldviews of those who discuss the existence of God, those who argue transcendentally debate which argument determines whose reasonings are most consistent with their worldview. In other words, it asks, "What presuppositions are necessary to make anything provable?" In the transcendental argument, you would argue that a debate is impossible without God. For God must exist, having created man in His own image, in order for man to be able to argue God's existence in plain, logical language. No other presupposition can account for the fact that logic exists and that man can use it to debate whether God exists. After all, logic is not part of the natural world. Logic is intangible and cannot account for itself coming out of an evolutionary world that exploded from nothing, came together by accident, created complex life from nothing by chance, and established order from chaos, with the laws of logic settling over the previously chaotic world (not to mention laws of physics, aesthetics, mathematics, and morality).

What the transcendental argument seeks to show is that this worldview, the naturalist worldview of the atheist, is absurd in that although it attempts to make sense of the created world, it fails miserably since it cannot explain why matters of science, morality, and logic exist. The only thing the atheistic worldview can account for is the material world, and most atheists claim to be materialists (aka, naturalists). As such, atheists cannot account for abstract or universal laws. Furthermore, the laws of logic must be excluded from the atheist's worldview because they are not material. Yet if we cannot account for the laws of logic, then why would we enter a debate where the foundation of a discussion must be logical? Why would an atheist demand a logical and intellectual debate when his worldview cannot even account for the laws of logic? Yet we cannot have a meaningful debate and throw out the laws of logic. If we did, our debate would sound like gibberish since nothing would need to make sense.

But this is the crux of the matter, for the Christian worldview can account for logic while the atheist's worldview cannot. The worldview of the Christian is therefore consistent with itself while the worldview of the naturalist is not. To be sure, the atheist *does* believe in the laws of logic. He is just unable to account for why those laws exist. Therefore when an atheist comes to a debate, he loses the debate by simply showing up, for by showing up, the atheist has to borrow from the Christian's worldview in order to make an argument!

The Great Debate

The debate in 1985 at the University of California, Irvine, between Dr. Gordon Stein, an atheist, and Dr. Greg Bahnsen, a Christian theist who used the transcendental argument for God's existence, was dubbed "the Great Debate." In that debate, Dr. Stein said, "The use of logic or reason is the only valid way to examine the truth or falsity of the statement which claims to be factual." Of course this is true, but how would Dr. Stein prove that logic or reason is the only way to prove factual statements? After Stein asserted this truth, Bahnsen observed that Stein "is now on the horns of a real epistemological dilemma. If he says that the statement is proven by logic or reason, then he's engaging in circular reasoning, and he's begging the question, which he staunchly forbids. If he says that the statement is proven in some other fashion, then he refutes the statement itself that logic or reason is the only way to prove things."

In his book *The Ultimate Proof of Creation*, Jason Lisle, using a phrase from Bahnsen, stated that Christianity is the only worldview that can account for "the preconditions of intelligibility" (the reliability of our memory and of our senses) in order to make any argument at all.[56] What this means is that in order to make sense of anything, atheists and theists alike must *assume* things like the laws of logic and the uniformity of nature. The uniformity of nature means that things behave in a predictable pattern with some regularity in time and space. In other words, we

---

[56] Lisle, 45.

can wake up each day with great confidence that the sun will rise, the laws of gravity still work, etc.

Of course, atheists and Christians alike understand these truths, but only the Christian worldview gives a clear reason for believing in the uniformity of nature and laws of science: *God has said that He will continue to govern and sustain the created order by His word until the end of time* (Gen. 8:22). Christians have a basis for believing that the future will be like the past and therefore have a basis for scientific research, which observes phenomena that behave according to a certain pattern. But no such confidence can exist in the atheistic worldview, for although they too can make predictions for the future based on the past, they cannot account for why that is.

Although Dr. Stein prided himself on showing how circular Christian proofs are for God's existence, he exposed his own willingness to use circular reasoning when he demanded from Bahnsen some evidence for God's existence. Bahnsen spoke kindly of the evidence of the created order itself that testifies to God's wisdom, power, plan, and glory. He spoke of the testimony of the solar system, the persuasion of the sea, and the amazing intricacies of the human body. He spoke of the evidence of history in how God delivered the Israelites from Egyptian bondage, the miracles at Passover night and the Red Sea, the visions of Isaiah, the Shekinah glory in the temple, the virgin birth of Jesus, His miracles, and His resurrection from the dead. Bahnsen also spoke of the evidence of special revelation, the wonder of the Bible as God's Word, unsurpassed in its coherence over time, its historical accuracy, and its life-renewing power. He concluded by saying, "There is no shortage of empirical indicators or evidences of God's existence from the thousands of stars of the heavens to the 500 witnesses of Christ's resurrection."

Dr. Stein, however, would have no part of Bahnsen's proof for God. Why? Because as a naturalist, his worldview precludes the very possibility of any of this empirical evidence counting as proof of God's existence. The religion of a naturalist begins with the presupposition that supernatural explanations are not valid in science. So whereas Stein was renowned for ridiculing Christians for explaining their worldview with the presupposition that miracles are possible (circular reasoning), he was guilty of the same circular reasoning (i.e., begging the question) given that he began his argument with the idea of such miracles being impossible. In advance, Dr. Stein was committed to disallowing any theistic interpretation of nature, history, or experience, which is just as much begging the question on his own part as it is on the part of the theist who appeals to such evidence. Bahnsen concluded that Stein "did not prove at all by empirical observation and logic his precommitment to naturalism. Rather, he assumed it in advance, accepting and rejecting all further factual claims and terms of that controlling and unproven assumption."

It might seem at this point that atheists and Christians are at a hopeless standstill in debating their worldviews. But that is not the case. Bahnsen suggested "that we can prove the existence of God from the impossibility of the contrary."[57] This is what the transcendental argument exposes about atheism, for it demonstrates that without God's existence, nothing can be proven. Van Til stated it this way:

> We must point out that [non-theistic] reasoning itself leads to self-contradiction, not only from a theistic point of view, but from a non-theistic point of view as well... It is this that we ought to mean when we say that we reason from the impossibility of the contrary. The contrary is impossible only if it is self-contradictory when operating on the basis of its own assumptions.[58]

The foolishness of atheism is seen in its inability to consistently provide a foundation for man's intelligence, or what Bahnsen called in the debate the "preconditions of intelligible experience." What's worse, the atheistic worldview cannot account for logic, morality, or science (which observes repeated occurrences of some law like gravity, laws of physics, etc.). Therefore, the impossibility of the contrary of a world that believes in God is just that—an impossible world.

---

[57] Greg Bahnsen, "The Crucial Concept of Self-Deception in Presuppositional Apologetics," *Westminster Theological Journal* 57, no. 1 (1995), 3.

[58] Cornelius Van Til, *A Survey of Christian Epistemology* (Philadelphia: Presbyterian and Reformed, 1969), 204.

The presuppositional approach to apologetics, the transcendental argument, has at least two advantages. First, it is scriptural in that it attempts to use Scripture while trying to lead someone who has suppressed the truth back to the truth. Second, it attempts to use Scripture to convince unbelievers that God's revelation of Himself is true and that by believing it, their worldview is not only consistent with their behavior, it is also life-changing and meaningful.

The Problem of Atheism in Light of the Transcendental Argument

As previously stated, it is not that atheists do not believe in the laws of logic and their universal applications; rather, they simply do know why they are able to do so. In order to escape the ultimate implications of this fact, namely that there is a God who imposes His universal standards of logic and reason, the atheist tries to maintain that these are merely "principles" or matters of general agreement among men. Yet, as Bahnsen stated in the debate with Stein, if the laws of logic could be reduced to mere principles, then it would be impossible to have any kind of rational discussion since either side of the debate could demand their own principles at any point during the discussion. One side would demand his principle of truth and the other side his own principle of truth—both of which would negate the other side of the discussion.

By denying God's existence, atheists undermine man's ability to reason, for by denying God, they deny the very foundation on which logic stands. Then they attempt to use logic to question the God who embodies logic. In essence, the atheist actually steals the laws of logic from the God who embodies them in order to disprove God. This is akin to breathing in the air in order to make an argument that air does not exist.

Atheism pretends to be a freethinking neutral way of looking at the world. Thus, it precommits itself to the idea of *naturalism*, namely that the physical world is all there is. There is nothing beyond it, there is no explanation for it, and it is not heading in some purposeful direction since there is no purpose for life. How could there be? There is no God, and the cosmos is all there is. Since the cosmos is not God, it has no plan or purpose for its inhabitants. But naturalists typically view themselves as being more than simply atheists or skeptics. In the words of one of their own, they are happy just to be full-fledged participants in the natural order and to play by nature's rules.[59]

Thus, they arbitrarily forbid any supernatural explanation for nature, history, personal experience, or the world itself, believing that none of these things are scientific or reasonable. In truth, naturalism is a purposeless belief system where all things began to exist with no purpose from absolutely nothing after nothing exploded with a big bang, creating all things in the known universe, and is gradually and randomly spreading thinner and thinner into nothingness again.

With this in mind, it is remarkable how active so many naturalists and atheists are in attempting to convince the world that there is no God. What purpose are they trying to serve? After all, if there is no Creator, and all things happened by accident, then there can be no purpose for life. Yet if there is no purpose for life, why do some atheists like Richard Dawkins make it their life's purpose to travel around the world and convince the world that there is no God? Why do they care? Furthermore, what exactly do they think is so appealing about their purposeless life of naturalism-atheism? There is no good news in atheism like there is in Christianity. Could it be they just want to create a world where everyone is as purposeless as they are?

In sum, the transcendental argument for the existence of God proves that Christian theism is consistent with itself while exposing all other worldviews that either discount God's existence or espouse many gods as hypocrisy. Thus, the transcendental argument for God's existence is a valid argument because:

1. Christian theism can account for the laws of logic because it holds that God exists and embodies logical thinking. Hence, it is consistent with itself. Naturalism, however, cannot account for the laws of

---

[59] Naturalism.Org. "Worldview Naturalism in a Nutshell," www.naturalism.org (accessed June 12, 2012).

logic. A naturalist-atheist certainly believes in the laws of logic, but he cannot account for those laws since they are immaterial, and in his world there is only material. Scientifically speaking, logic cannot evolve out of a world that was created by natural causes and through chance.

2. Laws of morality, though shared by both Christians and atheists, can only be accounted for if there is a God; hence, they are consistent only with Christian theism. Whereas a Christian knows why he obeys the law and strives to be good, an atheist simply cannot account for why he believes in right and wrong. In his atheistic world, there can be no right and wrong because morality does not evolve out of naturalistic beginnings. And since morality is also nonmaterialistic, it does not fit in the naturalistic world.

3. The Christian worldview can account for man having a purpose. In Christianity, God is to be glorified in all things, and it is the Christian's purpose to bring glory to God through obedience to Him. Hence, Christians preach morals and ethics that are clearly taught in the Bible, and it is their purpose to glorify God by bringing the good news to those who do not believe. For the atheist, however, there is no purpose to life since it came about by random chance. Yet atheists strive to be wealthy and healthy, they strive to be fulfilled, and some even make it their life's goal to convince everyone that there probably is no God. But why? If life has no purpose and all we do is rot in the ground after death, why have a purpose to do anything? Having a purpose is good, but it is consistent only in the worldview of Christian theism.

We must not make the mistake of accusing those who have naturalistic/atheistic worldviews of being unable to prove things. On the contrary, atheists are largely intelligent people who can prove many things, but their ability to prove anything at all is based on their ability to borrow from the Christian worldview, which begins with God's existence as the embodiment of logic and truth. In this, they show that they really do believe in God, although they are too spiritually blind to understand what they are actually doing. They are rebels against God who have willfully exchanged the truth of God for a lie (cf. Rom. 1:18–21). This is why they are fools, for only a fool would set out to disprove that which he knows to be true.

Chapter 4

THE COSMOLOGICAL ARGUMENT FOR GOD'S EXISTENCE

Existence seems pretty simple to understand, although philosophers have traditionally made it quite difficult at times as we will see in Descartes' ontological argument. But once a person figures out that they do indeed exist, or that anything exists at all, they might start to wonder *how* anything exists or even *why* anything exists. Possibly one of the most foundational questions in all philosophy is, "Why does something exist instead of nothing?" But before we look at *why*, the question of *how* must be addressed—how did the universe come into being? Of course naturalists believe it all occurred *naturally*, but although this is what they espouse, even their own scientists realize how absurd this is. Consider David Darling's thoughts on this issue:

> What is a big deal—the biggest deal of all—is how you get something out of nothing... Don't let the cosmologists try to kid you on this one. They have not got a clue either—despite the fact that they are doing a pretty good job of convincing themselves and others that this is really not a problem. 'In the beginning,' they will say, 'there was nothing—no time, no space, matter or energy. Then there was a quantum fluctuation from which...' Whoa! Stop right there. You see what I mean? First there is nothing, then there is something. And the cosmologists try to bridge the two with a quantum flutter, a tremor of

uncertainty that sparks it all off. Then they are away and before you know it, they have pulled a hundred billion galaxies out of their quantum hats.[60]

For the Bible-believing Christian, the answer is simple: God created it (Gen. 1:1). But this will not settle discussions with those, like Darling, who do not believe in the Bible as God's Word but have exchanged the truth of God for a lie. So, for the Christians who appreciate good science alongside our faith, there are answers we can give to those who ask us about the hope we have in Christ (cf. 1 Peter 3:15–16).

The Great S-U-R-G-E

Although the big bang theory is popular among secular scientists as well as Christians, it is not without its problems.[61] But for the sake of argument, we will assume it has enough validity to work with as a starting point for the discussion. In their book *I Don't Have Enough Faith to Be An Atheist*, Norman Geisler and Frank Turek use the big bang as a five-point acronym for discovering truth: "In the beginning, there was a great S-U-R-G-E."[62] Each letter represents a scientific argument for discovering truth over and against *relativism*—the doctrine that espouses that nothing is absolute—not knowledge, not truth, and not morality. All of these are said to exist in relation to societal norms and historical context. These scientific certainties, however, will guide the thinking of anyone seeking to discover truth.

1. Second law of thermodynamics. This is the study of matter and energy, and because it states that the universe is running out of usable energy, it will one

---

[60] David Darling, "On Creating Something Out of Nothing," *New Scientist*, vol. 151 (September 14, 1996). Quoted in Henry M. Morris, *Their Words Against Them* (San Diego: Institute for Creation Research, 1997), 25.

[61] Meta Research, "The Top 30 Problems with the Big Bang," http://metaresearch.org/cosmology/BB-top-30.asp (accessed June 15, 2012).

[62] Norman L. Geisler and Frank Turek, *I Don't Have Enough Faith to Be an Atheist* (Wheaton, IL: Crossway Books, 2004), 76-84.

day die. The law, however, cannot work if the universe is eternal as some, like astronomer Carl Sagan, have proposed.[63] But if it can be demonstrated that the universe is not eternal, then it must have had a beginning.

2. Universe is expanding. If we could watch an old reel-to-reel tape recording of the history of the universe in reverse, we would see all matter in the universe collapse back to a single point—a point mathematically and logically that is actually nothing. Note, however, that the universe is not expanding into empty space, but space itself is expanding, for there was no space before the big bang when there was nothing. It is also vital to realize that the universe did not emerge from existing material but from *nothing*, for there was no matter before the big bang, and if there was, it would have to be accounted for. In fact, chronologically, there was no "before" the big bang because there are no "befores" without time, and there was no time until the big bang. All came into existence at the big bang. Therefore the universe had a beginning.

3. Radiation from the big bang is the afterglow of light and heat from the initial big bang. Though no longer visible due to its wavelength being stretched by the expanding universe to wavelengths slightly shorter than those produced by a microwave oven, its heat is detectable. Therefore, it looks as if the universe had a beginning.

4. Great galaxy seeds. The slight variations in the temperature of the cosmic background radiation. These temperature ripples enabled matter to congregate by gravitational attraction into galaxies. The ripples found show that the explosion and expansion of the universe was precisely tweaked to cause just enough matter to congregate to allow galaxy formation, but not enough to cause the

---

[63]Carl Sagan, *Cosmos* (New York: Random House, 1980), 4.

universe to collapse back on itself. Any slight variation one way or the other, and none of us would be here to tell about it.

5. Einstein's theory of general relativity is the theory that demands an absolute beginning for time, space, and matter. It shows that all three are correlative in that they are interdependent, which means that one cannot exist without the others.

In lieu of these five points, there are three possible explanations for the universe: 1) It is eternal and has always existed; therefore, it needs no creator; 2) It created itself; 3) It was created by something or someone outside of itself.

Is the Universe Eternal?

The late American astronomer Carl Sagan (1934–1996) said, "The cosmos is all that is or ever was or ever will be."[64] This is an interesting statement from an intelligent scientist who observes phenomena in order that he might draw scientific conclusions. The question is, did Sagan observe so much that he was able to conclude that the universe itself is eternal and thus never had a beginning? Aristotle was also an intelligent man, but his conclusions were very different from Sagan's. Aristotle said:

> Our present position, then, is this: We have argued that there always was motion and always will be motion throughout all time, and we have explained what is the first principle of this eternal motion. We have explained further which is the primary motion and which is the only motion that can be eternal. And we have pronounced the first movement [or: "Prime Mover"] to be unmoved.[65]

One intelligent man believed the universe was eternal, and another intelligent man believed the universe had a first cause.

---

[64] Sagan, *Cosmos*, 4.
[65] Aristotle, *Physics*, Book VIII, chapter 9.

Other intelligent people hold views that are at odds with both of these men. What does all this mean? At the very least, it means that science is not necessarily going to answer these foundational questions, for no one was in the beginning to observe what actually happened. Conclusions people draw are therefore based on their worldview. The Christian worldview interprets scientific evidence through the lens of the Bible. Atheists like Carl Sagan interpret scientific findings through the lens of a world where there is no God, so the best conclusion he could draw was a universe that was eternal.

Addressing the issue of an eternal universe, Josh McDowell said:

> Most people who declare that the universe is eternal do not actually believe that the universe had no beginning. Usually they say it is "eternal" because they cannot imagine a time when the universe was not in existence. This universe is the only dimension with which they are familiar, and it seems impossible to think of a time when what is, wasn't.[66]

Sagan represents those who struggle to reconcile that which they have observed with scientific evidence and that which they believe by faith. Being an intelligent man, Sagan was well aware of the two most fundamental laws of physics. The first law deals with the conservation of energy. This means that the sum total of mass and energy in the universe is neither created nor destroyed. A tree, for instance, might begin as a seed, grow high into the sky, and later be cut down and ground into dust. It is neither created nor is it destroyed in its essence. It changed at various times of its existence, but it never ceased to be at any point, either before or after it was a tree.

The second law is called the law of *entropy*. Robert J. Spitzer, founder and president of the Magis Center of Reason and Faith, said:

---

[66] Josh McDowell, *Josh McDowell's Handbook on Apologetics*, electronic ed. (Nashville: Thomas Nelson, 1997).

Entropy is a technical concept that, basically, measures the degree of "disorder" or disorganization of a system. For purely probabilistic reasons, systems left to their own devices ("isolated systems") tend to evolve in a way that keeps the level of disorganization (entropy) constant or increases it.[67]

In short, entropy means *deterioration*, and the law of entropy entails that everything is moving toward decay and decline. Ashes do not reassemble to become trees, and old people do not reverse their age and become young again. Note the words of the founder of the Institute of Creation Science (www.icr.org), the late Dr. Henry Morris (1918–2006), who described the first two laws of physics and how they relate to the origin of the universe:

The basic principle of all physical science is that of the conservation and deterioration of energy. The law of energy conservation states that in any transformation of energy in a closed system from one sort into another, the total amount of energy remains unchanged. A similar law is the law of mass conservation, which states that although matter may be changed in size, state, form, etc., the total mass cannot be changed. In other words, these laws teach that no creation or destruction of matter or energy is now being accomplished anywhere in the physical universe... This law of mass and energy conservation is also known as the first law of thermodynamics and is almost without controversy the most important and basic law of all physical science... The second law of thermodynamics [law of entropy], of almost as great significance, enunciates the corollary law of energy deterioration. In any energy transfer or change, although the total amount of energy remains unchanged, the amount of usefulness and availability that the energy possesses is always decreased. This principle is also called the law of entropy increase, entropy being a sort of

---

[67] Robert J. Spitzer, *New Proofs for the Existence of God: Contributions of Contemporary Physics and Philosophy* (Grand Rapids: Eerdmans, 2010), 25.

mathematical abstraction which is actually a measure of the non-availability of the energy of a system... The same principle applies to all the stars of the universe, so that the physical universe is, beyond question, growing old, wearing out and running down. But this law certainly testifies equally to the necessary truth that the universe had a definite beginning. If it is growing old, it must once have been young; if it is wearing out, it must once have been new; if it is running down, it must first have been wound up.[68]

Because the universe is obviously in motion, something or someone had to have set it in motion. This is the *law of inertia*, which teaches that an object at rest will remain at rest unless acted upon by an unbalanced force.[69] Further, an object in motion continues in motion with the same speed and in the same direction unless acted upon by an unbalanced force. Throw the universal law of entropy into the mix, and clearly the universe and all it contains is not eternal, for that which is in motion will certainly fizzle out. After all, physicists regard "perpetual motion machines" as impossible.[70] This means that the universe had a beginning, for science has proven that it cannot be eternal. If it were eternal, it would be that which physicists know is impossible, namely, a perpetual motion machine.[71] Spitzer said, "The fact that stars are still forming today tells us that the universe has not run down completely—and that puts a limit on how long it has been around."[72]

So if the big bang theory is true, then who or what caused that which was at rest to explode, move toward organization, and then move toward disorganization as the law of entropy demands? Since the chief characteristic of matter is that it is always undergoing change, how can the universe, which is made up of changeable matter, be eternal in and of itself? It cannot, and since

---

[68] Henry M. Morris, *The Bible and Modern Science* (Chicago: Moody, 1968), 11–13.
[69] Sproul, 128.
[70] Spitzer, 26.
[71] Spitzer, 26
[72] Spitzer, 29.

it cannot, the universe cannot be eternal. It too is an effect with a cause, namely God.

One of the implications for a universe that is eternal is that it would be infinitely old. This means it would have used up all its useful energy and arrived at a temperature of absolute zero. Yet useful energy, like the sun, continues to exist! Therefore, the universe must be finite in duration. And because it is finite, it had a beginning—a time when all its energy was given to it by something or someone outside of it. That energy, per the law of entropy, is winding down to a time when it loses all its energy.[73] Hence, the universe is like a car running out of gas, running down into a state of disorder.

If the overall amount of energy stays the same (first law of thermodynamics), but we are running out of usable energy (second law of thermodynamics), then what the universe began with was not an infinite amount to sustain it for eternity. After all, it is impossible to run out of an infinite amount of anything. Therefore, the universe could not have existed forever in the past and will not exist forever in the future. Arthur Eddington said:

> The Law that entropy increases—the Second Law of Thermodynamics—holds, I think, the supreme position among the laws of Nature... If your theory is found to be against the Second Law of Thermodynamics I can give you no hope; there is nothing for it but to collapse in deepest humiliation.[74]

Even the big bang theory, widely held by most astronomers today as the answer to the universe's origin, supports the fact that the universe *came into existence* at some point in time (typically thought to be from 12–14 billion years ago[75]). Astronomers have

---

[73] Ian O'Neill, "The 'Astronomical Unit' May Need An Upgrade As the Sun Loses Mass," *Universe Today.* http://www.universetoday.com/12743/the-astronomical-unit-may-need-an-upgrade-as-the-sun-loses-mass/ (accessed June 13, 2012).

[74] Quoted in Geisler and Turek, 78.

[75] National Aeronautics and Space Administration, "How Old is the Universe?" *Universe 101.* http://map.gsfc.nasa.gov/universe/uni_age.html (accessed June 15, 2012).

observed the expansion of the universe and the fact that galaxies are moving away from each other at great speeds. Theoretically, if the process were reversed, like running a reel-to-reel tape backward, all things in the known universe would come back to a single point in time just prior to the big bang when the universe was supposedly birthed. Add to this the fact that the universe is aging and deteriorating (something that which is eternal cannot do!) due to the law of entropy (for which there are no known exceptions), and we are left with just one scientific conclusion: *the universe is not eternal.*

On the non-eternal universe, Spitzer concluded:

> In view of the extensive preponderance of evidence for a beginning of the universe (and the narrow and tenuous path which must be taken to get around it), it can be concluded that the evidence currently supports a reasonable likelihood of a beginning—a point at which the universe came into existence.[76]

Did the Universe Create Itself?

As previously noted, the law of noncontradiction is a law that must govern all intelligent and meaningful discussion. It is the presupposition that everyone comes to the table with before they discuss anything intelligently. With this in view, the question of whether the universe created itself is easily answered in the negative. For the universe to have created itself, it would have to have existed prior to itself in order to create itself. Therefore, the universe had to have existed and not existed at the same time, thus violating the law of noncontradiction. In other words, the universe would have to have first existed in order to have caused itself in spite of the fact that nothing can exist prior to itself in order to bring itself into being. Unless a person is willing to throw out the law of noncontradiction, this hypothesis is absurd.

---

[76] Spitzer, 44.

Was the Universe Created by Something or Someone Else?

In this third possibility, something or someone created the universe. Unless you regress backward infinitely trying to discover the first cause from things that are unable to cause anything—but being effects themselves—the creation itself had to have been the beginning of all things. Further, it would have to have been done *ex nihilo*—out of nothing—which is the only reasonable explanation for the existence of anything since it is the only option for creation since only God existed before the beginning of His creation.

This means that something had to have existed eternally that created all things. This being the case, God's existence is proven in a general sense, for only that which is defined as "God" can qualify as an uncaused, eternal, and omnipotent Being. Unfortunately, skeptics are not convinced, for they tend to accuse Christians of throwing God into the gaps, as it were, in situations like these when they are unable to explain some scientific phenomenon. They call this the "God-of-the-gaps."[77] Ironically, they are just as guilty of using evolution-of-the-gaps, for when something is unexplainable, they just explain it away with evolution.

If it is absurd to argue that the universe brought itself into being out of nothing, then is it any less absurd to conclude that an eternal Being brought it all into existence out of nothing? Although some skeptics actually define "nothing" as "something," it is true that nothing is what rocks think about; nothing is "no-thing." Since nothing is unable to cause anything, why is there something and not nothing? Can nothing, contrary to all common sense and scientific knowledge, actually become everything? Apologist Dan Story said:

> The Bible affirms that something, namely God, created the universe out of nothing. God didn't happen upon some matter and energy and fashion the universe out of it. God spoke, and the universe came to be (Gen. 1).

---

[77] Theopedia: An Encyclopedia of Christianity, "The God of the Gaps," http://www.theopedia.com/God_of_the_Gaps (accessed August 5, 2012).

There was no preexistent stuff out of which God created the world. Is that contradictory? No. Something (God) caused something else (the universe) to exist. That satisfies the law of causality and doesn't violate the law of non-contradiction. Therefore, if this philosophical case for God's existence is valid and sound, which it is, then there should be empirical (observable) evidence to support it, which there is.[78]

The Cosmological Argument

The cosmological argument for the existence of God uses God's general revelation of Himself to argue for His existence. Whereas God's general revelation of Himself is seen in the creation (cf. Rev. 1:18–19), His specific, special revelation of Himself is found in the Scriptures. On the two ways in which God reveals Himself, Story said:

> Scripture not only confirms God's existence, but it also includes very specific information about the nature of God. For example, the Bible states that God is holy, eternal, omniscient, omnipresent, omnipotent, and omnibenevolent. It tells us that God is triune—Father, Son, and Holy Spirit… General revelation is information about God found outside of the Bible. So it is accessible and understandable by *all* people at all times throughout history. It is a perpetual or continuous revelation of God. It shows that God exists, and it unveils some of His attributes, but it does not provide all the information the Bible does about God, such as details about His triune nature. General revelation occurs primarily through nature (Rom. 1:20; Ps. 19:1; Acts 14:16–17) and an intuitive moral consciousness God placed in all human beings (Rom. 2:14–15).[79]

---

[78] Dan Story, *Defending Your Faith* (Grand Rapids, MI: Kregel Publications, 1997), 25-26.

[79] Story, 26-27.

The cosmological argument assumes that some*thing* indeed exists, for we are able to observe it everywhere through God's general revelation. And since it does exist, we can argue that there must be a sufficient *reason* for what exists and/or a first cause that created what exists. We can take any object and move backward to find who or what made the object, but eventually we have to tackle questions like, "Who or what began the creating process?" and "Who or what is responsible for the first thing created through which all other created things have their existence?" Since it is the existence of the universe that confounds scientists and philosophers, and since its existence is certain, most philosophers begin with how or why it exists. Furthermore, since the universe exists and is so unfathomably large, those seeking to make an argument about God's existence should begin with the universe itself and the known laws of the universe to explain the universe.

Using the known law of cause and effect within the universe, the logic of the cosmological argument is as follows: 1) Every effect has a cause; 2) The universe is an effect; 3) Therefore, the universe has a cause. If the first two premises can be proven true, then the third one follows. Let's look at some of the evidence for the argument.

Apologist William Lane Craig, in *Reasonable Faith*, overviews the cosmological view according to Thomas Aquinas (1225–1274), who argued for the cause of the universe.[80] Aquinas argued that in light of the known and indisputable law of cause and effect, there had to be a first cause that begat the first effect, which begat more causes, etc. Noticing that within the world things are in motion, and knowing that things in motion have to be set in motion, Aquinas argued that the first cause set all things in motion. It is absurd to think that just because a thing has the potential for motion that it has the power to set itself in motion. Something outside it must set it in motion.

To take away the first cause, which Aquinas believed was God, is to be left only with those things that have the *potential* for motion. It would be Adam without God's breath of life in his nostrils, the planets without motion around the sun, the sun without heat, a series of gears in a watch without accurate time, or the parts

---

[80] Craig, 97-98.

of an engine without power. All these merely contain the potential for motion or life, but they need something to put them in motion. Therefore, the only way these existing things can be in motion is if an *uncaused first cause* gave them motion. This was Aquinas' "First Way" for arguing God's existence.

Aquinas' "Second Way" for arguing God's existence attempts to prove that in light of the known law of cause and effect, there must be a first cause that goes back to the very beginning of all things that explains all forms of existence.[81] Obviously nothing can cause itself, for it would have to first exist in order to cause its own existence, and that is absurd. Thus, all things that exist, insofar as they can be shown to be *effects* from a cause, must have a cause. Many attempt to explain one effect with a cause and then explain the previous effect with another cause. But arguing in this infinite regression of causes still leaves us wondering how it all began and what the first cause was. If there was indeed a big bang, for instance, how did *it* explode, and who or what lit the fuse on *it* (as it were) to make *it* explode? What exactly was "it" and where did "it" come from given that there was nothing in the beginning?

If the world began with crystals through the process of entropy, as Dr. Richard Dawkins surmises,[82] where did that all begin? And if, as Dawkins also proposes, everything that exists in our universe today exists because aliens seeded our universe for life,[83] then how did the aliens come to be? In other words, if it is possible that crystals or aliens are responsible for the genesis of the universe, who or what is responsible for their existence or the process through which they came into being?

---

[81] Craig, 97-98.

[82] Richard Dawkins Foundation for Reason and Science, "Entropy Alone Can Create Complex Crystals from Simple Shapes; Tetrahedra Packing Record Broken," http://richarddawkins.net/articles/4746-entropy-alone-can-create-complex-crystals-from-simple-shapes-tetrahedra-packing-record-broken (accessed June 5, 2012).

[83] William Hooper, "Richard Dawkins on Intelligent Alien Design," TheOligarch.Com.
http://www.theoligarch.com/richard-dawkins-aliens.htm (accessed July 20, 2012).

Aquinas argued that because all things that begin to exist have a cause, there must be a first cause. Geisler commented on Aquinas' first cause by concluding that it/He must be:

- Self-existent, timeless, non-spatial, and immaterial (since the First Cause created time, space, and matter, the First Cause must be outside of time, space, and matter). In other words, he is without limits, or infinite.
- Unimaginably powerful, to create the entire universe out of nothing.
- Supremely intelligent, to design the universe with such incredible precision.
- Personal, in order to choose to convert a state of nothingness into the time-space-material universe (an impersonal force has no ability to make choices).[84]

Aquinas' "Third Way" for arguing God's existence was to argue for an Absolutely Necessary Being based on the existence of contingent beings.[85] What this means is that because people (beings) come and go, they are not *necessary* beings, for they are contingent or dependent. Hence, they are not *essential* beings but *possible* beings. If they were necessary, they would always exist, but since they pass away, they are unnecessary. The logic for the Absolute Necessary Being should be argued for in the sense that all beings, including matter itself, cannot be contingent, for if all beings that exist are merely contingent, then it is possible that nothing would exist. So, if an infinite amount of time has passed from eternity past, nothing should exist. But we do exist! Therefore, since from nothing comes nothing, an Absolutely Necessary Being must exist for anything to exist. And He is the Necessary Being—*God*.

John Warwick Montgomery quotes from F.C. Copleston in his famous 1948 BBC debate with Bertrand Russell, the great historian of philosophy regarding the fundamental "argument from contingency" for God's existence. Copleston said:

---

[84] Geisler and Turek, 93.
[85] Craig, 98.

First of all, I should say, we know that there are at least some beings in the world which do not contain in themselves the reason for their existence. For example, I depend on my parents, and now on the air, and on food, and so on. Now, secondly, the world is simply the real or imagined totality or aggregate of individual objects, none of which contain in themselves alone the reason for their existence. There isn't any world distinct from the objects which form it, any more than the human race is something apart from the members. Therefore, I should say, since objects or events exist, and since no object of experience contains within itself the reason of its existence, this reason, the totality of objects, must have a reason external to itself. That reason must be an existent being. Well, this being is either itself the reason for its own existence, or it is not. If it is, well and good. If it is not, then we must proceed farther. But if we proceed to infinity in that sense, then there's no explanation of existence at all. So, I should say, in order to explain existence, we must come to a being which contains within itself the reason for its own existence, that is to say, which cannot not-exist.[86]

In sum, using Aquinas' Third Way, we must do three things: 1) Establish the contingency of the physical universe; 2) Show how the contingency of the universe entails the existence of a necessary being; 3) Show that this necessary being is God.

Another version of the cosmological argument is called the *kalam* cosmological argument, from al-Ghazali (1058–1111).[87] "Kalam" is an Arabic word that means "speech," and as Craig said, "It came to denote a statement of theological doctrine and ultimately the whole movement of medieval Islamic theology."[88] In essence, the argument gives one of two alternatives. Either the universe had a beginning that was caused by a personal Creator, or the universe had no beginning (is itself eternal), was uncaused, and

---

[86] John Warwick Montgomery, "Is Man His Own God?" *JETS*, 12:2, Spring 1969, 73.
[87] Craig, 96.
[88] Craig, 96.

is thus impersonal. The argument centers around three premises. First, the universe had a beginning. Second, the beginning of the universe was caused. Third, the cause of the beginning of the universe was personal, namely, God.[89]

These two versions of the cosmological argument for the existence of God attempt to answer *how* there can be something and not nothing. But G.W.F. Leibniz (1646–1716) moved beyond *how* the universe was created and used the cosmological argument in an attempt to answer the question, "*Why* is there something and not nothing?" According to Craig, the Leibnizian way sought a *sufficient reason* as to why anything exists at all.[90] Whereas Aquinas argued for the *necessity* of a first cause that created the universe, Leibniz believed the universe existed for a *reason*. So, can something happen without a sufficient reason, like the creation of the universe? If not, there must be a sufficient reason for the existence of the universe and all its contents.

Where the answer cannot be found is within the universe itself, for every individual thing itself within the universe is a contingent thing and does not have to exist. Therefore, none of the universe's contents can explain the reason for the universe. Of course, if we put every*thing* together as one collective object and tried to answer the question, we would still come up empty because the universe is simply the collection of contingent things and is therefore itself contingent. So the only place to find a sufficient reason for the universe is to look outside of it and to argue for a being that has its own sufficient reason for existing, whose existence is self-contained. Such a being would be responsible for the universe's existence and would have a reason for creating it.

So are the premises of the cosmological argument valid? Craig comments on the validity of the first premise of the cosmological argument, namely that all things that come into existence began to exist, saying:

---

[89] J. P. Moreland, "Does the Cosmological Argument Show There Is A God?", *The Apologetics Study Bible: Real Questions, Straight Answers, Stronger Faith,* ed. Ted Cabal, Chad Owen Brand, E. Ray Clendenen, et al. (Nashville, TN: Holman Bible Publishers, 2007), 806.

[90] Craig, 99.

From the very nature of the case, as the cause of space and time, this supernatural cause must be an uncaused, changeless, timeless, and immaterial being that created the universe. The being must be uncaused because there cannot be an infinite regress of causes. It must be timeless and therefore changeless because it created time. Because it also created space, it must transcend space as well and therefore be immaterial, not physical. Moreover, I would argue, it must also be personal, for how else could a timeless cause give rise to a temporal effect such as the universe? If the cause were a mechanically operating set of necessary and sufficient conditions, then the cause could never exist without the effect. For example, water freezes because the temperature (the cause) is below 0°C. If the temperature were below 0° from eternity past, then any water that was around would be frozen from eternity. It would be impossible for the water to *begin* to freeze just a finite time ago. So if the cause is timelessly present, then the effect should be timelessly present as well. The only way for the cause to be timeless and the effect to begin in time is for the cause to be a personal agent who freely chooses to create an effect in time without any prior determining conditions. For example, a man sitting from eternity could freely will to stand up. Thus, we are brought not merely to a transcendent cause of the universe but to its personal Creator.[91]

Likewise, J.P. Moreland believes that premise two of the cosmological argument, that the universe began to exist and hence had a cause, is also sound. He said, "This is confirmed by universal experience with no clear counterexamples. Alleged cases where something comes from nothing actually involve one thing coming into existence from something else (e.g., lead from uranium)."[92] Craig commented:

---

[91] William Lane Craig, "Why I Believe God Exists," in Norman L. Geisler and Paul K. Hoffman, *Why I Am a Christian: Leading Thinkers Explain Why They Believe* (Grand Rapids, MI: Baker Books, 2001), 64.

[92] Moreland, 806.

The typical objection raised against the philosophical argument for the universe's beginning is that modern mathematical set theory proves that an actual infinite number of things can exist. For example, there is an infinite number of members in the set {0, 1, 2, 3,...}. Therefore, there's no problem with an infinite number of past events. But this objection does not work. First, not all mathematicians agree that actual infinities exist even in the mathematical realm. They regard series such as 0, 1, 2, 3,... as merely *potentially* infinite; that is to say, such series approach infinity as a limit, but they never actually get there. Second, existence in the mathematical realm does not imply existence in the real world. To say that infinite sets exist is merely to postulate a realm of discourse, governed by certain axioms and rules that are simply presupposed, in which one can talk about such collections. Given the axioms and rules, one can discourse consistently about infinite sets. But that's no guarantee that the axioms and rules are true or that an infinite number of things can exist in the real world. Third, the real existence of an infinite number of things would violate the rules of infinite set theory... Trying to subtract infinite quantities leads to self-contradictions; therefore, infinite set theory just prohibits such operations to preserve consistency. In the real world, however, there's nothing to keep us from breaking this arbitrary rule.[93]

Therefore, it seems far more reasonable to affirm the cosmological evidence for God's existence than to deny it. Moreland said:

Evidence for premise three derives from the fact that since time, space, and matter did not exist earlier than the beginning of the universe, the universe's cause had to be timeless, spaceless, and immaterial. This cause cannot be physical or subject to scientific law since all such causes presuppose time, space, and matter to exist. The

---

[93] Craig, *Why I Am a Christian: Leading Thinkers Explain Why They Believe*, 65.

universe's immaterial cause was timeless, spaceless, and had the power to spontaneously bring the world into existence without changing first to do so. (If it had to change before bringing the world into existence, then that change, not the act of bringing the world into existence, would be the first event.) Such a cause must have free will, and since only persons have free will, it is a personal Creator.[94]

Of course, atheists are not convinced, believing that Christian apologists are once again guilty of the God-of-the-gaps fallacy, which says, "Just because something cannot be explained does not mean that God did it." Addressing this, Craig said:

> Such a response misconstrues the argument. In the first place, this argument is a deductive argument. Therefore, if the premises are true and the logic is valid, the conclusion follows, period. It doesn't matter if it's explanatory or not. The conclusion is entailed by the premises, so you can't object to the conclusion once you have granted the premises. Moreover, in no place does the argument postulate God to plug up a gap in our scientific knowledge. The scientific evidence is used only to confirm the truth of premise 2, which is a religiously neutral statement that can be found in any textbook on astronomy. God's existence is implied only by the conjunction of premise 1 with premise 2. Finally, the hypothesis of God is, in fact, genuinely explanatory, though it is not a scientific but a personal explanation. It explains some effect in terms of an agent and his intentions. We employ such explanations all the time. The truth of the matter is, as Oxford philosopher Richard Swinburne points out, there is no way to conclude from science anything about the first state of the universe since nothing preceded it. Personal explanations are all we have, and these are based upon our worldview. If a personal explanation does not exist, then there is simply

---

[94] Moreland, 806-07.

no explanation at all—which is metaphysically absurd, since on that account the universe just popped into being uncaused out of nothing.[95]

In sum, there can be absolutely no explanation for the universe unless there is an eternal Being; unless God exists. The universe and all that it contains exists because it is an effect created by a cause. But an eternal Being is by definition eternal and without a cause. Therefore, the first premise of the cosmological argument does not state that all things need a cause; rather, it states that every effect, or that which begins to exist, demands a cause. Something cannot come from nothing, yet God, because He did not begin to exist but has always existed outside of time and space, brought all things into being through His power. Atheists typically cry foul with this statement, saying it is a special pleading for God. Ironically, they have been guilty of this as well with reference to an eternal universe since they are responsible for claiming that the universe itself is eternal and uncaused (e.g., Carl Sagan). As to using the argument that an actual infinite entity cannot exist because there is no thing that is infinite, Craig said:

> God is not a collection of an infinite number of things. As a nonphysical being, He doesn't even have parts. When theologians speak of God's infinity, they are thus using the term in a *qualitative* not a *quantitative* sense. They mean that God is absolutely holy, uncreated, self-existent, all-powerful, all-present, and so forth. It's not a mathematical concept. Thus, there's no contradiction.[96]

Therefore, although atheists continue to rail against the cosmological argument,[97] it seems logical to conclude that the universe was not self-created, and it is not eternal. It is an effect that demands an ultimate cause. The universe was created ex nihilo by a necessary Being who is uncaused, changeless, dwelling

[95] Craig, *Why I Am a Christian: Leading Thinkers Explain Why They Believe,* 66.

[96] Craig, 67.

[97] Austin Cline. About.com, "Cosmological Argument: Does the Universe Require a First Cause?" http://atheism.about.com/od/argumentsforgod/a/cosmological .htm (accessed June 5, 2012).

outside of time, without material substance, personal in that He cares intimately for His creation, and absolutely holy. The Holy Bible calls this Creator *God*. The Hebrew Bible (the Old Testament) calls Him YHWH ("Yahweh"), which means "the one who is, that is, the absolute and unchangeable one."[98] This is God's personal name, the one He revealed to Moses (Exod. 3:15; cf. vv 13, 14; John 8:56–58), and the name that is never to be taken in vain (Exod. 20:2, 7).[99]

Certainly those who reject Him take His name in vain and sometimes use it as a punch line. It is not that they are smarter than those who believe in God, for intelligence does not settle the debate over God's existence. After all, there are intelligent people on both sides of the debate. Rather, it is our worldview that determines what we believe about God, a worldview shaped by our teachers, life experiences, and influences. Ultimately, God reveals Himself to those He has determined to save (cf. John 6:44; 14:6; Acts 13:48; Rom. 8:28–30).

There is nothing illogical about the idea of a self-existent, eternal being—of a being not caused by something else.[100] An eternal creator of the universe is neither illogical nor religious, but absolutely necessary to explain why anything exists. The law of causality demands that every effect has a cause, and the universe is clearly an effect. It and all its contents have been produced by something outside of itself. Therefore, the idea of an uncaused being is perfectly rational. This "aseity"—that which exists in and of itself—is uncaused, uncreated, and differs from everything in the universe that *does* have a cause.

---

[98] F. Brown, S.R. Driver, and C.A. Briggs, *A Hebrew and English Lexicon of the Old Testament*, 218.

[99] The name of God was so holy to the Jews that they refused to speak it, believing that their lips were too unholy to pronounce the holy name of God. Therefore, they used another word for God, *Adonai*, which means "Lord." Since the original Hebrew text did not contain vowels but only consonants, when the Masoretes added the vowel pointing system, they superimposed the vowels for Adonai over the four letter name of God YHWH. This eventually produced the name "Yehowah" or "Jehovah." Each time YHWH is used in the Hebrew text, English translators used LORD, using capital letters or small caps to distinguish it from other words or names with the same meaning.

[100] Sproul, 122.

Chapter 5

THE ONTOLOGICAL ARGUMENT FOR GOD'S EXISTENCE

The Bible teaches that everything that exists has its existence because God exists, for it is God who made everything that exists (Gen. 1:1). The ontological argument (from the Greek *ontos*, "being") for the existence of God, though it is perhaps the most controversial proof for God's existence,[101] basically says that if God is conceivable, then He actually exists.[102] God proceeds from the idea that He is an absolutely perfect and necessary being. It is an argument using mostly or only *a priori* reasoning and little reference to empirical observation.[103] William L. Rowe defined ontological arguments as those that start from the definition of God and, using only *a priori* principles, conclude with God's existence.[104]

The ontological argument was made famous by St. Anselm (1033–1109), theologian and Archbishop of Canterbury, in the second and third chapters of his *Proslogion*. It was Immanuel Kant (1724–1804), however, who dubbed it the ontological argument because he believed it made an illicit transition from thought to being (*ontos*).[105]

---

[101] Peter Kreeft and Ronald Tacelli, *Handbook of Christian Apologetics* (Downers Grove, IL: IVP, 1994), 69.

[102] Craig, *Reasonable Faith*, 95.

[103] Internet Encyclopedia of Philosophy, "Ontological Argument," http://www.iep.utm.edu/ont-arg/ (accessed August 5, 2012).

[104] William L. Rowe, *William L. Rowe on Philosophy of Religion: Selected Writings* (UK: Ashgate Publishing, 2007), 353.

[105] Geisler, *Baker Encyclopedia of Christian Apologetics*, 554.

Anselm is credited with developing two forms of the ontological argument.[106] His first argument is as follows:

1. God is by definition an absolutely perfect being.
2. An absolutely perfect being cannot lack anything.
3. But a being that exists has something that a being that does not exist lacks—namely, existence.
4. Therefore, an absolutely perfect being must exist.

The second form of Anselm's argument goes like this:

1. God is by definition a necessary being.
2. But a necessary being cannot *not* exist (otherwise, it would not be a necessary being).
3. Therefore, a necessary being necessarily exists.

Let us use an illustration of the perfect beast. If we tried to imagine such a creature, it would have a lean physique and strong muscles that set it apart from all other beasts. This beast would have sharp teeth, run faster than any other beast, and even be able to fly so that he rules over all other beasts both on land and in the air. The beast would also be amphibious so it rules over all sea-dwelling creatures. Its eyes would be sharper than an eagle's, its armor would make it impenetrable to any other predator, and so on.

To *conceive* of such a beast does not mean that it actually exists. It exists only in our minds, although a picture of it could be painted as well. Unless such a beast is found, it cannot be proven to actually exist. For the beast to exist only in our minds is one thing, but in order for the beast to be all it can be, it must actually exist. In sum, the perfect beast can only be perfect if it exists in reality and not just in the mind. Also, it must be shown to be a necessary beast in that it cannot *not* exist. If it does not actually exist, then it is neither necessary nor perfect.

Anselm believed that God, by definition, is "that than which nothing greater can be conceived."[107] Furthermore, he proposed

---

[106] Norman L. Geisler and William D. Watkins, *Worlds Apart: A Handbook on World Views*, 2nd ed. (Grand Rapids, MI: Baker Book House, 1989), 54-55.

that to merely conceive of such a being makes that being less than God, for it is *necessary* for God to not only have conception in the mind but to have true existence. In other words, it is greater to exist in reality than to exist only in the mind, like the example of the so-called perfect beast. Therefore, God must exist in reality, for if He did not, He would not be the greatest possible being since He would exist only in the mind.

Because Anselm believed that God is a necessary being (unlike the imaginary perfect beast), he believed only in the case of an absolutely perfect being, which would have to be a necessary being, provided it is true that if a being is conceivable, then it must exist outside the mind too. All contingent beings, like humans or the perfect beast example, do not *have* to exist. It is conceivable that we do not exist at all. Only a necessary being cannot not exist. Therefore, God must exist.[108]

But does this prove God's existence in reality? Someone might say that before the essence of God can be discussed, His existence must be proven, or the discussion would be futile. Yet it is certainly rational to discuss ideal characteristics of someone or something before it is known if that someone or something is real and then later ask whether it exists.[109]

Rene Descartes' Ontological Argument

All arguments begin somewhere, at some *a priori* point, for no one begins a discussion without certain presuppositions. Atheists begin their arguments with no God, and the converse is true for Christians. Even taking the middle road of agnosticism is an *a priori* stance. Anselm's ontological argument begins with the assumption that God is a perfect and necessary being, and it concludes that God must exist both in the mind and in reality; otherwise, He would not exist at all.

---

[107] Philosophy of Religion, "Anselm's Ontological Argument," http://www.philosophyofreligion.info/theistic-proofs/the-ontological-argument/st-anselms-ontological-argument/ (accessed June 5, 2012).

[108] Geisler, *Baker Encyclopedia of Christian Apologetics*, 555.

[109] Geisler, 555.

The French mathematician Rene Descartes (1595–1650), known as the father of modern rationalism,[110] wondered about the origin of the idea of God. In doing so, he concluded that only God Himself could have caused the idea of His existence to exist in the minds of the people He created. Kreeft and Tacelli summarized and simplified Descartes' complicated argument as follows:

1. We have ideas of many things.
2. These ideas must arise either from ourselves or from things outside of us.
3. One of the ideas we have is the idea of God—an infinite, all-perfect being.
4. This idea could not have been caused by ourselves, because we know ourselves to be limited and imperfect, and no effect can be greater than its cause.
5. Therefore, the idea must have been caused by something outside us which is nothing less than the qualities contained in the idea of God.
6. But only God Himself has those qualities.
7. Therefore, God Himself must be the cause of the idea we have of Him.
8. Therefore, God exists.[111]

In Descartes' day, there was a growing concern regarding truth and the Church's ability to know and discern truth. After all, the Church had held for centuries that the earth was the center of the solar system, yet Copernicus, Galileo, and Kepler had shown that the sun was the center of the solar system, not the earth—a truth that met with great resistance from the Church. With this in mind, Descartes began to wonder about all the other things assumed to be true that might simply be illusions, like the illusion of an oar bending when it goes into the water. Being a mathematician, he wondered if answers regarding truth in the field of philosophy and theology could be as concrete as they were in the field of mathematics.

---

[110] J. D. Douglas, Philip Wesley Comfort, and Donald Mitchell, *Who's Who in Christian History* (Wheaton, IL: Tyndale House, 1992), 531.
[111] Kreeft and Tacelli, 68.

For Descartes, the best route to discovering the answers he sought was to doubt everything, even his own existence, which he thought might be an illusion. And if his life was an illusion, then God's existence might also be in question since God exists in the minds of humans. In short, Descartes sought to undo the common assumptions held by people until those assumptions could in fact be proven true. It is important to note that Descartes was not attempting to overthrow the Church's authority, but to show how the Church's authority might properly merge with current philosophical considerations.[112] Therefore, Descartes' skepticism was the avenue for him to discover truth about himself, mankind, and ultimately God. What he would discover about himself, first and foremost, would lead the way for others to be able to ask and answer, "Do any of us truly exist, or are we just daydreams in the minds of gorillas jumping through the forest?"

By doubting everything held to be true, Descartes concluded through his thought processes that his own thoughts proved his existence. He said, "No matter how skeptical I become, the one thing that I cannot doubt, whenever I'm doubting, whatever it is that I am doubting, is that I am doubting. There is no way I can escape the reality of doubt."[113] Believing that his own ability to doubt pointed toward cognition, he wrote:

> Just as doubt requires a doubter, just as thought requires a thinker, if I am doubting, I must conclude, rationally, that I am thinking; and if I am thinking, then I must *be*. I must exist, because that which does not exist cannot think, that which cannot think cannot doubt, and since there is no doubt that I am doubting, it would mean also that I am thinking; and if I am thinking, I am existing… *I think, therefore, I am.*[114]

Descartes became as convinced of this philosophy as he was about mathematics, and he concluded that the mere doubt of his existence *proved* his existence. Thus, illusion had to be discarded

---

[112] William Edgar and K. Scott Oliphint, *Christian Apologetics, Past and Present, vol. 2: A Primary Source Reader* (Wheaton, IL 2011), 169.
[113] Quoted in Sproul, 104.
[114] Quoted in Sproul, 105.

as a possibility for whether anything exists. Descartes concluded that if anything exists at all, God must exist as that which first existed in order to bring about any existence.[115]

Contrary to Descartes' conclusions, some believe that the self is indeed an illusion. Siddhārtha Gautama (aka Buddha, the *enlightened one*) began a speculative religion that was a reformation within Hinduism, itself a religion of speculations and superstitions. Buddha's basic beliefs are summed up in the "Four Noble Truths": 1) Life is suffering; 2) Suffering is caused by desires for pleasure and prosperity; 3) Suffering can be overcome by eliminating desires; 4) Desire can be eliminated by the Eightfold Path.[116]

This path is both a system of religious education and the moral precepts of Buddhism. It includes right knowledge (Four Noble Truths), right intentions, right speech, right conduct (no killing, drinking, stealing, lying, or adultery), right occupation (none that cause suffering), right effort, right mindfulness (denial of the finite self), and right meditation, which is Raja Yoga.[117] What this results in for the Buddhist is *nirvana*—the realization of the self *as illusion*,[118] the highest spiritual level a human can attain.[119] This level of enlightenment entails that all suffering ceases, not in reality, but in the mind. For a mind that has reached nirvana no longer sees or feels any kind of suffering. Although many adhere to this belief system, the ontological musings of Descartes expose their absurdity. Furthermore, some might surmise that existence is not real, but no one lives as if this is actually true.

Since an explanation for all that exists obviously cannot be explained as illusion, that still does not mean God created it. This is where the ontological argument merges with the cosmological

---

[115] Sproul, 105.

[116] Walter Martin, *The Kingdom of the Cults* (Minneapolis, MN: Bethany House, 1985), 262.

[117] Norman L. Geisler and Ronald M. Brooks, *When Skeptics Ask* (Wheaton, IL: Victor Books, 1990), 134.

[118] Erwin Fahlbusch and Geoffrey William Bromiley, *The Encyclopedia of Christianity,* vol. 4 (Grand Rapids, MI; Leiden, Netherlands: Wm. B. Eerdmans; Brill, 1999-2003), 906.

[119] Story, 201.

argument for God's existence. His existence is not proven by the ontological argument, but existence seems to be substantiated by the logic of the argument. If we grant that our existence is proven by the ontological argument, then we are back to the questions we asked in the cosmological argument, namely, how is there something and not nothing? After all, man is an effect from a cause, so what is the ultimate cause of man and the universe where he dwells? Is the universe eternal? Is the universe self-created? Or is the universe the creation of an ultimate Creator?

To summarize those conclusions, the problem with the idea of a self-created universe is that for this to be true, the law of noncontradiction must be shelved since the universe would have to both be and not be at the same time.[120] In other words, it would have to be in existence in order to form itself. This is obviously absurd, for nothing produces nothing since it equates to *no-thing*. For something to be self-existent, like the elements that exploded all things into existence in the big bang, it would have to possess the power of being within itself—which is uncreated. Second, the problem with the view that the universe itself is eternal and that it is made up of the eternal particles that exploded in the big bang, how can the particles that formed it, which are not eternal, come together and form something eternal? This is absurdity on top of absurdity because the particles that came together to ignite the big bang are neither eternal nor self-existent. Therefore, self-creation fails to explain reality. The only other option, unless you choose to opt for *illusion*, is that man and the universe where he lives were created by God, the eternal, necessary Being.

So, scientifically speaking, the universe and the self can neither be illusion nor self-created. That leaves only one other option, short of acknowledging a Creator: *chance*. But "chance" is not a cause; it is a *word* used to describe mathematical possibilities. It has no power of its own. Chance is *no*thing. It is what rocks dream about. Chance has no being and no power, but has only to do with odds under unstable circumstances.[121] Bereft of being, chance cannot be a valid explanation for the universe since it is powerless. Add powerlessness to nothing, and nothing

---

[120] Sproul, 110.
[121] Geisler and Turek, 125.

happens. Therefore, those who use chance as an explanation for the universe are basically saying, "We not only do not know how the universe came into being, we are not willing to listen to any good scientific explanations for how it might have."

The Importance of the Ontological Argument

The ontological argument is important because contingent beings like humans, since we are not necessary beings, need to have an explanation for our existence. We need to know the cause that accounts for our effect. Since we are contingent and not necessary or eternal beings, we must have had a beginning, so we can only be explained by a cause. An infinite regress that takes us back to the first human still does not answer where that first human originated or why he was created.

Anselm and Descartes both wondered why, if God does not exist, He exists so prevalently in the minds of humans from the earliest of generations. Dr. Albert Mohler, president of Southern Baptist Theological Seminary in Louisville, Kentucky, asks atheists this very question, wondering why, if the mind is nothing more than a chemical and neurological machine developed through hundreds of thousands of evolutionary processes, generations of people have believed in a supernatural deity.[122] He said:

> Natural selection explains that those characteristics which confer some survival advantage are passed on, while those which do not eventually die out. Thus those creatures with larger brains have succeeded where those with smaller brains have not. Those who have the ability to walk have survived where those who had not such ability did not. So why did those who believed in God survive while those who did not believe did not? If you hold to a purely natural understanding of religion like Dennett and Dawkins, there is only one answer. You have to say that there must have been some evolutionary advantage at some point to believing in God... Somehow

---

[122]   Albert Mohler, *Atheism Remix* (Wheaton, IL: Crossway, 2008), 46.

all this must produce replicators who replicate more successfully. Dennett's solution to this problem is to say that while belief in God must have conferred evolutionary advantage somewhere back in time, it does so no longer. Thus, Dennett suggests, our great task in this generation is to rid ourselves of what was once an advantage but is now an evolutionary disadvantage.[123]

Since the Bible answers the question of origins, the innate idea of God inside every human being, and why there is something and not nothing, the issue is settled for those who believe that the Bible is God's Word. Unlike Dennett's fluctuating evolutionary theology, God never changes. Atheists and skeptics, however, typically deny anything the Bible teaches if it assumes God's existence or presumes to speak for God since they do not necessarily believe in God. Cabal said:

> When a fool says in his heart that there is no God (Psalm 14:1), he demonstrates that he understands what is meant by the term God, namely "that than which nothing greater can be conceived." And anything that can be conceived *not* to exist is not God. Thus God cannot be conceived *not* to exist.[124]

But the question remains, *if there is no God, how did everything that is come into being*? And if God is not an effect stemming from a cause, how did He come to be? With foundational questions like these, apologists are faced with the task of arguing for God's existence *outside* of the Bible since to the unbeliever, a Christian who argues from the Bible is arguing in a circle (e.g., "I believe in an all-powerful Being because the Bible teaches this truth"). Therefore, Christian apologists must use the laws of logic and the creation itself—God's general revelation of Himself—to argue first for existence and show how our existence

---

[123] Mohler, 46-47.

[124] Ted Cabal, "Notable Christian Apologist: Anselm," *The Apologetics Study Bible: Real Questions, Straight Answers, Stronger Faith*, ed. Ted Cabal, Chad Owen Brand, E. Ray Clendenen, et al. (Nashville, TN: Holman Bible Publishers, 2007), 801.

logically leads to a Creator. The ontological argument is worth the time to study, although in and of itself, it does not convert atheists into Christian theists.

So Who Made God?

"In the beginning was the Word, and the Word was with God, and the Word was God" (John 1:1). This passage says that God was in the beginning, and He was with the Word—the pre-incarnate Son of God, Jesus Christ (cf. John 1:14). Genesis 1:1–2 says that God existed prior to the universe and He created the universe. Therefore, if God created the universe, then He had to have existed before the universe. Though we might wonder who created God, ultimately the question of what or who caused God is foolish, for God is eternal and by definition is uncreated and without a beginning. Paul Copan summarized the reasons for believing in God's eternality:

> First,…science clearly leads us to conclude that the universe began to exist…, it was birthed at some point in time…, is expanding… that the second law of thermodynamics (energy tends to spread out) has no known exceptions, [so] we can only conclude from scientific observation that the universe had a beginning. And since scientific observation has led us to conclude that nothing times nothing equals nothing, we can only conclude logically that the universe did not create itself, for being cannot come from nonbeing. Therefore, there had to be an eternal Being, a Creator, who has the essence of being within Himself, who created the universe. Secondly, everything that exists does not have to have a cause. Only effects have causes, and an eternal necessary being is certainly not an effect…To say "Everything needs a cause" would necessarily exclude an uncaused God. Thirdly, an uncaused entity like God is both logical and intelligible. Fourthly, uncaused things are not uncommon…Logical laws are real; we can't think coherently without using them. Moral laws or virtues

(love, justice) are real. But none of these began to exist. They are eternal and uncaused. Finally, the question, 'Who made God?' commits the category fallacy, for to imply that all things, even God, must be caused is illogical.[125]

Alvin Plantinga commented on the absurdity of asking why God exists, saying,

> Now it becomes clear that it is absurd to ask why God exists. To ask that question is to presuppose that God does exist; but it is a necessary truth that if He does, He has no cause. And it is also a necessary truth that if He has no cause, then there is no answer to a question asking for His causal conditions. The question "Why does God exist?" is, therefore, an absurdity.[126]

To conclude this argument from existence, the ontological argument does not prove God exists. It is simply an argument for God's existence, and it points directly at God as the Creator. This argument has endured centuries of evaluation, and it is perhaps the most controversial argument for the existence of God.[127] Geisler summed it up this way:

> The only feasible way to make the ontological argument valid is to assume or affirm that something exists. And once one argues, "Something exists, therefore God exists," he has really argued cosmologically. The ontological argument by itself, without borrowing the premise, "Something exists," cannot possibly prove the existence of God. For it is always logically possible that nothing ever existed and hence it is not logically

---

[125] Paul Copan, "If God Made the Universe, Who Made God?" *The Apologetics Study Bible: Real Questions, Straight Answers, Stronger Faith,* ed. Ted Cabal, Chad Owen Brand, E. Ray Clendenen, et al. (Nashville, TN: Holman Bible Publishers, 2007), 869.

[126] Alvin Plantinga, "Necessary Being," in *The Analytic Theist: An Alvin Plantinga Reader* (Grand Rapids, MI: Eerdmans, 1998), 223.

[127] Kreeft and Tacelli, 69.

necessary to affirm that God exists. On the other hand, neither has anyone made a successful ontological disproof of God, making it logically impossible that there is a God... If one could somehow validate a theistic argument by importing the undeniable premise that "something exists" and arguing from this that "something necessarily exists," it still is a long way from this to the simple and absolutely perfect Being of Christian theism. It is interesting to note that three views of God have been concluded from the same kind of ontological argument, and others feel a fourth may be inferred. Descartes and Leibniz concluded a theistic God. Spinoza argued to a pantheistic God. Hartshorne ended with a panentheistic God. It is also suggested that, apart from importing some kind of Platonic premise, the ontological argument yields polytheistic gods. Even many atheists are willing to recognize the universe is somehow necessary, but in no way do they identify it with God. Since the positions are mutually exclusive, it follows that they cannot all be true... In order to defend theism, one must apparently go beyond the ontological argument. For the ontological argument alone apparently does not designate which kind of God (or gods) is found at the conclusion.[128]

---

[128] Geisler, *Baker Encyclopedia of Christian Apologetics*, 564.

Chapter 6

THE TELEOLOGICAL ARGUMENT FOR GOD'S EXISTENCE

A fourth argument for the existence of God is based on God's general revelation of Himself through His perfect and completed creation. It is called the *teleological* argument, from the Greek word *telos*, which means "perfect; complete; mature."[129] The logic of this argument is as follows: 1) Every design has a designer; 2) The universe is intricately designed for life; 3) Therefore, the universe has a designer. Christians know Him as God, the Creator of heaven and earth. William A. Dembski said:

> The design argument is like this. It looks at certain features of the natural world and concludes that they exhibit evidence of a designing intelligence. But just as the *Mona Lisa* can tell us only so much about its creator (da Vinci), so the natural world can tell us only so much about its Creator (God). The design argument allows us reliably to conclude that a designing intelligence is behind the order and complexity of the natural world. In particular, the design argument is silent about the revelation of Christ in Scripture. It follows that the design

[129] Johannes P. Louw and Eugene Albert Nida, vol. 2, *Greek-English Lexicon of the New Testament: Based on Semantic Domains*, electronic ed. of the 2nd edition. (New York: United Bible societies, 1996), 243.

argument cannot "prove the Gospel" or "compel someone into the kingdom."[130]

The argument from design has always been particularly popular among scientists. "It is the most empirical of the arguments for God," said Frederick Ferré, based on "observational premises about the kind of order we discover in nature."[131] Physicist-astronomer-philosopher-theologian Isaac Newton (1642–1727) was a believer in the Creator God based on the universe's intricate design. He wrote, "This most beautiful system of the sun, planets and comets, could only proceed from the counsel and dominion of an intelligent and powerful Being."[132]

The Design Observed in the Universe

Certainly the universe is full of intricate design. The fact that man is able to live at all on the earth is due to the earth's unique ability to allow for human life. In other words, the earth has been uniquely tweaked, as it were, like no other known planet, star, or solar system, to allow for life as we know it. How is this possible? Walter Bradley said:

> First, we need a sufficient diversity of elements, combined with a relative abundance of certain critical elements, to make possible the production of complex "molecular machines" capable of processing energy, storing information, and replicating molecules such as RNA, DNA, and protein. Second, at least one element in this complexity of life must be capable of serving as a

[130] William A. Dembski, "Does the Design Argument Show There Is A God?" *The Apologetics Study Bible: Real Questions, Straight Answers, Stronger Faith*, ed. Ted Cabal, Chad Owen Brand, E. Ray Clendenen, et al. (Nashville, TN: Holman Bible Publishers, 2007), 1327.

[131] Frederick Ferré, "Design Argument," *Dictionary of the History of Ideas*, vol. 1 (New York: Charles Scribner's Sons, 1973), 673.

[132] Isaac Newton, "General Scholium," in *Mathematical Principles of Natural Philosophy* (1687) in *Great Books of the Western World*, Robert M. Hutchins, ed. (Chicago, IL: Encyclopedia Britannica, n.d.), 369.

ready connector, reacting with essentially all elements to form bonds that are stable but not too stable to be broken during "reuse"; carbon is such an element. Third, we must have an individual element or compound that is liquid at certain temperatures on planet earth and very abundant and that can serve as a universal solvent. This liquid must be capable of dissolving most elements and/or compounds essential to the chemistry of life; that describes water. Fourth, we need long-term sources of energy that fit with the chemical energy in the carbon bonds so that this energy can fuel the chemical reactions we find in the carbon-based, chain molecules that are essential to life. At least 50 such requirements have been identified, all necessary for life to exist in our universe.[133]

According to Robert J. Spitzer, the universe is governed by five kinds of constants: 1) constants of space and time; 2) energy constants; 3) individuating constants; 4) large-scale constants; 5) fine structure constants.[134] He said:

> If the values of any of these constants were a little higher or lower, the universe could have been constituted by multiple black holes, by a single black hole, by diffuse non-interacting particles, etc. All these scenarios would prohibit the development of any life form.[135]

This means that the universe has been fine-tuned for life on earth, a phenomenon some scientists call the *anthropic principle*. The term "anthropic" is Greek for "man," so anthropic principle refers to the nature of earth's allowance for man to live, breathe, eat, and reproduce. No other known planet, star, or solar system has ever been discovered that allows for life of any nature,

---

[133] Walter L. Bradley, "Does Science Support the Bible?" *The Apologetics Study Bible: Real Questions, Straight Answers, Stronger Faith,* ed. Ted Cabal, Chad Owen Brand, E. Ray Clendenen, et al. (Nashville, TN: Holman Bible Publishers, 2007), 831-32.

[134] Spitzer, 53.

[135] Spitzer, 53.

especially life for man. Geisler and Turek list 15 of these numerous anthropic principles:

1. Oxygen Level—On earth, oxygen comprises 21 percent of the atmosphere. That precise figure is an anthropic constant that makes life on earth possible. If oxygen were 25 percent, fires would erupt spontaneously; if it were 15 percent, human beings would suffocate.

2. Atmospheric Transparency—If the atmosphere were less transparent, not enough solar radiation would reach the earth's surface. If it were more transparent, we would be bombarded with far too much solar radiation down here.

3. Moon-Earth Gravitational Interaction—If the interaction were greater than it currently is, tidal effects on the oceans, atmosphere, and rotational period would be too severe. If it were less, orbital changes would cause climatic instabilities. In either event, life on earth would be impossible.

4. Carbon Dioxide Level—If the CO_2 level were higher than it is now, a runaway greenhouse effect would develop (we'd all burn up). If the level were lower than it is now, plants would not be able to maintain efficient photosynthesis (we'd all suffocate—the same fate the astronauts are trying to avoid).

5. Anthropic Constant 5: Gravity—If the gravitational force were altered by 0.00000000000000000000000000000 00000001 percent, our sun would not exist, and, therefore, neither would we. Talk about precision!

6. If the centrifugal force of planetary movements did not precisely balance the gravitational forces, nothing could be held in orbit around the sun.

7. If the universe had expanded at a rate one millionth more slowly than it did, expansion would have stopped, and the universe would have collapsed on itself before any stars formed. If faster, then no galaxies would have formed.

8. Any of the laws of physics can be described as a function of the velocity of light (now defined to be 299,792,458 meters per second). Even a slight variation in the speed of light would alter the other constants and preclude the possibility of life on earth.

9. If water vapor levels in the atmosphere were greater than they are now, a runaway greenhouse effect would cause temperatures to rise too high for human life; if less, an insufficient greenhouse effect would make the earth too cold to support human life.

10. If Jupiter were not in its current orbit, the earth would be bombarded with space material. Jupiter's gravitational field acts as a cosmic vacuum cleaner, attracting asteroids and comets that might otherwise strike earth.

11. If the thickness of the earth's crust were greater, too much oxygen would be transferred to the crust to support life. If it were thinner, volcanic and tectonic activity would make life impossible.

12. If the rotation of the earth took longer than twenty-four hours, temperature differences would be too great between night and day. If the rotation period were shorter, atmospheric wind velocities would be too great.

13. The 23-degree axis tilt of the earth is just right. If the tilt were altered slightly, surface temperatures would be too extreme on earth.

14. If the atmospheric discharge (lightning) rate were greater, there would be too much fire destruction; if it were less, there would be too little nitrogen fixing in the soil.

15. If there were more seismic activity, much more life would be lost; if there was less, nutrients on the ocean floors and in river runoff would not be cycled back to the continents through tectonic uplift (so even earthquakes are necessary to sustain life!).[136]

---

[136] Geisler and Turek, 98-106.

Dennis Sciama, professor of astrophysics at Cambridge, said, "If you change just a little bit, say the charge of an electron, then the way the universe develops is so changed that it is very likely that intelligent life would not be able to develop."[137] Likewise, Dr. David Deutsch, professor of mathematics at Oxford, said:

> If we nudge one of these constants just a few percent in either direction, then stars burn out within a million years of their formation. No time for evolution. And if we nudge it in the other direction, then no elements heavier than helium form... so no carbon, no life, not even any chemistry; no complexity at all. And if we could alter the relative masses of just the two subatomic particles, the proton and the neutron, by just a fraction of a percent, atoms would be unstable. There would be no stars, no light, no warmth, no structure at all, just chaos.[138]

No scientist can deny the anthropic principle. English astronomer Fred Hoyle, who spent his life working at the Institute of Astronomy at Cambridge, said, "I do not believe that any physicist who examined the evidence could fail to draw the inference that the laws of nuclear physics have been deliberately designed with regard to the consequences they produce inside stars."[139] Even renowned atheist Stephen Hawking estimated that if the rate of the universe's expansion one second after the big bang had been smaller by even one part in a hundred thousand million-million, the universe would have collapsed into a hot fireball.[140]

Likewise, British physicist P. C. W. Davies calculated that the odds against the initial conditions being suitable for later star formation (without which planets could not exist) is one followed by more than a thousand billion-billion zeroes.[141] Davies also

---

[137] The Anthropic Principle, DVD, directed by Paul Davies (England: BBC LTD Productions, 1988).

[138] *The Anthropic Principle*, DVD, directed by Paul Davies (England: BBC LTD Productions, 1988).

[139] *The Anthropic Principle*.

[140] Stephen W. Hawking, *A Brief History of Time* (New York: Bantam Books, 1988), 123.

[141] Quoted in Geisler and Hoffman, 68.

estimates that a change in the strength of gravity or of the weak force by only one part in 10,100 would have prevented a life-permitting universe.[142] And Roger Penrose of Oxford University calculated that the odds of the big bang's low entropy condition existing by chance are on the order of 1 out of 1010(123). Around 50 such quantities and constants are present in the big bang that must be fine-tuned in this way if the universe is to permit life. And it is not just each quantity that must be finely tuned; their ratios to one another must be also finely tuned.[143] Therefore, improbability is added to improbability to improbability until our minds are reeling in incomprehensible numbers.

Clearly, the scientific evidence for the genesis of the universe does not at all point toward a chance explosion in the beginning that, over time and by chance, spread out and formed a completely sensible universe complete with life and laws—both moral and physical. The tweaking of the universe, and most notably the earth, seems clearly to point to some intelligent designer. Jay W. Richards, research fellow at Acton Institute, said:

> Think of the following features of our earthly home: the transparency of the earth's atmosphere in the visual region of the spectrum, shifting crustal plates, a large moon, and a particular location in the solar system, and our solar system's location within the Milky Way galaxy. Without each of these assets, we would have a hard time learning about the universe. It is not idle speculation to ask how our view of the universe would be impaired if, for example, our home world were perpetually covered by thick clouds. After all, our solar system contains several examples of such worlds. Just think of Venus, Jupiter, Saturn, and Saturn's moon, Titan. These would be crummy places to do astronomy. We can make similar comparisons at the galactic level. If we were closer to our galaxy's center or one of its major, and dustier, spiral arms, for instance—the extra dust would impede our view

---

[142] Geisler and Hoffman, 68.

[143] Craig, *Why I Am a Christian: Leading Thinkers Explain Why They Believe*, 68.

of the distant universe. In fact, we probably would have missed one of the greatest discoveries in the history of astronomy: the cosmic microwave background radiation. That discovery was the linchpin in deciding between the two main cosmological theories of the 20th century. Underlying this debate was one of the most fundamental questions we can ask about the universe: is it eternal, or did it have a beginning?[144]

These evidences may not prove that God exists, but for anyone seeking truth and a cogent explanation for the origins of the universe, they certainly make a better argument for the existence of God than they do against His existence.

The Design Observed in the Building Blocks of Life

God's design can be seen in the vastness and complexity of the universe, as the writer of Psalm 19 proclaimed. But it can also be observed in the tiniest of organisms such as the cell. Bruce Alberts, president of the National Academy of Sciences, said:

> We have always underestimated the cell... The entire cell can be viewed as a factory that contains an elaborate network of interlocking assembly lines, each of which is composed of a set of large protein machines... Why do we call [them] machines? Precisely because, like machines invented by humans to deal efficiently with the macroscopic world, these protein assemblies contain highly coordinated moving parts.[145]

---

[144] Jay W. Richards, "The Contemporary Argument for Design: An Overview," in *Passionate Conviction*, ed. Paul Copan and William Lane Craig (Nashville, TN: B&H Publishing, 2007), 74-75.

[145] Bruce Alberts, "The Cell as a Collection of Protein Machines," *Cell* 92 (February 8, 1998).

Nancy Pearcey and Charles Thaxton imagined the cell enlarged to the point where people could walk around inside of it to observe its intricacies:

> The cell would resemble a fully automated modern factory. We would see a vast range of products and raw materials continually passing through conduits in an orderly fashion to various assembly plants. We would see robot-like machines—tens of thousands of different kinds—in charge of production. These are the proteins. Some of them (enzymes) act as catalysts, regulating the cell's processes like little robots with stopwatches. In fact, we would see analogues to nearly every feature of our own advanced machines. Much of the terminology needed to describe this fascinating molecular reality we would have to borrow from late twentieth-century technology.[146]

Ariel Roth explained that the intricacy of the cell would contain about 3,000 *million* pairs of the DNA genetic alphabet (A-T-C-D).[147] The information would be overwhelming since just *one* single DNA molecule contains enough information to fill one volume of an encyclopedia. The amount of information contained in a single human cell, not just a DNA molecule inside the cell, is equivalent to all 30 volumes of the *Encyclopedia Britannica* several times over. And all that is not inside a fully formed human, but inside *one single cell*! What is known about the simplest of life-forms is that they contain the information-equivalent of 1,000 encyclopedias.[148] Furthermore, the complex human life-form not only has *trillions* of cells, it is also producing millions of new cells each second. So where did all that information originate? It seems to point logically to a designer.

Michael J. Behe, associate professor of biochemistry at Lehigh University in Pennsylvania, author of *Darwin's Black Box:*

---

[146] Nancy Pearcey and Charles B. Thaxton, *The Soul of Science: Christian Faith and Natural Philosophy*, Turning point Christian worldview series (Wheaton, IL: Crossway Books, 1994), 221.

[147] Ariel Roth, *Origins* (Hagerstown, MD: Herald, 1998), 66. Quoted in Geisler and Turek, 145-46.

[148] Geisler and Turek, 26.

the Biochemical Challenge to Evolution, argued that the extraordinary complexity of those biochemical processes comprising a cell are compelling evidence for design and hence for a designer. He reasons that since they do nothing until all their components are fully in place, it is impossible to imagine how the evolutionary idea of natural selection could have created them from simpler processes since effective simpler processes do not exist. He calls his argument the argument from *irreducible complexity.*[149] Behe explained, "A system or device is irreducibly complex if it has a number of different components that all work together to accomplish the task of the system, and if you were to remove one of the components, the system would no longer function."[150]

Using a simple mousetrap to illustrate his principle, Behe said that the irreducible complexity of a mousetrap is that it needs a wooden platform to which all the other parts are attached: a metal for crushing, a spring with extended ends to press against the platform and the hammer when the trap is charged, the catch that releases when a mouse touches it, and a metal bar that connects to the catch and holds the hammer back when the trap is charged. If any one of these parts is taken away or not precisely positioned, the mousetrap is useless since it cannot work without all its parts. So it is with all irreducibly complex objects like a single cell.

If a simple mousetrap cannot evolve over time without intelligent manipulation, how could a single cell, with its intricate design and information, suddenly appear in the proverbial primordial soup and evolve over time, with chance guiding it, to form life as we know it? And if it did, what is the origin for all the information inside that cell? Scientifically speaking, since we know that nothing that complex can be created on earth without a designer, why would we relegate such intricacies to evolution and chance? Those who hypocritically call Christians nonscientific are

---

[149] Ben M. Carter, "Communication As General Revelation: The Anti-evolutionary and Pro-Trinitarian Implications of Communication Phenomena," *Journal of Christian Apologetics,* Volume 2, no. 1 (Plymouth, MI: Michigan Theological Seminary, 1998), 80-81.

[150] Quoted in Lee Strobel, *The Case for a Creator* (Grand Rapids: Zondervan, 2004), 239.

actually the guilty parties. Believing the cell just appeared by chance takes far more faith than believing it was created.

It is important to note that it is not just the cell that is irreducibly complex, *but the very parts of the cell* themselves are irreducibly complex.[151] There is the bacterial flagellum—the tail-like projection that protrudes from the cell body of certain prokaryotic and eukaryotic cells. This tail both steers the cell and senses chemicals and temperatures outside the cell.[152] Behe said:

> While cilia act like oars to move cells, it was discovered in 1973 that the flagellum performs like a rotary propeller... Only bacteria have them... Just picture an outboard motor on a boat and you get a pretty good idea of how the flagellum functions, only the flagellum is far more incredible. The flagellum's propeller is long and whip-like, made out of a protein called *flagellin*. This is attached to a drive shaft by hook protein, which acts as a universal joint, allowing the propeller and drive shaft to rotate freely.[153]

Citing Edward M. Purcell, Behe said, "Several types of proteins act as brushing material to allow the drive shaft to penetrate the bacterial wall and attach to the rotary motor."[154] Behe addressed who might be steering the cell:

> It turns out it has sensory systems that feed into the bacteria flagellum and tell it when to turn on and when to turn off, so that it guides it to food, light, or whatever it's seeking. In a sense, it's like those smart missiles that have guidance systems to help them find their target, except there's no explosion at the end! And the flagellum is irreducibly complex. Genetic studies have shown that

---

[151] Strobel, 255.

[152] Wikipedia, "Flagellum." http://en.wikipedia.org/wiki/Bacterial_flagellum #cite_note-0 (accessed June 15, 2012).

[153] Quoted in Strobel, 253.

[154] Edward M. Purcell, "The Efficiency of Propulsion by the Rotating Flagellum," *Proceedings of the National Academy of Sciences USA* 94 (October 1997).

between 30 and 35 proteins are needed to created a functional flagellum. I haven't even begun to describe all of its complexities; we don't even know the roles of all its proteins. But at a minimum you need at least three parts— a paddle, a rotor, and a motor—that are made up of various proteins. Eliminate one of those parts and you don't get a flagellum that only spins at five thousand RPMs; you get a flagellum that simply doesn't work at all.[155]

If each one of the cell's parts is irreducibly complex, this means it could not have been built by a process of simple steps over long periods of time (i.e., through evolution). In order for the cell to function, it has to have all its complexity *all at once* (like the mousetrap), for if it lacked any of its moving parts, it would not work half-way and evolve until it fully worked. It would be useless, for anything less than a fully functioning cell renders it nonfunctional. The same is true with the eye, the heart, the liver, etc. Being irreducibly complex, human organs could not have evolved over time. They were created *as is* by the Almighty God, who, in His wisdom, created the cell so complex and so wonderful that it confounds and astonishes those who look into it with a microscope.

So with all that information existing all at once inside the cell, it seems scientific to conclude that something or someone created it, for science teaches us that intelligence does not spring forth from chaos or some primordial soup. In fact, the odds of a one-cell animal emerging by purely natural process is 1 in $10^{40,000}$![156] That means there is a *chance* it could happen, but the odds are astronomically against it. Behe said that the probability of getting just one protein molecule (which has about 100 amino acids) by chance would be the same as a blindfolded man finding one marked grain of sand in the Sahara Desert three times in a row. Regardless, one protein molecule does not equate to life. To get life, you would need to get about 200 of those protein molecules together.[157]

---

[155] Quoted in Strobel, 255.

[156] Geisler, *Baker Encyclopedia of Christian Apologetics*, 681.

[157] Geisler and Turek, 125.

Clearly, there are multiple reasons for believing in an Intelligent Designer of the universe. And believing this logical probability seems to take far less faith than believing life, with all its intricate design, spontaneously appeared by chance. Scientifically speaking, irreducible complexity means that new life cannot come into existence by the Darwinian method of slight, successive changes over a long period of time.[158] Therefore, the design we see points to a Designer.

Observing Design from Deoxyribonucleic Acid (DNA)

The discovery of DNA by Francis Crick and James Watson in 1953 was quite an impressive scientific discovery. DNA contains the information for life. That such an extraordinary information storage system exists, and that the DNA molecules have somehow come to be encoded with the exact information needed for life, is the climax to a remarkable witness from science, and it points to God's providential care for His creation.[159]

The discovery of DNA, and how to interpret the existence of DNA, is akin to the argument of William Paley (1743–1805) that every watch requires a watchmaker. His argument asks, "What if you were to stumble upon a watch in an open field? Would you surmise that it naturally grew from a tree and fell on the ground or that it grew from the earth? Did the rain or wind form the watch, or was it a long process of natural forces that came together over time to make the watch?" These questions would be absurd, for anyone stumbling upon an intricately designed timepiece in an open field would know that someone had left it there and not assume that time and weather had produced the watch.

Updating Paley's example and using DNA instead of a watch, Pearcey and Thaxton proposed that we "could say that ascribing DNA to physical-chemical causes would be like finding a 100 terabyte storage device filled with files of information on someone's desk and ascribing its contents to the effects of wind

---

[158] Geisler and Turek, 145-46.
[159] Bradley, "Does Science Support the Bible?" 831-32.

and erosion. If books and computer programs require an intelligent origin, so too does the message in the DNA molecule."[160]

Darwinist Richard Dawkins, professor of zoology at Oxford University, admitted that the message found in just the cell *nucleus* of a tiny amoeba is more than all 30 volumes of the *Encyclopedia Britannica* combined, and the entire amoeba has as much information in its DNA as 1,000 complete sets of the *Encyclopedia Britannica!*[161] In his book *The Blind Watchmaker*, a sarcastic pun directed at Paley's example of the watchmaker, Dawkins admits that design is found in the existence of life, for he said, "Biology is the study of complicated things that give the appearance of having been designed for a purpose."[162] Yet just two pages later, despite acknowledging "the intricate architecture and precision-engineering" in human life and in each of the trillions of cells within the human body, he rejects the idea that life points to a designer. Commenting on Dawkins' conclusions, Geisler and Turek said, "Apparently, Dawkins refuses to allow observation to interfere with his conclusions. This is very strange for a man who believes in the supremacy of science, which is supposed to be based on observation."[163]

Dawkins, being an informed scientist, knows that there are no known natural laws that create information, yet he will not concede a Designer simply because his worldview will not allow it. But he knows what all scientists know—that only *intelligence* can create information. For instance, it is common sense for humans to conclude that a collection of research, such as found in a set of encyclopedias, was put together by intelligent authors. No intelligent person would ever conclude that it just came together by chance. No one walks into a library and assumes for a moment that the books and the information they contain came together by chance. So why would anyone abandon common sense knowledge based on observable realities in the here and now and propose that in the beginning a wealth of knowledge simply appeared in the DNA inside a cell that led to life?

---

[160] Pearcey and Thaxton, 243-44.
[161] Richard Dawkins, *The Blind Watchmaker* (New York: Norton, 1987), 17-18, 116.
[162] Dawkins, 1.
[163] Geisler and Turek, 119.

If science is defined as knowledge that stems from observable and testable evidence, then how can Darwinism be dubbed as such when nothing of which it purports with reference to the origins of life has been observed? Furthermore, since Darwinism requires more and more time for chance to bring all things together as they are, in spite of the fact that science has proven that more time actually begets greater chaos, it seems clear that Darwinism a religion. What's more, it is a religion of blind faith that attempts to pass itself off as good science. And it is being passed off as fact in just about every school system in the world, even many so-called Christian schools and universities!

The late Carl Sagan was amazed at God's creation in spite of the fact that he rejected God as the Creator of the universe and of mankind. He said:

> The information content of the human brain expressed in bits is probably comparable to the total number of connections among neurons—about a hundred trillion... If written out in English...that information would fill some 20 million volumes, as many as in the world's largest libraries. The equivalent of 20 million books is inside the heads of every one of us. The brain is a very big place in a very small space... The neurochemistry of the brain is astonishingly busy, the circuitry of a machine more wonderful than any devised by humans.[164]

In spite of this thoughtful observation, however, Sagan refused to give glory to God. It seems that if he had stumbled upon Paley's watch, he would have concluded that the wind, rain, and other natural processes had formed it. In fact, Sagan went to his grave "viewing the whole universe as nothing more than molecules in motion," believing that some extraterrestrial entity would one day be able to explain to us our purposes and our origins.[165] Even Francis Crick, who discovered DNA, answered the question of

---

[164] Sagan, 278.

[165] Ravi Zacharias, *The End of Reason: A Response to the New Atheists* (Grand Rapids, MI: Zondervan, 2008), 34.

how life began by saying, "Probably because a spaceship from another planet brought spores to seed the earth."[166] That is certainly an answer to the question, but it is difficult to find anything scientific about it. His *a priori* rejection of God's existence means that he has to come up with some answer, and spaceships and aliens appear to provide that option.

Although Darwinists speak of new life-forms that are being created, scientifically speaking, it is impossible for any new life-form to form without preexisting life. This brings the argument right back to the cosmological argument, which logically concludes that there had to have been a first cause, an eternal and necessary being that created and began the life process. But whether speaking of huge entities like the beginning of the universe from nothing, or speaking of miniscule entities like the cell and DNA, for those with a Darwinistic worldview, the universe and life simply appeared and fought its way into its present form. Yet even this fails to explain how the selection of the superior over the inferior occurs without intelligence. If the process of evolution is by definition without intelligence, how can any "selecting" be taking place?[167]

To be sure, the survival of the fittest idea is indeed true, but everything that survives remains what it inherently is. For example, although bacteria grow stronger against antibiotics over time, they remain bacteria no matter how much time they have to grow stronger. Micro changes obviously occur within a species, called *microevolution*. Darwinists, however, are not promoting this particular scientific fact. They espouse the idea of *macroevolution*, which theorizes that new life-forms are created from one species into another, as from a dinosaur to a bird or from a tree to a human. Geisler and Turek cited five reasons why this is absolutely impossible:

- **Genetic limits**—These are built into a species. For example, dogs, though varied in size and shape, have always remained dogs.

---

[166] Zacharias, 34.
[167] Geisler and Turek, 140.

- **Cyclical change**—Changes simply shift back and forth within a limited range, like the beaks on the finches Darwin observed on the Galapagos Islands. The finches had varying beak sizes related to the weather, to be sure, but finches remained finches!
- **Irreducible complexity**—Something composed of several well-matched, interacting parts that contribute to its basic function would cease functioning if any one of the parts ceased to function. Intermediates are nonfunctional. Darwin himself feared this might be found to be true. He said, "If it could be demonstrated that any complex organ existed which could not possibly have been formed by numerous, successive, slight modifications, my theory would absolutely break down."[168]
- **Nonviability of transitional forms**—Transitional forms could not survive. As in the case of dinosaurs turning into birds, how could a creature survive that no longer has scales but does not quite have feathers? Even feathers are irreducibly complex.
- **Molecular isolation**—Whereas the DNA similarity between apes and humans may imply an ancestral relationship, this just points to a common Creator.[169]

Observational evidence—science—reveals that intricate design points to a designer, for all known *effects* must have had a *cause*. As the design becomes more intricate, so too does the designer. For instance, naturally speaking, you might observe some weathering on a rock that resembles a letter of the alphabet or maybe even two letters side by side. But no one would stop at a roadside historical marker, read it, and then conclude it got there through weathering or through a series of earthquakes and volcanoes. Likewise, although theoretically, you might surmise that a million monkeys with laptop computers could produce a piece of literature worth reading, no one picks up a piece of

---

[168] Charles Darwin, *The Origin of Species* (New York: New York University Press, sixth ed., 1998), 154.
[169] Geisler and Turek, 142-151.

literature—even a children's book—and concludes anything less than that an intelligent source wrote the book. All this simply means that when we consider the universe and what it says through scientific study, we can only conclude that an Intelligent Designer created it. From observing the universe to the cell, there is no question there is a God!

Atheist and evolutionist Julian Huxley once said, "The reason we accepted Darwinism even without proof, is because we didn't want God to interfere with our sexual mores."[170] What is most interesting about Huxley's comment is that he did not justify his evolutionist beliefs based on science but on morality. In other words, he and his colleagues opted for Darwinism over God in order to live out their fleshly desires. Had they accepted God's existence, they knew that their lifestyles would be condemned by Him. But by disregarding God, they could live as they pleased. Likewise, Lee Strobel, an atheist-turned-Christian, said, "I was more than happy to latch onto Darwinism as an excuse to jettison the idea of God so I could unabashedly pursue my own agenda in life without moral constraints."[171] So, straight from the mouths of those who exchanged the truth of God for a lie is the admission that Darwinism was not a scientific truth in their minds, but rather a worldview that provided an avenue through which they could live out their selfish desires without any regard for God.

In sum, the universe's fine-tuning can be explained through one of three ways: through natural processes, chance, or intelligent design. The first two options are based on odds that essentially equate to zero. Option three is not only scientifically defensible, it agrees with the teachings of Scripture and basic common sense. Atheist-turned-Christian Alister McGrath said that only Christianity makes sense of this shower of information provided by the universe, that only Christianity "gives us a way of bringing order and intelligibility to our many and complex observations of the natural world, human history, and personal experience. It

[170] Quoted in D. James Kennedy, *Skeptics Answered* (Sisters, OR: Multnomah, 1997), 154.

[171] Lee Strobel, *The Case for Faith* (Grand Rapids: Zondervan, 2004), 91.

allows us to integrate them as interconnected aspects of a greater whole."[172]

The intricate design of all things—from the vast universe to the smallest of life's building blocks—points to a Creator and Designer. Christians know Him as God, who created the world through His Son Jesus Christ (Gen. 1:1; cf. Col. 1:17).

---

[172] Alister McGrath, *Mere Apologetics: How to Help Seekers & Skeptics Find Faith* (Grand Rapids: Baker Books, 2012), 93.

Chapter 7

THE MORAL ARGUMENT FOR GOD'S EXISTENCE

The moral law is that which all people understand as a distinction between right and wrong. J. Budziszewski said, "Everyone knows certain principles. There is no land where murder is virtue and gratitude vice."[173] Certainly no one advocates cowardice over bravery, hate over love, or treason over faithfulness. In other words, everyone knows there are absolute moral obligations, something that is binding on all people, at all times, in all places. Murder, for instance, is known worldwide as immoral behavior. We are incapable of knowing know that killing an innocent person is wrong. Cold, unfeeling murderers may not feel remorse for their brutal acts of murder, but not one of them does not know that what they did was wrong. So, if there is an absolute moral law even for just one law like murder, then there must be an absolute Moral Law Giver.

Although God's moral law is obviously written in His special revelation (i.e., the Scriptures, cf. Exod. 20:1–17), God has placed that sense of moral justice within the human race in contradistinction to all of his other creatures (cf. Rom. 2:14–15).[174] Therefore, the moral law is part of God's general revelation of Himself to mankind, for mankind alone acknowledges his sense of right and wrong. Since man has an intellectual and a moral nature, his Creator must be an intellectual and moral Being, a Judge, and a

---

[173] Budziszewski, 208-209.
[174] Paul P. Enns, *The Moody Handbook of Theology* (Chicago, IL: Moody Press, 1997), 184.

Lawgiver. This is how the moral argument for God's existence endeavors to know where man's moral sense of justice derives. After all, man's conscience speaks to him about rights and wrongs—about *shoulds* and *oughts*—from his early childhood. Thus, they are not self-imposed, but rather imply the existence of a Moral Governor to whom we are responsible.[175] What is noteworthy about those who deny the moral law points to a moral Lawgiver is that those who declare they reject any absolute standard, in the next breath exhort us to do better![176]

Clark Pinnock commented that although other arguments for God's existence:

> …supply grounds for believing in a transcendent, personal God, the moral argument goes further. It addresses itself to a most fundamental question which concerns humanists and Christians alike. Both groups are eager to sustain an ethic of moral obligation to our fellow man. But on what basis does such a noble commitment securely rest? How is it to be sustained, or even explained? The moral dimension of human experience raises very readily the question of God whom Christians believe constitutes the only ground that can support the kind of moral commitment which is needed today.[177]

What Is the Moral Law?

The logic of the moral argument is as follows: 1) Every human being is conscious of laws of right and wrong (even those who say there is no such thing as right and wrong are in fact stating a law they believe to be true!); 2) Every law has a lawgiver; 3) Therefore, there must be a supreme moral lawgiver.

---

[175] William Evans and S. Maxwell Coder, *The Great Doctrines of the Bible*, Enl. ed. (Chicago: Moody Press, 1998), 17.

[176] Charles Caldwell Ryrie, *A Survey of Bible Doctrine* (Chicago: Moody Press, 1995).

[177] Clark Pinnock, "The Moral Argument for Christian Theism," Volume 131. *Bibliotheca Sacra* (Dallas, TX: Dallas Theological Seminary, 1974), 115.

Moral laws do not describe what *is* but what *ought* to be. In other words, moral laws are not descriptions of *how* man behaves but *how man ought to behave.* Yet in the atheist-naturalist worldview, there can absolutely be no "oughts." In fact, the atheistic worldview actually explains morality away,.[178] In a naturalistic world where survival of the fittest is how the present situation came into being, there should be absolutely no law against one man killing another insofar as it benefits the other man's existence. This is not to say that atheists believe this. In fact, most atheists and naturalists are quite moral, and in many cases are far more moral than professed Christians! However, they cannot account for their morality based on their worldview. Since man cannot explain these moral "oughts" without assuming he was created with an innate sense of them, the moral law has to transcend the natural order and thus require a transcendent cause. Any explanation of where these moral laws originated will stand on the foundation of a law that governs the argument it attempts to prove.

Immanuel Kant (1724–1804), in his *Critique of Practical Reason* (1788), developed a moral argument for God, immortality, and freedom. He reasoned that man's sense of moral duty, which is the universal and necessary principle in all moral judgments, presupposes the freedom to act out of duty rather than desire for happiness. And since duty and happiness are not always conjoined in this life, it is necessary to postulate another life in which happiness does reward virtue, and a divine lawgiver and judge to guarantee that outcome. But God, immortality, and freedom are the presuppositions we uncover, not conclusions that we demonstrate.[179] Kant believed it was the innate sense of "oughtness"—that inherent sense of right and wrong—that exists in all humans as signified by their feelings of guilt over doing wrong or pride after doing right.[180] He felt that if there was no

---

[178] Mark D. Linville, "The Moral Poverty of Evolutionary Naturalism," *Contending with Christianity's Critics: Answering the New Atheists and Other Objectors,* ed. Paul Copan & William Lane Craig (Nashville, TN: B&H Publishers, 2009), 58.

[179] J. D. Douglas, Philip Wesley Comfort and Donald Mitchell, *Who's Who in Christian History* (Wheaton, IL: Tyndale House, 1992), 394-95.

[180] Sproul, 148-149.

God, then there would be no ultimate ground for doing good and shunning evil. He thus believed heavily in justice, believing that good behavior should be rewarded and wrong behavior should be punished. This led him to believe that perfect justice must exist somewhere, and he concluded that "somewhere" was with God.[181]

In Kant's mind, God had to be morally perfect in order to dispense perfect justice. He was thus an all-powerful and all-knowing God. And if this God existed, then His creation was endowed with the idea of moral absolutes inherently. Kant did not promote that these moral absolutes existed through empirical evidence but through man's innate understanding. He espoused that because this moral code existed in the minds and hearts of all humans, God also existed necessarily. There would be no hope for humans if He did not exist.[182]

If the universe is, as the late Carl Sagan believed, "all that is or ever was or ever will be,"[183] then everything exists *by pure chance*. Aside from this belief being indefensible through scientific evidence found in the universe itself, chance cannot explain the moral conscience found in humans. If Sagan was right, then who could say that murder, lying, adultery, rape, and theft are wrong? If chance governs all things, then there should be no rules or ethics, for no morality can exist within a world of chance.

Furthermore, how could humans demand rights in light of their own inherent dignity if they are simply products of a valueless cause-and-effect series of events that evolved over time by chance? If man's morality evolved over time and by chance, all we could do is *describe* how humans actually function; we could not *prescribe* how humans *ought* to behave.[184] Yet that is what we do in each and every society around the world. In short, we could never make absolute statements about right and wrong if the world was created and governed by chance. The idea is not only unscientific, it is absurd.

---

[181]   Sproul, 148-149.
[182]   Sproul, 149.
[183]   Sagan, 4.
[184]   Paul Copan, "A Moral Argument," *Passionate Conviction: Contemporary Discourses on Christian Apologetics,* ed. Paul Copan & William Lane Craig (Nashville: B&H Publishers, 2007), 88.

Out of a universe composed of atoms and molecules, it is striking that personal, rational, and moral creatures such as humans should arise. What can account for this extraordinary fact? Naturalism says that personality, rationality, and morality have all arisen by chance out of impersonal, irrational, and amoral being. If this were actually true, then the evolutionary stream would have risen much higher, qualitatively speaking, than its source. But any such theory falls far short of full rationality and scientific observation, for science has taught us that a cause does not produce an effect that contains in itself qualities altogether lacking in the cause. If the world contains personal, rational, and moral creatures, as it does, it can only be because the cause of the world is personal, rational, and moral.[185]

Are There Moral Absolutes?

Dan Story said:

Comparative studies in anthropology and sociology reveal a universal standard of behavior in all people, regardless of their culture, religion, or their period in history. Not only Western culture, but also Eastern societies of Hindus and Buddhists and Egyptians have had a similar concept of right and wrong. Even primitive cultures have exhibited this universal awareness of what is evil, this innate sense of right and wrong that helps people everywhere judge the injustice of others and themselves. This generic moral code is manifested worldwide in prohibitions against murder, stealing, lying, rape, cheating, and so on.[186]

The moment someone engages another person in the moral law argument for the existence of God, moral laws are presupposed by both parties, even if one party assumes there are no moral absolutes, for that in itself is a moral stance. The very foundation

---

[185] Pinnock, 117.
[186] Story, 29.

of any argument is a law in which to argue; otherwise, there is no argument to be made. This means that the moral law is irrefutable.

Although it is a self-defeating statement to claim that "there are no absolutes," for one must make an absolute statement in their attempt to refute absolutes, the claim *there are no moral absolutes* is not self-defeating. Yet because those who deny moral absolutes tend to value their moral right to deny them, the statement leaves them open to exposure. For instance, if someone said, "I do not believe in moral absolutes," and an alert apologist responded with, "Only dim-witted Nazis believe there are no moral absolutes," the first person would, no doubt, be highly offended for having been insulted for giving their opinion. This is because the statement's offensive nature devalues the person and their right to their own opinion, however ridiculous it may be. Yet is that not the issue? When a person who believes there are no moral absolutes values their right to their own opinion, are they not espousing the moral law?

People who believe there are no moral absolutes also believe they have a moral right to their opinion, but they often fail to realize this until they are insulted by their own viewpoint. Their offended sensibilities and complaints actually reveal that they too believe in moral absolutes, for they value their right to say that there are none. In other words, even those who deny all *values* nevertheless *value* their right to make that denial. And therein lies the inconsistency. Moral values are practically undeniable.[187]

C. S. Lewis said:

> The moment you say that one set of moral ideas can be better than another, you are, in fact, measuring them both by a standard, saying that one of them conforms to that standard more nearly than the other. But the standard that measures two things is something different from either. You are, in fact, comparing them both with some Real Morality, admitting that there is such a thing as a real Right, independent of what people think, and that some people's ideas get nearer to that real Right than others. Or put it this way: if your moral ideas can be truer,

---

[187] Geisler and Turek, 173.

and those of the Nazis less true, there must be something—some Real Morality—for them to be true about.[188]

With the issue of tolerance being so widespread today and considered the highest moral road we can take, Lewis' logic can be used to argue *against* tolerance as the highest ideal. After all, those who espouse tolerance are espousing one moral idea over all the others while trying to include all the others! Geisler and Turek commented:

> Tolerance itself is a moral principle. If there is no Moral Law, then why should anyone be tolerant? Moreover, the plea to be tolerant is a tacit admission that the behavior to be tolerated is wrong. Why? Because you don't need to plead with people to tolerate good behavior, only bad. No one needs to be talked into tolerating the behavior of Mother Teresa, only the behavior of some relativists. Likewise, no one makes excuses for acting like Mother Teresa. We only make excuses when we act against the Moral Law. We wouldn't do so if it didn't exist.[189]

Those who oppose the moral argument for God's existence oppose it as a subjective argument, and they tend to oppose it *absolutely*. In doing so, they become guilty of making their own subjective judgment since they judge the moral argument to be wrong. This is truly a post-modern way of thinking, although thankfully, it is not the way society is governed. If we had a truly post-modern culture, the ethic that would govern us would be that no one could make right-wrong judgments because there is no moral law. This is why post-modernism is impossible, for to make the judgment that there are no right-wrong statements is to make a right-wrong statement since it judges right-wrong statements to be wrong.

---

[188] C. S. Lewis, *Mere Christianity* (New York: Collier Books, 1943), 25.
[189] Geisler and Turek, 181.

If one view of morality is subjective, then so is the other for judging it. What becomes evident is that the detractors of the moral argument argue in a circle by claiming to make an objective statement about moral laws, for they are implying there is a moral law in their effort to deny it. They make "nothing but" statements that require "more than" knowledge.[190] So they obviously hold to some absolute standard, albeit an arbitrary one. While denying moral absolutes, these people *demand* to be treated fairly, with civility, and with dignity. If they are insulted, have their car stolen, are lied to, or are physically struck, they will demand justice based on the moral absolutes they deny in debates but rely on for fair treatment.

Though not all moral laws are agreed on from one person to the next, some basic moral laws are fundamental to all humans. The way people react when some injustice has been done to them reveals their moral values. For instance, someone may advocate lying to achieve a certain end, but if that same person is lied to, they typically do not take it so well. Another example is sexual promiscuity. Many people claim it is a fact of life and ought not be judged (note the moral stance of *ought* in that statement). Yet those same people would disapprove of their spouse cheating on them or their young daughter living a loose life.

The same is true with abortion. Although many believe the unborn are not human and can thus be aborted under the principle of a woman's right to choose (note the absolute moral belief that a woman should have the right to choose), the underlying moral issue is murder. If pro-choicers and abortionists could be persuaded that these children are fully human while in their mother's womb, would not abortion cease due to it being murder? After all, even abortionists oppose the senseless death of children, the raping of women, and other such atrocities. No society tolerates these things.

Furthermore, no society rewards cowardly behavior like running away from a battle or betraying the confidence of another. Why? Because a moral law is inherent within all humans.

---

[190] Douglas Russell, "Obstacles to Evangelism in Contemporary China," *Christian Apologetics Journal* Vol. 6 (Matthews, NC: Southern Evangelical Seminary, 2007), 73.

Certainly, some of the parameters of morality are gray areas to humans and up for debate, but there is indeed agreement within the human race that the moral law exists. Since there is without question a moral law inherent within us, since naturalism has no explanation for moral laws, and since the revelation of an all-powerful and loving God is both logical and historical, it stands to reason that *the moral law has its origin with God.*

Friedrich Nietzsche's Arguments Against the Moral Law

Friedrich Nietzsche (1844–1900) denied the existence of both the moral law and moral absolutes. Being a nihilist (believing in no authorities and no objective truths), he sat at the opposite end of the moral spectrum from Immanuel Kant, who believed in both the moral law and a transcendent God, though he was not a Christian. Nietzsche boldly claimed that: 1) "God is dead"[191] and man killed Him;[192] 2) "Truths are illusions"[193]…"there is no truth."[194]

Thus, according to Nietzsche, man is free to create his own ethic and transcend the traditional beliefs of right and wrong. He is free from the slave morality of those who believe in God's existence.[195] Sproul noted that although Nietzsche believed that alternatives to theism were grim (no justice, no absolutes, etc.), he still saw no reason to assume the existence of God. He felt that Kant's view of God, and certainly anyone else who believed in God, was a hindrance to their ability to rise above the

---

[191] Friedrich Nietzsche, *The Gay Science*, nos. 108, 125, in *The Nietzsche Reader*, ed. Keith Ansell Pearson and Duncan Large (Oxford Blackwell Publishing, 2006), 219, 224.

[192] Nietzsche, 224.

[193] Friedrich Nietzsche, "On Truth and Lies in a Nonmoral Sense," in *The Nietzsche Reader*, no. 1, 117.

[194] Friedrich Nietzsche, *The Will to Power*, trans. Walter Kaufmann and R.J. Hollingdale, ed. Walter Kaufman (New York: Random House, 1967), 549, 291.

[195] Hendrik van der Breggen, "Awakening from the Nightmare: A Critical Overview of Friedrich Nietzsche's Philosophy," *Christian Research Journal* 34, no. 1 (January 2010), 38.

meaninglessness of life. Clearly, Nietzsche understood that once God is dead, natural rights, morality, and the idea of progress become total shams.[196]

In spite of all Nietzsche's psychotic ramblings about there being no truth and no God, vehemently claiming that there are no facts, "only interpretations,"[197] Hendrik van der Breggen cogently observed that "If there are only perspectives (interpretations), then the thesis that there are only perspectives is a perspective too—one among many."[198] With this self-defeating philosophy, it is amazing that Nietzsche wrote so much given that he apparently did not believe anything he said or wrote. If a man does not believe in truth, why write? Why philosophize? Why tell anyone anything? If his philosophy is that there is no truth, then there is no reason to espouse anything, for in doing so, he espouses some perceived truth, whether it is true or not.

Atheism in its purest form naturally leads to nihilism—the rejection of all religious and moral principles with the conclusion that life is without meaning. But because most atheists *do* believe in human rights and their own personal dignity (biblical doctrines that reflect the mind and character of God), atheists have to *borrow* from theism to justify how they live and what they live for. After all, what sense does human dignity make if humans are mere accidents? Even atheists like Karl Marx, who called religion an opiate for the masses, and Sigmund Freud, who believed religion was a crutch for weak people, had a *purpose* they thought everyone should pursue. These two men were educated and opinionated, defending their view that people invented religion to help them deal with their fears. They believed that they offered hope to a hopeless and pathetic world that believed in God. Yet their atheistic worldview was inconsistent with the way they taught and wrote, for their writings promoted purpose and a better life.

Charles Darwin, and all other evolutionists for that matter, must have struggled with man's ability to reason given their belief that man evolved from a dim-witted monkey. It is self-defeating to claim that there is no moral agent who created the universe and all

---

[196] Sproul, 154.
[197] Nietzsche, *The Will to Power*, 267.
[198] van der Breggen, 40.

it contains, while at the same time assuming a trustworthy reasoning process to arrive at the conclusion that man cannot trust his reasoning since it comes from unreasoning origins![199] But this is not self-defeating for Bible-believing Christians. We know the Scriptures teach that all have an innate sense of right and wrong (Rom. 2:14–15) given to us by our Creator. Pinnock commented:

> The Christian message is tailor-made to solve the problem of morality. There seems to be a wide discrepancy between our inward inclinations and the moral law. What man obviously needs is divine redemption in which there is the possibility of a significant degree of righteousness in this world and a promise of perfect righteousness in the world to come. We desperately need a healing power from beyond ourselves. This condition is richly fulfilled in the Christian gospel: 'For the grace of God has appeared for the salvation of all men' (Titus 2:11).[200]

For the Bible-believing Christian, there is indeed a Moral Lawgiver, the Lord God Almighty, who gave Moses His perfect moral code in the Decalogue (Exod. 20:1–17) sometime around 1450 BC. Amazingly, these laws are as applicable today as they were over 3,500 years ago. Sins like murder, lying, and stealing are still considered immoral behavior and thus punished by the law of the land. Only God can be considered the source of such moral ideals. The fact that human moral codes still reflect God's laws points to the existence of God—the Moral Lawgiver.

Geisler and Turek summarize the moral argument in eight points:

1. The moral law is *undeniable* because those who deny it tend to value their right to deny it, for while they desire everyone to value them as people, they deny that there are values for all persons.

---

[199] Copan, 89.
[200] Pinnock, 119.

2. We know the moral law exists by our reactions, for if people are treated unfairly, they will appeal to the moral law for fair treatment.

3. The moral law is the basis for human rights. Under what other law would the Nazi war criminals have been tried in Nuremburg for violating basic human rights? If these morals did not transcend the laws of the German government, there would be no grounds for condemning the Nazis.

4. The moral law is the unchanging standard of justice, for to know evil is to assume a moral good.

5. The moral law defines a real difference between moral positions, for to promote moral relativism we have to conclude that there's no moral difference between a person who lives to do good to others vs. one who lives to hurt others.

6. The moral law tells us what is absolutely wrong because we inherently know what is absolutely right. To say that abortion is right, for instance, is to say that women have the right to choose. But does not standing for one's "right" to do or believe something imply a moral absolute to have such a right?

7. The moral law is the grounds for political and social dissent. In government and in Hollywood, people espouse their opinions on just about every issue—from abortion rights to fiscal policy. But if there is no God, there can be no objective grounds for holding to any position. There is no *right* to an abortion, for example, because without God there are no rights. So by rebelling against the Moral Law, atheists undermine their grounds for rebelling against anything.

8. If there were no moral law, then we wouldn't make excuses for violating it. Even the issue of tolerance reveals the Moral Law, for tolerance itself is a moral principle that demands toleration for something considered not true.[201]

---

[201] Geisler and Turek, 172-181.

The words of Clark Pinnock cogently conclude the moral argument for God's existence:

> What we do maintain is that only religious belief renders the existence of the moral dimension *understandable*. It alone can explain what transpires in that area of human experience. Apart from belief in God, the moral order is an impenetrable mystery... Surely it is plain that humane values are not likely to persist if the naturalistic view of the world should become dominant. By leaving God out of the picture, secularism undermines the very foundation on which even its own ethical concerns must rest. It is totally self-stultifying. The Christian faith, on the other hand, supplies a superb basis for a truly ethical concern for other people. By all means let us dedicate ourselves to the good of all mankind. But let us do it within the framework which truly sustains so noble a commitment.[202]

---

[202] Pinnock, 119.

Chapter 8

DOES THE EXISTENCE OF EVIL PROVE THERE IS NO GOD?

In Ravi Zacharias' book *The End of Reason: A Response to the New Atheists*, he addresses atheist Sam Harris' questions about what God was doing during hurricane Katrina which struck New Orleans in 2005, devastating the city and people inside it. Harris, like most atheists, puts the God he rejects on trial when he asks why the Christian God allows evils like hurricanes, rape, and the senseless torture of innocent children.[203] In essence, when anyone asks such a question, they are making a value judgment about what they think is right and wrong. And when disasters occur, they wonder why such things would be allowed to occur if a loving God actually exists.

To be fair, this issue confuses even the most faithful of Christians, but when avowed atheists pose the question, they are saying essentially that they see no moral order at work. Furthermore, if a God could be proven to exist, they would judge Him based on the fact that He would ever allow evil to exist and torment seemingly innocent people.

Since this is an issue that arguably everyone ponders at some point in their life, it demands a proper and biblical response. Therefore, an apologist worth his salt (i.e., any educated Christian) should be able to turn the table on this issue and use the argument against God's existence as an argument *for* God's existence. The late C. S. Lewis, atheist-turned-Christian, wrote:

---

[203] Zacharias, 50.

> [As an atheist] my argument against God was that the universe seemed so cruel and unjust. But how had I got this idea of just and unjust? A man does not call a line crooked unless he has some idea of a straight line. What was I comparing this universe with when I called it unjust?[204]

Lewis was admitting that there was indeed a moral law in his mind even when he questioned God's existence, for even those who deny a supreme moral lawgiver believe in moral absolutes (cf. Rom. 2:14–15). They tend to judge the Christian God by their own moral absolutes without realizing from where their moral absolutes derive. Dan Story said:

> By identifying what is evil, atheists implicitly acknowledge that God is. We could not know what evil is, in any universal sense, unless a moral standard exists outside of us. Without a moral absolute—namely— independent of human consciousness, there would be no criteria to determine what is right or wrong, whether what is wrong today will be wrong tomorrow, whether what is wrong for me is also wrong for you, and whether what is wrong in my culture is also wrong in yours. I could not justify telling you what you ought to do unless there was an absolute standard of moral behavior independent of individual persons and cultures.[205]

Once again, the problem with the atheistic worldview is that it has to borrow from the Christian worldview to make these kinds of moral judgments. The atheistic worldview cannot in any way account for why moral laws exist. The Christian worldview, however, exists quite peacefully alongside a holy God, the Moral Lawgiver. If atheists were consistent with their worldview, they would let science be their guide and *welcome* the murder of anyone who stands in the way of another. The survival of the fittest is a scientific fact that they believe has led to the present day

---

[204] Lewis, *Mere Christianity*, 45.
[205] Story, 29.

population—from bacteria all the way up to people. If only the strong have survived up to the present day, then insofar as the murder of another benefits the survival of the murderer, how can it be wrong? As Ravi Zacharias said, "Atheists cannot have it both ways. If the murder of innocents is wrong, it is wrong not because science tells us it is wrong but because every life has intrinsic worth—a postulate that atheism simply cannot deduce."[206]

If God Exists, Why Does He Allow Evil?

Bible-believing Christians know that evil exists because sin exists and man is responsible for sin being in the world, which results in death (Rom. 5:12). In fact, *man* chose to bring sin into God's perfect creation. In the beginning, while Adam was living in a world without sin, without sunburn, without thorns, even without any need for clothing, God told him, "From any tree of the garden you may eat freely; but from the tree of the knowledge of good and evil you shall not eat, for in the day that you eat from it you shall surely die" (Gen. 2:16–17). Yet Adam and his wife transgressed God's command and ate from that forbidden tree (Gen. 3:1–19). Therefore, sin entered the world through them and was passed on to their offspring and to the earth itself (cf. Rom. 5:12–14). From that day to the present, sin has plagued mankind—from natural disasters to sickness and death.

People complain about evil being in the world, but since we have all sinned and continue to sin, we need look no further than our own mirror if we want someone to blame. Today's evils, therefore, exist because of our rebellion against God. And we now live with the consequences of our sinful actions. Yet God in all of His mercy and grace has come to us in Jesus Christ to relieve us of the penalty for sin. All those who receive Christ as Lord and Savior, who submit to Him in faith, are saved from God's wrath. Although they continue to live in a world plagued with sin and its consequences, they have been forgiven for their transgressions and are able to look past this world into their eternal future with Christ.

---

[206] Zacharias, 52-53.

Since atheists object to the Christian explanation of why evil, suffering, and death exist, it is up to the apologist to answer their questions philosophically. It is no less valid to answer a person philosophically insofar as what we say is in accordance with truth. After all, truth is truth, and God is the Author of all truth, whether that truth is found in the Bible or not.

The problem of evil for the atheist is an intellectual problem. This is in accordance with the Bible's teaching which says that unregenerate man's problem is his intellect, for he is dead in his trespasses and sin (cf. Eph. 2:1–5). And the dead mind, which cannot discern matters of the Spirit, is unable to comprehend the existence of evil alongside a holy God. First, the atheist will use his depraved intellect to argue that the Bible speaks of a holy God, but the Bible contradicts itself since that holy God *allows* such atrocious evils and may even instigate them. The atheist cannot accept such a God, so he rejects Him outright. Second, the atheist will use natural disasters that devastate people (i.e., hurricanes, earthquakes, tsunamis, etc.) and atrocities like the existence of innocent, starving children to conclude that a holy God cannot exist alongside such evils.

Craig notes two tasks that face the apologist with regard to explaining the existence of evil. First, he must answer the atheist's misguided logic, which says it is logically impossible for God to exist alongside evil. Second, the apologist must answer *probabilistically* in the sense that although it might seem improbable that God and evil exist alongside each other, it is conceivable.[207]

Is it Logical that God and Evil Exist Alongside Each Other?

In the struggling mind of the atheist, he believes that if there really is an eternal, all-powerful God, He can create any world He chooses to create. Furthermore, it stands to reason in the atheist's mind that this omnibenevolent God would prefer a perfect world

---

[207] William Lane Craig, *Hard Questions, Real Answers* (Wheaton, IL: Crossway Books, 2003), 80-81.

with no sin or evil. The fact that the existing world is *not* that world means there is no God. An atheist might not promote a world of puppets created by God that did everything He programmed them to do, but atheists believe it would be a holy God's *preference* for all of His creatures to make the right choices all the time. And with His power, this God would have created such a world.

Eighteenth century skeptic David Hume said, "Is [God] willing to prevent evil but not able? Then He is impotent. Is He able but not willing? Then He is malevolent. Is He both able and willing? Whence then is evil?"[208] Dissecting Hume's argument, Craig said that his two assumptions are not necessarily true. First, it is not necessarily true that an all-powerful God would want to create just any possible world, especially a world where His created people were not given a free will (which man clearly has). Second, God's omnipotence does not mean that He can do logical impossibilities, such as make a round square or *make* someone *freely choose* to do something. Thus, if God grants people a genuine free will, and in their free will they choose to rebel against Him (as was the case in the Garden of Eden in Genesis 3), then God cannot be said to have failed; only His free-thinking creatures did.[209]

If God created people who choose evil, and clearly He has, then the only way He could prevent their choosing of evil would be to remove their free will. Thus, it is *possible* that this world that God created contains free creatures who create their own evils with their free will. Furthermore, if God's created order included the creation of angels, who also have a free will, and who have powers that transcend those possessed by mankind, then natural evils might be explained by those angels who chose to rebel against God (demons) as the agents behind those natural evils. Logically speaking, God would no more remove their free will than that of humans.[210]

---

[208] David Hume, *Dialogues Concerning Natural Religion* (Indianapolis, IN: Bobbs-Merrill, 1980), 198. Quoted in Craig, *Hard Questions, Real Answers,* 82.

[209] Craig, 83.

[210] Craig, 83.

Any mention of demons being responsible for natural disasters and the like will sound foolish to an atheist, but at this point of the discussion about God and evil existing alongside each other, all the apologist is concerned with is whether it is logical that God and evil can exist together. We are not yet talking about realities or probabilities, just logic. Logically speaking, all that has been said is that there is a God who created both man and angels, giving both a freewill with which they exercised freely in rebellion against God. *And that is why there is evil in the world.* It is not relevant if someone objects to this scenario as improbable, for this half of the argument is only concerned with logic.

In Hume's second assumption, he supposes that if God is all good, He would not allow suffering. Yet this too is not necessarily true. If we use experience to conclude that God has used pain and suffering in people's lives to bring about some greater good, then God cannot be scrutinized for being evil in allowing such. After all, who learns anything of substance during the easy times of life? Is not character built during the tough times? Note the words of C. S. Lewis who surmised about a patient enduring a surgery. He said, "The goodness of the surgeon is that he is diligent to cut on the human body to fix the patient's problem. How could he be good if he succumbed to the patient's plea to stop because it hurt? He could stop the surgery, but how could that help the patient?"[211] God *can* exist alongside evil, even using it for His purposes.

Something that most people would agree on, both Christians and atheists, is that good seems to outweigh the bad in the world where we live. Though there are many things to fret about, cry about, and even go to war over, the world does seem more good than bad, more worth living in than it does not living. Therefore, the apologist might argue that God has created a world that has the absolute most good it can have for the least amount of evil. Yes, God created the perfect world in the beginning and gave man the opportunity to exist within it. But when man sinned, God sovereignly implemented the present scheme that is in keeping with His ultimate purposes for His created world. It is God's purpose to reveal Himself by demonstrating His mercy, grace, and

---

[211] C. S. Lewis, *A Grief Observed* (London: Faber & Faber, 1985), 55-56. Quoted in Craig, *Hard Questions, Real Answers,* 84.

love. Therefore, by allowing His created people to rebel by their own free will, and yet still demonstrating His love, mercy, and grace toward them, God is able to demonstrate that which is in keeping with His overall purposes.

To summarize whether it is logical that God and evil exist alongside each other, the apologist only has to show that God and evil *can* coexist as a logical possibility. And if God can use evil for His own divine purposes, then He can logically exist alongside evil. If the objector aims to show it is logically impossible for God and the evil in the world to both exist, then he has to prove that God cannot have morally sufficient reasons for permitting the amount and kinds of evil that exist. The burden of proof, therefore, moves from the Christian to the atheist.

Is it Probable that God and Evil Exist Alongside Each Other?

The second part of the argument that Craig suggests is to demonstrate whether it is *probable* that God and evil can exist side by side.[212] Without doing any exposition of a biblical text or talking about any theological system in depth, it seems clear just from reading various prophecies in the Bible (Ezek., Dan., Matt., 2 Thess., Rev.) that God not only foresaw that sin would enter His creation, God is also using sin and evil to bring His ultimate plan and purpose to a conclusion. All of history is moving toward God's ultimate goal, and God is using all means to do this, even evil. Therefore, the presence of evil in the world that God created is neither a surprise nor a hindrance to God, but is an opportunity for Him to bring His perfect plan to completion. He will be glorified for His mercy and grace upon sinful people, and He will be glorified for the justice He metes out on those who have sinned without receiving His grace—the grace He offered through His Son, Jesus Christ.

If God decreed before the foundation of the world that salvation be granted to some (cf. Acts 13:48; Eph. 1:4–12; Rev. 13:8; 17:8), then the horrific death of Christ on the cross was

---

[212] Craig, 89-112.

necessary to atone for their sins. Likewise, if God decreed that Israel would once again become a state in 1948 after almost 1900 years of being trodden down by Gentiles, then the Holocaust was His avenue to finally bring Israel to statehood. And if God decreed before time began that He would display His love, mercy, and grace to a sinful people, then in His sovereign plan He chose to use evil to reveal His love, mercy, and grace. After all, without evil and the sin mankind is born into, how could God show His love, mercy, and grace?

We certainly do not have all the answers as to why evil is allowed to exist, but we can not only see the logic in it, we can also show the *probability* that God exists alongside evil by simply showing that God has a morally sufficient reason to permit it. Man may want to judge God for what God does or for what He allows, but if God is real, then at the very least He understands all the events that unfold before His watchful eyes. Maybe God could have gone about establishing the state of Israel in a less violent way than the Holocaust, but can a fallible man honestly determine what a holy God should do and how a holy God must act? Not at all (cf. Rom. 9:20).

Craig lists four Christian doctrines that increase the probability that God and evil can indeed coexist in this world.[213] First, *the chief purpose of life is not happiness, but the knowledge of God.* Many evils occur in life that may be utterly pointless with respect to the goal of producing human happiness. But they may not be pointless with respect to producing a deeper knowledge of God. It may well be the case that natural and moral evils are part of the means God uses to draw people into His kingdom, and man may question this. But who is man to answer back to God? Shall what is molded say to its molder, "Why did you make me like this?"

Second, *mankind is in a state of continual rebellion against God and His purpose,* and he has been ever since he sinned in the Garden of Eden (Gen. 3). The Christian is thus not surprised about the moral evil in the world. On the contrary, the Scriptures indicate that God has given those who choose to remain in their sin over to

---

[213] Craig, 94-101.

sin. God does not interfere to stop mankind, but allows human depravity to run its course (cf. Rom. 1:24).

Third, *God's purpose is not restricted to this life—a life that spills over beyond the grave into eternal life.* The apostles and the martyrs of the Church from the first century to the present have suffered intensely, for this is how God molded their character and made them into the men He designed them to be (cf. Phil. 1:29). God molds and makes His people after His likeness through difficult trials and tribulations. His faithful followers learn to look back on their sufferings and praise Him for them.

Fourth, *the knowledge of God is an incommensurable good.* Since suffering brings Christians closer to God, causing their knowledge of Him to increase, the evils they suffer are necessary and ultimately good. It may well be the case that God is not so much concerned with the evils people endure, but with their attitudes in the midst of them. In order to bring people to salvation or into a deeper relationship with Him, God may permit intense suffering.

Taken together, these considerations make it neither illogical nor improbable that God and evil can exist alongside each other. None of these arguments actually *prove* God's existence, but neither do they disprove it. Though atheists would likely disagree, it seems that these arguments point far *more* toward God's existence alongside evil than not.

The conclusions we might draw from this are the following: 1) If God does not exist, then objective moral values do not exist; 2) Evil exists; 3) Therefore, objective moral values exist; 4) Therefore, God exists. Since man is morally guilty before God, the question is not how God can justify Himself to man, but how man can be justified before God. The answer: through trusting in the Son of God—Jesus Christ—by exchanging his slavery to sin with submission to Christ as Lord and God.

Chapter 9

DO MIRACLES PROVE GOD'S EXISTENCE?

If it is true that there is indeed a God, an eternal and necessary Being who created all things out of nothing, then it is logical that He not only has the ability to perform miracles but that He *does* perform miracles, at times working through certain people to perform them. The Bible reveals that there *is* only one God (Deut. 6:4–9) and one of the ways He communicates His being is through the special avenue of miracles—events that signify a supernatural intervention because of their inexplicable nature to contradict the laws of nature. If a worldview does not allow for God, then it also does not allow for miracles. Ronald Nash said:

> For a naturalist, the universe is analogous to a closed box. Everything that happens inside the box is caused by, or is explicable in terms of, other things that exist within the box. *Nothing* (including God) exists outside the box; therefore, nothing outside the box we call the universe or nature can have any causal effect within the box...The major reason, then, why naturalists do not believe in miracles is because their worldview prevents them from believing. The worldview of Christian theism affirms the existence of a personal God who transcends nature, who exists "outside the box." Christian supernaturalism denies the eternity of nature. God created the world freely and *ex nihilo* (out of nothing). The universe is contingent in the sense that it would not have begun to exist without God's creative act and it could not continue to exist without

God's sustaining activity. The very laws of the cosmos that naturalists believe make miracles impossible were created by this God. Indeed one of naturalism's major problems is explaining how mindless forces could give rise to minds, knowledge, and sound reasoning.[214]

Atheist Antony Flew called miracles "something which would never have happened had nature, as it were, been left to its own devices."[215] In brief, a miracle is a divine intervention into the natural world. It is a supernatural exception to the regular course of the world that would not have occurred otherwise.[216] The miracles in the Bible certainly fit this definition, having three specific traits: 1) They are perceivable by both believers and unbelievers; 2) They appear to either intervene or facilitate the normal sequence of natural laws through which God governs the universe; 3) They are performed for the purpose of executing a divine act, validating a religious truth, or illustrating a religious principle.[217]

If there is a God and if He performs miracles, He would conceivably use them to convince everyone that the person He is working the miracle through is one of His authentic messengers. In other words, in order for God to reveal Himself and His glory to man, He would work a miracle through a person and speak through that person, saying, "Thus says the LORD." Moses is a prime example. God not only chose him to lead Israel out of Egyptian bondage (Exod. 3:7–10), He displayed His power through Moses in order to show His glory to the Israelites. Likewise, for Moses to be heard by Pharaoh, Moses needed to show he was truly speaking for God, so God worked miracles through him (7:9). Thus, Moses authenticated to Pharaoh and Israel that God was working through

---

[214] Ronald Nash, "Are Miracles Believable?" *The Apologetics Study Bible: Real Questions, Straight Answers, Stronger Faith,* ed. Ted Cabal, Chad Owen Brand, E. Ray Clendenen, et al. (Nashville, TN: Holman Bible Publishers, 2007), 96.

[215] Antony Flew, "Miracles," in *The Encyclopedia of Philosophy,* Paul Edwards, ed., vol. 5 (New York: Macmillan and the Free Press, 1967), 346. Quoted in Norman L. Geisler, *Miracles and the Modern Mind: A Defense of Biblical Miracles* (Grand Rapids, MI: Baker Book House, 1992), 14.

[216] Norman L. Geisler, *Miracles and the Modern Mind: A Defense of Biblical Miracles* (Grand Rapids, MI: Baker Book House, 1992), 14.

[217] Story, 152.

Him. The same is true for the New Testament apostles, who also performed signs and wonders to confirm that they were indeed God's chosen messengers who spoke God's revelation (2 Cor. 12:12; Heb. 2:3–4; cf. Acts 9:32–42).

God, insofar as He exists, might also use miracles to authenticate the validity of Jesus of Nazareth who came to explain the nature of God (cf. John 1:18). Some examples of this are Jesus' miraculous conception and virgin birth (Luke 1:35), His signs and wonders (John 5:36; 11:41–42), and His resurrection from the dead (Matt. 12:38–40). Jesus performed hundreds of miracles, though not all are recorded in the Bible (cf. John 21:25). Those that are recorded serve the purpose of revealing Jesus Christ as God's only Son. They not only met the physical needs of those who benefitted from them, they served to authenticate Jesus as the Messiah (John 10:37–38).

Therefore, if miracles can be proven, then they prove that God exists since they are acts of God that confirm the truth of God. Miracles are thus events that are both *morally* and *theologically* compatible with a theistic God.[218]

The Denial of Miracles

Naturalists deny that miracles can occur, for their worldview does not allow for miracles since they cannot be explained naturally. Jesus Seminar cofounder John Dominic Crossan, a staunch adversary of the possibility of miracles, said, with reference to Jesus curing diseases, that Jesus "did not and could not cure that disease or any other one."[219] As to Christ's resurrection from the dead, Crossan said, "I do not think that anyone, anywhere, at any time brings dead people back to life."[220] But it is not as though Crossan believes that strange, unexplainable things cannot occur. For example, if Christ's resurrection could be proven to him, or a naturalist like him, he would simply give nature credit for allowing

---

[218] Geisler, *Christian Apologetics*, 282.
[219] John Dominic Crossan, *Jesus: A Revolutionary Biography* (San Francisco: HarperCollins, 1994), 82.
[220] Crossan, 95

something that he cannot currently explain. That is why he said Jesus' resurrection would be the "supreme 'nature' miracle."[221] Commenting on the absurdity of this, Geisler said:

> The arguments against miracles, however, beg the question, for they presuppose that miracles are impossible either in principle or in practice. Rather than *looking* at the evidence for or against miracles, they end up *legislating* in advance the impossibility of the miraculous. They say in effect: "whatever happens in the natural world is a natural event." But some things that happen *in* the natural world may have a supernatural origin. In point of fact, if there is a God who can act (viz., a theistic God), then acts of God (i.e., miracles) are automatically possible. Thus, all arguments for God's existence need to be exhausted first.[222]

The clear reason why people reject miracles is not because they have taken all the miracle accounts that exist both inside and outside the Bible and scrutinized them to the point of concluding their impossibility. They have simply decided that miracles are impossible in spite of any evidence to the contrary. A naturalist might say, "I do not believe in miracles because I am a naturalist, and miracles do not happen in a naturalistic world." This faith system of the naturalist, therefore, negates miracles not because they have disproved them, but because their worldview will not allow them to believe in anything outside the natural, material world.

Miracles are not scientific per se, for a miracle cannot be tested and retested to determine whether it occurred (if it could, it would cease to be a miracle!). This is because miracles are historical events, taking place in time and space, and science is unable to prove historical events. Since the Bible is a document filled with historical accounts of various events, the authenticity of

---

[221] John Dominic Crossan, *The Historical Jesus: The Life of a Mediterranean Jewish Peasant* (San Francisco: HarperCollins, 1991), 404.

[222] Geisler, *Christian Apologetics*, 282.

the miraculous events it records requires historical investigation, not scientific. As Edward John Carnell said:

> Laws of nature are a description of what *happens*, not a handbook of rules to tell us what *cannot happen*. In choosing his laws of nature, therefore, the scientist should first consult history, and after deciding by historical evidence what has happened, should then choose his laws within the limits of historical actuality. The non-Christian thinker, intent on repudiating miracles, proceeds by a reverse method. He chooses his law without regard to historical limits, and then tries to rewrite history to fit his law. But surely this method is not only the reverse of the Christian method, it is clearly the reverse of rational procedure as well.[223]

Two men whose circular reasoning regarding the impossibility of miracles is easy to expose are Benedict Spinoza (1632–1677) and David Hume. Spinoza, a naturalist, deduced that: 1) Miracles are violations of natural laws; 2) Natural laws are immutable; 3) It is impossible to violate immutable laws; 4) Therefore, miracles are impossible. But Spinoza begs the question in that he defines natural laws as being immutable—that they cannot be overpowered, interrupted, or interfered with. If the universe had a creator—whether God or chance—and it is a miraculous and unrepeatable creation no matter which belief you choose, then the laws of nature are clearly not immutable! In reality, natural forces are muted every day. As Geisler and Turek said:

> When a baseball player catches a falling baseball, he is overpowering the force of gravity. We do the same whenever we fly planes or blast off into space. In such cases, gravity is not changed, it is simply overpowered. If finite beings like us can overpower natural forces, then

---

[223] Edward John Carnell, *An Introduction to Christian Apologetics* (Alhambra, CA: Green Leaf Press, 1948), 258. Quoted in Story, 159.

certainly the infinite Being who created those forces can do so.[224]

Much like Spinoza, Hume rejected any and all accounts of miracles, believing they could not occur. He defined a miracle as:

> ...a transgression of a law of nature by a particular volition of the Deity or by the interposition of some invisible agent... A violation of the laws of nature; and as a firm and unalterable experience has established these laws, the proof against a miracle, from the very nature of the fact, is as entire as any argument from experience can possibly be imagined.[225]

Hume believed: 1) Natural law is by definition a description of a regular occurrence; 2) A miracle is by definition a rare occurrence; 3) The evidence for the regular is always greater than that for the rare; 4) A wise man always bases his belief on the greater evidence; 5) Therefore, a wise man should never believe in miracles.

Hume did not believe that natural laws had ever been violated, for certainly no one had ever witnessed such. This was proof enough for Hume to deny all miracles. Therefore, all of Jesus' miraculous signs and wonders, including His resurrection from the dead, were nonsense to Hume. For him, those who claimed to have witnessed a miracle by Jesus Christ were very likely mistaken since the evidence against an alleged miracle will always outweigh the evidence supporting it, and a wise man will conclude that a miracle has never occurred.

First, like Spinoza's circular argument, Hume's is no less so. As C. S. Lewis wrote, "We know the experience against [miracles] to be uniform only if we know that all the reports of them are false. And we can know all the reports to be false only if we know already that miracles have never occurred. In fact, we are arguing

---

[224] Geisler and Turek, 204.

[225] David Hume, *An Enquiry Concerning Human Understanding* (LaSalle, IL, 1955), 126-27.

in a circle."[226] Second, Hume's belief in nature's immutability was a philosophical assumption that, if true, means that no baseball player can ever catch a ball flying down from the sky, and no airplane could ever defy gravity by getting off the ground.

Third, Hume's assertion that it is impossible to demonstrate the existence of God is nothing but a presupposition that proves nothing. It merely assumes without any proof. Fourth, Hume apparently would never believe an account of someone winning the lottery or a golfer getting a hole-in-one because he refused to believe in assertions that are not the norm. No matter how strong the evidence might be against that which is the norm, Hume refused to believe. Dan Story said, "If Hume's approach to miracles were applied to other areas of historical inquiry, it would effectively destroy most of the historical facts we take for granted."[227]

If we took Hume's third argument, namely, "the evidence for the regular is always greater than that for the rare," all we would need to do is find one counter-example to show the absurdity of his logic. As already stated, winning the lottery is certainly a rare occurrence, as is a hole in one. Yet they happen every day! But what about the creation of the universe? Whether you believe God created it or it came about by chance when nothing exploded into everything, it is still an example of something that has occurred only once, and it is unrepeatable. Yet it happened! So if Hume's logic could be proven, then Hume himself could not be. Why? Because David Hume was only born once, and in his own words, a wise man always bases his belief on the greater evidence. Yet Hume clearly believed he existed. And if he questioned that, he certainly did not live as if he did not exist. Geisler and Turek remarked:

> The reluctance to deal directly with the flaws in Hume's argument tells us that disbelief in miracles is probably more a matter of the will than of the mind. It seems as though some people uncritically cling to David Hume's argument because they simply don't want to

---

[226] C. S. Lewis, *Miracles* (New York, NY: Macmillan, 1978), 102.
[227] Story, 156-58.

admit that God exists. *But since we know that God exists,
miracles are possible. Any argument against miracles that
can be concocted, including that of David Hume, is
destroyed by that one fact.* For if there is a God who can
act, there can be acts of God (miracles). So in the end, it's
not miracles that are hard to believe—David Hume's
argument is hard to believe! We might say it's a "miracle"
so many people still believe it.[228]

We should note two kinds miracles in the Bible: providential
miracles in which God acts within natural laws and miracles of
creation whereby God alters or interrupts natural laws.[229]

Providential miracles occur when God interrupts the natural
flow of history or nature without actually violating natural laws
(cf. Gen. 19:24–25; Exod. 14:15–31; Matt. 17:24–27; Acts 16:26;
James 5:17–18). For example, 2 Kings 19:20–35 says that as a
result of Hezekiah's faith and prayer, God destroyed the Assyrian
army camped outside the walls of Jerusalem—185,000 men (cf.
Isa. 37:21–38)! That many men dying all at once would obviously
be unnatural, so it is by definition a miracle. Without Hezekiah's
prayer and God's divine intervention, Jerusalem would have been
sacked that day by the Assyrians. What is interesting is that the
Greek historian Herodotus also spoke of this event. His
explanation, however, was that the Assyrian army was infected by
a sudden outbreak of a fierce plague caused by rats. Story said,
"Although the event is miraculous in that it was a direct
intervention of God, it nevertheless may have involved natural
phenomenon functioning in a normal fashion but at just the
appropriate time."[230]

Miracles of creation include the might acts of God in which
distinctive and astonishing events occur that temporarily set aside
or transcend known natural laws. Examples in this category
include the creation of the world out of nothing (Gen. 1:1), Jesus
changing water into wine (John 2:1–9), feeding thousands of
people with only five loaves of bread and two fish (John 6),

---

[228] Geisler and Turek, 209-10.
[229] Story, 152.
[230] Story, 152.

granting sight to the blind (John 9), and raising Lazarus from the dead (John 11:17–44).

The importance of miracles cannot be overstated for Christians. The two miracles of Christ's incarnation and His resurrection from the dead provided the foundation for Christianity, for if either one of them are proven false, Christianity dies with them (cf. 1 Cor. 15:12–19). When Jesus was asked for a sign to reveal His true identity, His response was that "no sign will be given...except the sign of Jonah the prophet; for just as Jonah was three days and three nights in the belly of the sea monster, so will the Son of Man be three days and three nights in the heart of the earth" (Matt. 12:39–40). Jesus' answer, therefore, pointed to His divinity. As God incarnate, He was predicting His miraculous resurrection from the dead (cf. Rom. 1:4). And without His resurrection from the dead, Christianity would be a joke (cf. 1 Cor. 15:12–19).

As we conclude our brief overview of miracles, we must remember that if God exists, then miracles are possible. And if miracles are possible, and they have been witnessed, then they are like any other historical event. They must be investigated rather than denied outright. When people refuse to believe in miracles, they confuse the *believability* of miracles with the *possibility* of miracles. But probability must never conflict with evidence. When there is evidence for something, it cannot be negated based on a worldview. In other words, if there is evidence for a miracle, then probabilities for it not occurring cannot negate it, except in the mind of someone whose worldview refuses to believe in miracles. In such a case, the nonbeliever in miracles is lost in absurdity, for he begs the question of miracles by claiming up front that miracles cannot occur and attempts to prove such by disregarding all evidence to the contrary. It is downright comical that these people tend to accuse Christians of circular reasoning!

Chapter 10

THE TRANSITION FROM MERE THEISM TO CHRISTIAN THEISM

All arguments for the existence of God are just that—arguments attempting to provide cogent reasons as to why we can believe there is a God. In keeping with the goal of studying apologetics, we study these arguments to learn what we believe, why we believe it, and how to share what we believe with confidence. By God's grace, we might actually share these truths with others and have an opportunity to lead them to Christ.

Therefore, we cannot stop with arguments for theism. We must continue our reasonings about the Christian faith and point others toward *Christian theism*. There are many theistic faiths, but there is only one true God. And since other theistic belief systems affirm God's existence or the existence of a plurality of gods, Christian theists have the task of leading them out of their absurd beliefs and into all truth, for it is the truth of God that sets us free (John 8:32). With that in mind, let us examine a few of the many theistic belief systems and why they fall short in their explanation of who God truly is.

Having already shown that belief in God is scientific, logical, and intellectual, we can easily judge against the atheistic worldview that does not believe in God. Furthermore, we have shown that believing in no God provides a worldview that has to borrow from the Christian worldview in an effort to make sense of itself (which it fails to do). Therefore, we will begin with the absurdity of atheism as a worldview and proceed logically to Christian theism as the only worldview that makes sense of everything we are given to observe.

Christianity in a World of Religions

Because there are so many religions in the world today, it makes sense that people are confused as to which one might be true, if any. Obviously, a person could begin with any religion, but C.J. Hazen gives four reasons why apologists should defend Christianity as the place to begin talking truth to unbelievers and skeptics.[231]

First, the uniqueness of biblical Christianity is that it actually *invites* scrutiny while encouraging people to investigate its claims—about God, man, and the universe itself. What's more, because Christianity hinges on investigative truth, it is both testable and scientific. Essentially, Christianity hangs on one vital point: *the bodily resurrection of Jesus of Nazareth from the dead three days after his crucifixion by the Roman authorities.* The Apostle Paul wrote, "If Christ has not been raised, our preaching is useless and so is your faith" (1 Cor. 15:12ff.). Contrary to the Christian faith, religions like Hinduism, Buddhism, and Mormonism espouse the so-called truth of their faith in *feelings*— from Nirvana in Buddhism to the "burning in the bosom" of Mormonism. Not so with Christianity, for although there are inner feelings associated with it, the claims of Christianity are scientific in that they can be investigated historically and taught with logic and reason. Better yet, the truths espoused in the Christian faith can be shown to be true whether you experience a feeling or not.

Second, evangelists should begin with Christianity in order to note that salvation is presented as a *free* gift from God for those who trust in Him alone. Nothing is required except faith. In other religions, however, if God is even a part of them, the deity himself must be *appeased* through great efforts on the seeker's part. Adherents to other religions must strive, sometimes heroically, to change their thoughts, feelings, and behaviors, all in an effort to appease their desired god. One of the problems with this kind of

---

[231] Craig J. Hazen, "Christianity in a World of Religions," in *Passionate Conviction: Contemporary Discourses on Christian Apologetics,* ed. Paul Copan and William Lane Craig (Nashville: B&H Publishers, 2007), 140-153.

religion is that its followers have no way to gauge their progress to know whether the god is actually pleased.

Third, the beliefs of biblical Christianity are fully consistent with the laws of the universe—laws of logic, science, and reason. Contrary to how Christianity is often presented, it does not require blind faith. On the contrary, Christianity paints a picture of the world that is in perfect keeping with the way the world really is. Consider the problem of evil in the world today. To even label something as evil is to make a judgment based on what seems to be right to the person making the judgment. In the Christian worldview, right and wrong are clearly spelled out in the Bible and *in the hearts of all men* (cf. Rom. 2:14–15).

Hinduism and Buddhism, for instance, have no written moral code, so not only is evil undefined, these religions are actually relegated to a *state of mind*, specifically *illusion*. Therefore, they cannot necessarily label the Holocaust as evil because the horrors associated with it were only an illusion. Without a moral code, there can be no right and wrong, and in these religions, only when suffering is understood properly can it be overcome. You just relegate it to illusion and ignore it as the Buddha espoused. In Christianity, however, evil and suffering are part of the fallen world where sin is running its course through man's rebellion against God. Once sin is understood, evil and suffering are simple to explain.

Fourth, all evangelist-apologists should note that in Christianity, *Jesus is the epicenter* of their faith. Oddly enough, Jesus is respected by most other faiths as a great prophet, and He is often co-opted into them as a model for goodness. Even in Islam, Jesus is exalted, at times even higher than Muhammad. But as the epicenter of Christianity, the religion stands or falls solely on His existence as God incarnate, risen from the dead, and coming again. Thus, if all these religions incorporate Jesus and His teachings and life, ought not the seeker of truth begin with Jesus of Nazareth in their quest to understand which religion is true and which ones are false?

Atheism

Atheism is the worldview that claims there is no God or gods; hence, a-theism (no-god). Geisler noted that atheism, as a worldview, fails to provide adequate answers for some major questions about reality.[232] First, an atheist assumes that the personal arose from the impersonal. That is, matter plus chance and time gave rise to the mind, instead of an intelligent mind of God or the gods giving rise to time and matter. Second, atheism asserts that the potential gives rise to the actual instead of the actual giving rise to the potential, in spite of the fact that potentials must be actualized by some actualizer. Third, atheism cannot answer the question, "Why is there something instead of nothing?" Since there is something, who or what gave it when it did not have to be given? If nothing existing at all is actually possible, then why is there something and not nothing? Since an eternal and necessary being is necessary for anything to exist at all—a Being who transcends all the created parts—then why do atheists reject a Creator? But if the universe is unnecessary, then why does it exist? Atheism has no adequate answer for these questions. In the final analysis, atheism must hold the absurd conclusion that something comes from nothing, that is, that nonbeing is the ground on which being rests. This seems highly unreasonable.

In lieu of these unanswered questions, atheism's arguments against the existence of God have proven to be invalid, often self-defeating, and often revealing a complete lack of understanding of what the theist is arguing for. Many of their arguments can actually be used to reason *for* the existence of God. Contrary to their accusations that theists ignore science and common sense, atheists must believe that something comes from nothing, that potentials actualize themselves, and that matter generated mind. When atheists argue for the creation of the universe occurring by chance, they presuppose a design without realizing it. You cannot speak meaningfully of a universe that is totally random without borrowing from the logical Christian worldview, which presupposes the existence of God who embodies logic.

---

[232] Geisler, *Christian Apologetics*, 213-234.

In other words, speaking about chance must be done with meaningful and logical sentences, phrases, and paragraphs— communication that cannot be articulated in a world that came together from randomness. Chance does not embody logic, meaning, morals, or design. Yet that is what atheists would have us believe. In the end, it takes at least as much faith to believe the tenets of atheism as it does the foundations of Christianity. In fact, it takes far more faith to adopt the faith of an atheist than to believe in the Creator God.

Buddhism

Whereas biblical Christianity claims that ultimate reality *can* be known, granted from the transcendent God who is both personal and knowable, Buddhism does not. It is an example of an atheistic faith. Often lacking in logic and words to defend its claims, Buddhism is a maze of man-made ideas that differ starkly from the Christian faith. Believing that suffering is man's greatest enemy, Buddhism seeks to overcome this enemy by striving to learn to deal with it in various ways.

Buddhism espouses that: 1) Life is suffering; 2) Suffering is caused by desire; 3) The cessation of desire eliminates suffering; 4) The stopping of desire comes by following "the Middle Way" between the extremes of sensuousness and asceticism.[233] A true Buddhist who has reached *nirvana*, therefore, is one who never cries, never laughs, never cares for another human who is suffering, and never cares whether anyone else reaches nirvana (their ultimate state of being). To have any expectations for another person is to leave yourself open for disappointment, which leads to suffering. Buddhism in all its forms is as hopeless a faith as there ever was.

Harold Netland gives five reasons why Christianity is superior to Buddhism.[234] First, the historicity of Jesus is far more

---

[233] Ron Carlson and Ed Decker, *Fast Facts on False Teachings* (Eugene, OR: Harvest House, 1994), 23-24.

[234] Harold Netland, "The East Comes West (or Why Jesus Instead of Buddha?)," in *Passionate Conviction: Contemporary Discourses on*

attestable than the historical Buddha. In Buddha's case, there is not even a consensus as to when he lived. Worse yet, his existence means nothing to the belief system, which is atheistic. Therefore, Buddhism would not change at all if Buddha himself was a mere myth. Not so with Jesus, for without Him there is no Christianity. Second, since Jesus believed that God existed and Buddha denied His existence, they are worlds apart. In fact, Buddha was an atheist who believed that the concept of God was what caused all suffering. Third, Jesus and Buddha disagree over the root problem that plagues mankind. Whereas Jesus came to die for man's sins, Buddha diagnosed man's problem not as sin, but as ignorance and the lack of understanding of the true nature of reality. Fourth, Buddhism teaches that man is responsible for attaining his own liberation, but Jesus and the writers of the New Testament said that no man can save himself, only God can. Fifth, Buddha died (as do all other religious leaders), but the historical Jesus was witnessed alive after His death due to His resurrection from the dead—even by His enemies!

Deism

Initially, the term "deism" was used by the Swiss theologian P. Viret in 1564 when he spoke with abhorrence of people who called themselves deists to emphasize that, in contrast to atheists, they believed in God even though they accepted nothing of Christ and His teaching.[235] The term "deist" (from where "deity" derives) comes from the Latin *deus* (a god or God). Whereas theists claim that God is active in His creation, deists, while claiming to believe in God's existence, do not believe that He intervenes in the universe.

Deists believe the universe is logical proof that there is a God; hence, they believe strongly in God's natural, or general, revelation. All men know this God through what has been made and seen, and they are responsible and accountable to this Maker.

Christian Apologetics, ed. Paul Copan and William Lane Craig (Nashville: B&H Publishers, 2007), 154-169.

[235] Fahlbusch and Bromiley, *The Encyclopedia of Christianity,* vol. 1, 788.

In a sense, deists believe God spun the world into existence, then He abandoned it, caring nothing at all for what He had created. They believe that God is in no way responsible for any problems that occur among men or the natural disasters that plague us. Worst of all, they do not believe that God ever inspired a work like the Bible. For Him to have done that, God would have had to interact with His people, and deists do not believe God interacts with people. Consequently, deists who might pray would never pray to God for any direct intervention in the lives of His created people.[236]

One of the inconsistencies with deism is that deists affirm that God created the universe out of nothing, yet they do not affirm miracles. Therefore, given that the creation of the world is an inexplicable event—one that has never been observed nor able to be observed—why would deists deny that God neither works in His creation nor performs miracles? Clearly, God cares enough for men to create them so wonderfully and to make their world so inhabitable. Likewise, God's personal interactions with His created beings not only seem possible but probable. If the desire to have personal communication between the supernatural and the natural realm flows from God as personal, then not to perform miracles of personal communication (viz., revelation) would show God to be something less than personal, and if He were less than personal, would He not cease to be God?

A God concerned enough to create men in the beginning would logically be concerned enough to intervene on their behalf, and this is in keeping with His omniscience and omnibenevolence. Furthermore, since the Bible speaks of God personally interacting with man, the pinnacle of His creation, to deny the Bible's accuracy in this regard is to relegate all of its contents to man-made ideas—an accusation most deists would reject, for deists believe that God did have something to do with the Bible. How else could man have known enough to record the history of God's works?

Unconfirmed to any church affiliation, deists can be found in all denominations around the world, from Christian churches to the

---

[236] Terrence Tiessen, *Providence and Prayer: How Does God Work in the World?* (Downers Grove, IL: InterVarsity Press, 2000), 31-32.

Church of Freethought. They are made to feel most comfortable in churches where the Bible is not necessarily taught but referenced and where congregants are motivated to do good, to work for the betterment of society, and to be all they can be without relying on God or expecting Him to listen to or answer their prayers.

Pantheism

"Pantheism" (from *pan,* "all," and *theos,* "god") is a doctrine or belief that God is simply Nature, the sum total of the universal system.[237] Two important aspects are the notions that: 1) All things are God, the divinizing of the world; 2) God is all things.[238] Geisler notes six fundamentals about pantheism.[239] First, pantheism is an all-embracing view of the sum total of reality. In this sense it is both metaphysical and comprehensive. Second, pantheism has put special emphasis on an ultimate dimension of reality, namely *unity.* Third, pantheism appropriately stresses that God is really *in* the world, at least within the depths of the human soul. Fourth, pantheism acknowledges that only God is *absolute* and *necessary.* Everything else is less than ultimate and absolute in the supreme sense in which God is. Fifth, pantheism demands that some form of intuitive knowledge is essential to knowing God who is the ultimate principle (person) in religion. Sixth, pantheists believe that God cannot be expressed in positive terms with limited meaning.

What seems most obvious about the pantheistic worldview is that it is actually unaffirmable and hence, absurd. For no finite individual reality exists as an entity that is different from God since God is all and is in all. Pantheism therefore, in its strictest sense, is self-defeating because a pantheist must affirm that because God is, I am not. In other words, a person must exist in order to affirm that he does not exist! This is obviously ridiculous. Second, granting that there are no real finite selves or "I's," then there is no such thing as an I-Thou relationship between finite

---

[237] Duffield and Van Cleave, *Foundations of Pentecostal Theology,* 60.
[238] Fahlbusch and Bromiley, *The Encyclopedia of Christianity,* vol. 1, 26-27.
[239] Geisler, *Christian Apologetics,* 171-191.

beings (i.e., humans) nor between men and God. Therefore fellowship and worship are impossible in pantheism. All alleged I-thou or I-I relations reduce to I, and "I" is god. Third, pantheism cannot explain the existence of evil, for if God is all, then God is evil. Fourth, if God is all or sharing the same limits or scope in His being with the universe, then pantheism is metaphysically indistinguishable from atheism. Both hold in common that the whole is a collection of all the finite parts or aspects. The only difference is that the pantheist decides to attribute religious significance to the *all* while the atheist does not.

One example of a pantheistic religion today is Mary Baker Eddy's Christian Science Church. Adopting the idea that the self is not real but actually an illusion, an idea taken from Hinduism, Mary Baker Eddy (1821–1910) believed that all things in the universe *are God*.[240] Believing that the world is just an illusion (*maya*), she taught that in order to overcome the illusion of matter, pain, and evil, man must learn to believe that all is God, including ourselves, so that the illusion will have no grip on us.[241] Even in her own day, Eddy was not without her critics. Mark Twain is said to have sarcastically asked her, "Nothing exists but mind?" "Nothing," Eddy answered. "All else is substance-less, all else is imaginary." Twain said, "I then gave her an imaginary check, and now she is suing me for substantial dollars. It looks inconsistent."[242]

A second example of a pantheistic religion today is Hinduism. Because Hinduism has so many various sects within the religion itself, it is difficult to generalize what all Hindus believe, but one certainty within their faith is that whatever they learn, they must learn from a guru, not from their scriptures. The gurus espouse *samsara*—man's need for liberation from his eternal cycle of reincarnation. This endless cycle is the result of karma, that which goes around comes around. Hindus live and die in their sins and are born over and over again into various forms in order to

---

[240] Ron Rhodes, *Find it Quick: Handbook on Cults and New Religions* (Eugene, OR: Harvest House, 2005), 59-60.
[241] Norman L. Geisler and Ronald M. Brooks, *When Skeptics Ask* (Wheaton, IL: Victor Books, 1990), 43.
[242] Quoted in Geisler and Brooks, *When Skeptics Ask*, 38.

work through their karma. Their salvation, or liberation (*moksha*), "is obtained when the individual expands his being and consciousness to an infinite level and realizes that *atman* (the self) is the same as Brahman (the One absolute being from which all else proceeds). In other words, each Hindu must realize that he is God."[243] This is accomplished through various forms of Yoga, ceremonies, sacrifices, fasting, and pilgrimages.

Hindus strive to be able to say, "I now understand that I am God." Yet Hinduism, being a form of pantheism, makes the impossible statement of coming to believe they are God when God can only be One, and by definition, He can never arrive at a belief about being God since He has always been God. Yet the claim of godhood is the heart of all Hindu thought and religion.[244]

One of the most notable inconsistencies with Hinduism as it relates to Jesus Christ is that Hinduism does not assist people who are in need or who are suffering. They firmly believe that karma is the reason for their condition. In other words, they are suffering because of sins they committed in a previous life, and they must suffer for them in order to escape the endless cycle of karma. Hindus believe that helping someone who is suffering is actually hurting them! Yet Jesus not only helped those who were sick and hurting, He also prayed for them and loved them. Jesus said, "Love your neighbor as yourself" (Matt. 22:39) and "Whoever has the world's goods, and sees his brother in need and closes his heart against him, how does the love of God abide in him?" (1 John 3:17).

Whereas Hindu gurus are necessary to understand the Bhagavad Gita and the Upanishads (the Hindu scriptures), God's Word is plain enough to be understood by all who read it. The study of the Bible is encouraged (cf. 1 Tim. 2:15). Additionally, whereas Hinduism calls its people to empty their minds through meditation, God calls His people to fill themselves with His Word (Col. 3:16-17; cf. Eph. 5:19) and to pray that His will be done (Matt. 6:10).

Finally, the Christian faith is superior to the Hindu faith because God grants salvation to those who call upon Jesus Christ

---

[243] Geisler and Brooks, 132.
[244] Geisler and Brooks, 132.

for salvation, and He does so without judging any meritorious works of the one calling to Him for salvation. The Hindu, however, is lost in the cycle of karma and reincarnation until he someday reaches *moksha.* Until that time, he is left alone to work his own way out.[245] How much greater it is to be saved by faith alone in the God who guaranteed that He would give His Spirit to all who ask as a down payment guaranteeing our future redemption (cf. Eph. 1:13–14; 1 John 5:13).

A third example of pantheistic religion in our society today is the New Age movement. New Age theology is generally thought to be the same as ancient Gnosticism, a heretical movement that John the Apostle wrote his letters (1,2,3 John) to combat.[246] Having many of its roots in Buddhism and Hinduism, New Agers have always denied that Jesus Christ is God. In the late first century, its adherents worked to convince early Christians that Jesus was not truly a man but only *seemed* to be one. Like all false religions, it has morphed through the centuries and evolved up to the modern day.

According to Ron Carlson and Ed Decker, the New Age movement's belief about God is that there is no personal God, just a cosmic force of male-female polarity (yin-yang). New Agers espouse that Jesus evolved from a man into an Ascended Master, and that the impersonal Christ rested on Jesus for a time just like it rests on many others at various times. New Agers reject the Bible as God's Word, believe salvation to be accomplished through occult disciplines, believe that death is a myth since reincarnation keeps the soul alive forever in various capacities, and deny monotheism.[247] The roots of the movement go back to the serpent in the Garden of Eden. John MacArthur said:

> Ancient   Gnosticism   also   elevated   women, considering Eve to have been a spirit-endowed woman who actually saved Adam *from* the bungling male deity called God. Similarly, salvation for all of mankind will be

---

[245] Geisler and Brooks, 133-34.
[246] Daniel L. Akin, "1, 2, 3 John," in *The New American Commentary*, vol. 38 (Nashville: Broadman & Holman Publishers, 2001), 29.
[247] Carlson and Decker, 182-183.

brought through female power. Dame Wisdom, the Heavenly Eve, was a mystical goddess who was the source of all wisdom. She was presumed to have entered the serpent in the Garden of Eden and instructed Eve in the ultimate wisdom of self-actualization and self-fulfillment, a wisdom she passed on to Adam. As Peter Jones observes, gnosticism took redemptive history and stood it on its head, like an upside-down satanist cross in a black mass.[248]

L. Russ Bush offers some insights into the New Age movement as it contrasts with Christian theism.[249] First, many of the New Age movement's principles have sprung forth from Hinduism and Buddhism and have evolved into concerns about a new consciousness about time, man's place in the universe, and the nature of reality. The New Age movement's god is a pantheistic god who does not transcend the universe but is himself a part of the universe and made of the universe. Second, the New Age movement does not believe in sin per se, although they do speak of salvation from their physical bodies, which they believe were created by a foolish sub-god. Salvation for its adherents results from enlightenment, moving from ignorance to illumination—not faith in Jesus Christ. Finally, the New Age movement believes in reincarnation whereby an individual gets in touch with his divine nature and works off previous problems from a former life.

New Agers can be recognized by their optimism about the future. From Transcendental Meditation and yoga classes offered by big businesses to the plethora of "seeker churches" in religion where relaxation and nonthreatening atmospheres free from biblical content rule the day, the New Age movement is evident everywhere. While the people hunger for answers to their problems, the New Age philosophies just tell them to be tolerant of all. In short, the New Age movement is an alternative to biblical Christianity, although it utilizes many of Christianity's ethics and

---

[248] John MacArthur, "Titus," in *The MacArthur New Testament Commentary* (Chicago, IL: Moody Press, 1996), 80.

[249] L. Russ Bush, *"Christ in the New Age," Passionate Conviction: Contemporary Discourses on Christian Apologetics,* ed. Paul Copan and William Lane Craig (Nashville: B&H Publishers, 2007), 170-186.

beliefs to make it into a form of godliness, except without the true godliness that comes by grace, through faith in Jesus Christ.

Panentheism

In contrast to pantheism, where God has the same boundaries and is identified with the universe, *panentheism* (from Greek *pan* "all," *en* "in," and *theos* "God") is the belief that the Being of God includes and penetrates the whole universe, so that every part of it exists in Him, but, contrary to pantheism, God's Being is more than, and is not exhausted by, the universe.[250] A panentheist believes that the universe exists within God, who in turn pervades, or is "in," the universe.[251] According to Geisler, as a worldview, panentheism defines God on one hand as a finite being who is, in actuality, identified with the changing and temporal world. On the other hand, the finite god of panentheism has a potential that reaches beyond the changing and temporal world into the eternal world. In other words, the god of panentheism is growing in his perfection with man's cooperation. Similar to pantheism, panentheism stresses the immanence of God, and similar to theism, it attempts to preserve some meaningful sense in which God is transcendent to the known world. The god of panentheism is a bipolar god who is at various extremes at various times.[252]

Panentheists, like deists, can be found in many different denominations. Those who deny God's sovereign power and His omniscience believe that God is learning as He goes. Its adherents believe that God is *dipolar*—having eternal potential while seeking temporal actualization. The Nation of Islam serves as an example of panentheistic beliefs. Louis Farrakhan speaks of God (Allah) as being self-created out of eternal darkness. He said:

> The Hon. Elijah Muhammad taught us God is self created. The Holy Qur'an says He is not begotten. If God is not begotten, then God is the Originator of Himself. In

---

[250] Cross and Livingstone, 1221.

[251] Fahlbusch and Bromiley, *The Encyclopedia of Christianity,* vol. 1, 21-22.

[252] Geisler, *Christian Apologetics*, 192-212.

the process of God's self creation, He had to overcome many things... He has to overcome frustration with the pace of His own evolution, and the disappointment of that pace gave rise to patience.[253]

The Superiority of Christian Monotheism Over All Other Faiths

The atheistic proposition "God does not exist" is either meaningless since we do not know what "God" means in the statement, or it is self-defeating because it supposes that we know what "God" means in the very statement affirming that we do not know what "God" means. So theism is the logical alternative to the futile nature of atheism. But this does not give theists the logical freedom to automatically assume God exists. Although it might be logically necessary to conceive of a necessary and supreme Being, it does not follow that such a Being necessarily exists. Yet simply thinking that God exists necessarily does not actually *prove* that He exists. For instance, when we think of a square, we have to think of it as having four sides, but that does not mean that squares necessarily exist. If they do, however, they must have four sides. For his part, a nontheist is only obligated to show that it is logically possible that a necessary Being does not exist. Hypothetically, it is a logical possibility that nothing ever existed at all, including God.

Of course, it is ridiculous to believe that nothing exists since it is unaffirmable to assert such an idea. We would have to exist in order to reason that we do not exist. Yet a nontheist may aptly reply that this is true only because you are really beginning with the actual existence of the person in order to affirm that something exists. But affirming that something exists in order to deny that nothing exists is not the same as arguing from the mere *inconceivability* of God's nonexistence. The requirement is just theoretical and not actual. And if there is no actual necessity that God exists, then it is possible that such a Being does not exist

---

[253] Quoted in Norman L. Geisler and Abdul Saleeb, *Answering Islam: The Crescent in Light of the Cross*, 2nd ed. (Grand Rapids, MI: Baker Books, 2002), 334.

(although no atheistic argument has ever been able to demonstrate that a necessary, eternal being does not exist). Theists, therefore, by appealing to the undeniability that something exists in order to prove that God exists, bring in the cosmological argument for God's existence, an argument that demands a first cause. That argument, however, is based on the *a priori* idea that something already exists. It says in effect, "I exist." Therefore, we cannot deny that something necessarily exists.

What actually happens in this scenario is that the *a priori* argument that something exists is based on an *a posteriori* conclusion from effect to cause. This means that there is no rational *a priori* way to prove God's existence. In short, since we have to begin the argument with our own *a priori* existence, the *a priori* argument is no longer *a priori*. Logically, this means that the *a posteriori* argument for God's existence is also invalid since experience is never logically necessary. The opposite of any state of affairs in the world is always logically possible. We cannot attempt to prove God's existence without reference to some belief based on experience or observations. So is God's existence provable?

Geisler proposed that through a combination of the *a priori* self-evident principle of existential causality and the undeniable *a posteriori* fact that something contingent exists, we can indeed give overwhelming evidence for God's existence. Geisler said:

> First of all, this is not based on logical necessity; it admits that reality cannot be established by logical necessity. It acknowledges that it is logically possible that nothing ever existed including God. Hence there are no rationally inescapable proofs for the existence of God. The contrary to any state of affairs is always logically possible. Second, not everything from experience lacks certainty. I am certain that I exist; I cannot deny that I exist without affirming that I exist in that very denial. Hence, it is undeniable (though not logically necessary) that something exists. For even though my nonexistence is not inconceivable, it is unaffirmable. Finally, the principle of existential causality is self-evidently true. It may be stated this way: "Everything that passes from

potentiality to actuality does so under the influence of some actuality" which is what "every effect has a cause" means. Once one understands that an "effect" is something that is caused and a "cause" is that which can produce an effect, then the principle of causality is as self-evident as "all bachelors are unmarried men." One need do no more than examine the nature of the subject and predicate to see that the predicate is reducible to the subject; they are both saying the same thing. Thus, the basic theistic argument in sum: 1) every effect has a cause; 2) the world is an effect; 3) therefore, the world has a cause.[254]

Conclusion to the Arguments for God's Existence

What we have been able to surmise up to this point, firstly, is that truth can be known. We know it through philosophical reasoning using logic, sifting through empirical evidence, using scientific methods, and drawing conclusions. Secondly, drawing from the first principle, we would have to logically deduce that the opposite of truth is untruth; it is false. Thirdly, the transcendental, cosmological, ontological, teleological, and moral arguments for God's existence give us ample, though not exhaustive, evidence that God exists. Not only is there far more evidence for God's existence in these arguments than there is for His nonexistence, to say that God does not exist is to use logical principles and language that cannot be accounted for by God's nonexistence. Fourthly, we conclude that God exists. Finally, if God is eternal, uncreated, omnipotent, omniscient, omnipresent, omnibenevolent, and immutable, then there can only be one of Him. For by definition, this all-everything God can only be one. If there were two of them, they would either be non-distinguishable since they would have no limits to define one over the other, or one would have to lack what the other has. Yet God lacks nothing since He is

---

[254] Geisler, *Christian Apologetics*, 235-258.

God! Therefore, there can only be one Supreme Being; there can only be one God.

Now we turn our attention to the only three religions that affirm this, three religions that are not only theistic but monotheistic: Islam, Judaism, and Christianity. Which one, if any, is the one true religion?

Chapter 11

ISLAM, JUDAISM, OR CHRISTIANITY?

At the end of the long line of absurd religions—from atheism to panentheism—there are only three that proclaim faith in monotheism: Islam, Judaism, and Christianity. Deciding which one of these is *the* true faith is not difficult. Although each one rightly believes there is only one God, they are mutually exclusive. Given the exclusive tenets of their respective beliefs, it would be illogical and hence absurd to conclude that each one is a path in and of itself to the true God. Their mutual exclusivity means that if one is right, the others must be wrong.

The Theism of Islam

The religion of Islam, which means "submission," was founded by Muhammad (AD 570–632), who began having visions by the time he was 40. Believing that the angel Gabriel was speaking to him in these visions, Muhammad supposedly wrote them down in what is known as the Qur'an (aka, the Koran). Geisler commented:

> According to Islamic tradition different fragments of the Qur'an were revealed to Muhammad verbatim by the angel Gabriel over a period of 23 years (25:32; 17:106). After each such occasion the prophet would recite the

words of revelation to those present (thus the word 'Qur'an,' which means reading or reciting).[255]

Since it is known that Muhammad was illiterate and unable to write,[256] many speculate that what was later written in the Koran was the work of another prophet of Islam, though this is only speculation.

The Koran is actually in agreement with the Bible in that God created the universe and He transcends it. Great respect is given in the Koran for Moses and even for Jesus, although the Koran denies that Jesus was God in the flesh, that He died a substitutionary death for mankind, and that He rose from the dead three days after He was crucified.[257] Where the Koran and the Bible begin to diverge starkly is after Genesis 16. In the Holy Bible, it is in Genesis 17 that God selects Abraham's son Isaac to be the son of promise while his other son, Ishmael, is rejected by God in Genesis 16. Whereas Hebrew Scripture exalts Isaac as the one through whom God's promises will begin to be fulfilled, the Koran opts for Ishmael as God's chosen one.

Carlson and Decker outline the six beliefs of Islam: 1) There is one true God named Allah. 2) Angels exist as servants of God, Gabriel being the highest of all angels who appeared to Muhammad. In addition, each person has two angels with him at all times, one who records bad deeds and one who records good deeds. 3) Allah has spoken through many prophets, including Moses, David, and Jesus. But his greatest prophet is Muhammad, and his words, as they are written in the Koran, supersede all previous prophets. 4) The Koran is the holiest of books, and it supersedes all other holy books. 5) A day of judgment is coming, and each person will be judged by their deeds, whether good or bad. 6) Allah's decree is final, and he ordains every man's fate.[258]

Similarly, Geisler and Brooks summarize Muhammad's teachings in five points: 1) Allah is the one true God. 2) Allah has sent many prophets, including Moses and Jesus, but Muhammad is

---

[255] Geisler and Saleeb, 91-92.
[256] Carlson and Decker, 106.
[257] Walter Martin, *The Kingdom of the Cults*, 366.
[258] Carlson and Decker, 110.

the last and greatest of all. 3) The Koran is the supreme religious book, taking priority over the Law, the Psalms, and the Injil (Evangel) of Jesus. 4) There are many intermediate beings (angels) between God and us, some of whom are good and others are evil. 5) Each man's deeds will be weighed on a balance to determine if he will go to heaven or hell in the resurrection. The way to gain salvation includes reciting the Shahadah several times a day—"There is no God but Allah; and Muhammad is his prophet"—prayer five times a day, a month of fasting each year, almsgiving, and a pilgrimage to Mecca.[259]

The problem with Muhammad's god is that he was originally part of a pantheon of gods that the Arabs worshiped in Mecca. Carlson and Decker wrote:

> Every Arab tribe has its sacred magic stones which they believed protected the tribe. Muhammad's particular tribe had adopted the black stone and had set it up in the Kaaba (their house)... The dominant religion just prior to Muhammad was Sabianism, a religion in which heavenly bodies were worshipped. The moon was viewed as a male deity, and a lunar calendar was used. Fasting was later adopted as one of the five pillars of faith in Islam. Fasting in Ramadan, in the ninth month, already preexisted in the Arab culture before Muhammad was even born... Muslims claim that Allah is the same God as Christians worship, just under another name. Yet if you look at the history of it, it is very different. The term "Allah" is a purely Arabic term used in reference to an Arabian deity. In fact, Allah was known to pre-Islamic Arabs...one of the many deities that already existed in Mecca. The tribe into which Muhammad was born was particularly devoted to Allah, which was the moon god. It was represented by a black stone which was believed to have come down from heaven... In Arabia the sun god was viewed as female, and the moon was viewed as the male god. In pre-Islamic times, Allah, the moon god, was married to the sun god, and together they produced three goddesses

---

[259] Geisler and Brooks, 130-32.

called The Daughters of Allah. The were viewed as being at the top of the pantheon of Arabian deities, those 360 idols in the Kaaba, at Mecca. When Muhammad took control of Mecca, he destroyed all the idols in the Kaaba except the stone deity, Allah. Do not ever accept that Allah is just another name for the true and living God!... The symbol of the worship of the moon god, Allah, in pre-Islamic Arab culture throughout the Middle East was the crescent moon. Today the crescent moon is on top of every flag of an Islamic nation.[260]

Emir Fethi Caner noted four key points that Christians must beware of regarding the differences between Islam and Christianity. First, there must be a recognition between the doctrine of the God of the Bible versus the god of Islam in the Koran. Second, the Christian must understand Christ in His fullest revelation, for although Muslims hold a high view of Jesus, they reject His resurrection and His deity. They have been taught that although the Bible was originally written without errors, it has been corrupted greatly through the centuries by Jews and Muslims. Barbara Pemberton said:

> Charges against the OT include false reports of immorality (David and Bathsheba), missing doctrines (afterlife in the Torah), and incompatibility with science. The Evangel has been corrupted with inaccurate historical references, discrepancies in the Gospel accounts, and fabrications (such as the crucifixion). Christians and Jews allegedly suppressed or removed biblical predictions of Muhammad. For example, Psalm 84:4–6 is said to be about Muhammad, who overcame his childhood disadvantages by God's grace. Jesus supposedly predicted the coming Prophet Muhammad when He spoke of the "Counselor" in John 14. Islam rejects the concept of human participation in the process of revelation that shows in the varieties of biblical books (Gospels, Letters, etc.). Jesus' original message is deemed lost. Muslims

---

[260] Carlson and Decker, 106.

believe that Gospel authors, writing long after Jesus, altered the message to promote their own points of view. Paul's letters are supposed to promote a "mystical" Christ and "false" doctrines such as the resurrection. Another Muslim argument against biblical reliability is the lack of a record that the original texts passed from one generation to the next.[261]

Yet because Muslims can offer no proof of this accusation, they should take caution not only as to *what* source or sources they choose to trust for their path to salvation, but also *why* they choose as they do. After all, if the Almighty God would allow His words to be corrupted in the Bible, it is just as likely that He has allowed the words of the Koran to suffer the same fate. Third, Christians must be able to teach the one way of salvation through Christ in contrast to the works-based salvation of Islam. Fourth, Christians must be able to argue the question of epistemology: "How do you know what you know?"[262]

It is certain that a person can no more be both a Christian and a Muslim than he can a Jew and Muslim. The differences between the two contrast like night and day. While Islam embraces monotheism, like Christianity and Judaism, and Muhammad used many of the people cited in the Bible when he created the Koran, such as Noah (Surah 6:84), Jacob (Surah 2:132), and Jesus (Surah 3:45–47), their commonalities end here. Ergun Mehmet Caner said:

> Like Mormonism, Islam teaches that both Christianity and Judaism are false religions, and that Islam through the Qur'an is the only true faith. The God of Islam is remote, and not intimate (Surah 112). Allah does not have a son (Surah 2:116), is not a Trinity (Surah

---

[261] Barbara B. Pemberton, "How Does the Bible Relate to Islam?" *The Apologetics Study Bible: Real Questions, Straight Answers, Stronger Faith,* ed. Ted Cabal, Chad Owen Brand, E. Ray Clendenen, et al. (Nashville, TN: Holman Bible Publishers, 2007), 1602.

[262] Emir Fethi Caner, "Islam and Christianity," in *Passionate Conviction: Contemporary Discourses on Christian Apologetics,* ed. Paul Copan and William Lane Craig (Nashville: B&H Publishers, 2007), 187-204.

5:72), and does not love unconditionally (Surah 8:53). In Islam, Jesus is simply a prophet, and emphatically is not the Son of God (Surah 5:72), and the angel Gabriel is the Holy Spirit (Surah 2:193)... Indeed, these differences cover the entire theology of Christianity. In Islam, there are "angels" that are created from fire (called *jinn*, Surah 72), a Tree of Zaqqum in hell (Surah 3:62–67), and virgin servants in heaven (Surah 4:57). In fact, even the creation in Islam is corrupted. In Islam, Satan's fall was due to his unwillingness to bow to Adam (Surah 2:34).[263]

Whereas the Bible teaches that Jesus was not only the Son of God but God Almighty (John 1:1–4, 14; Col. 2:9), Muslims deny that Jesus was divine. Whereas the Bible teaches that Jesus died on the cross for the salvation of all those who place their trust in Him alone (Matt. 26:28; John 19:20), Muslims believe it was actually Judas Iscariot who died in Jesus' place on the cross. As to Islam's relation to Judaism, whereas the Hebrew Scriptures teach that Abraham's son Isaac was God's chosen line for His covenant to bring redemption to His people (Gen. 17:18–20; cf. Rom. 9:7; Gal. 4:22–23), Muslims believe that Ishmael was God's chosen instrument. Whereas the Hebrew Scriptures teach that God is loving and knowable, befriending men like Abraham (Gen. 18:22ff.; Isa. 41:8; cf. John 3:16), in the Koran, Allah is unknowable and impossible to approach or comprehend.

Muhammad cannot compare to Jesus Christ. The Christian God loves, died for our sins, and offers salvation by grace through faith. The god of Islam did none of that, and the best his writings can offer is the wish that a person's good deeds outweigh their bad deeds and that Allah is in a good mood when he judges them! In addition, unlike Muhammad, Jesus was not a polygamist, He never plundered a single caravan (Muhammad plundered hundreds of them), and He performed miracles in front of hundreds (cf. 1 Cor. 15:6), even thousands (cf. Matt. 14:31-21), of eyewitnesses.

---

[263] Ergun Mehmet Caner, "Is Allah Identical to the God and Father of Our Lord Jesus Christ?" in *The Apologetics Study Bible: Real Questions, Straight Answers, Stronger Faith*, ed. Ted Cabal, Chad Owen Brand, E. Ray Clendenen, et al. (Nashville, TN: Holman Bible Publishers, 2007), 1754.

Finally, whereas Muhammad never claimed to be God, Jesus not only proclaimed it, He proved it by fulfilling prophecy, rising from the dead, and ascending into heaven to intercede on behalf of those who call to Him. Caner summarized the issue by saying, "Islam rejects the fatherhood of God, the divinity of the Son, and the person of the Holy Spirit. You cannot change the nature of the God of the Bible without changing the 'god' you are presenting. It is not the same God."[264]

The Theism of Judaism

From Deuteronomy 6:4, which reads, "Hear O Israel! The LORD is our God, the LORD is one!" the Jews believe in only one God, Creator of heaven and earth. Their Hebrew Scriptures date back to the creation of the world, and they believe that although Moses was not alive during the historical narratives of Genesis, he compiled everything handed down to him from the day of creation of the world, recorded by Adam, to the Hebrews' enslavement in Egypt when he was born (ca. 1500 BC). After the Hebrews departed Egypt, God spoke to Moses, and he wrote down what became known as the five books of Moses: Genesis, Exodus, Leviticus, Numbers, and Deuteronomy.

Moses' very existence, however, dates over 450 years back to Abraham with whom God made an everlasting covenant. In Genesis 12, 13, 15, 17, and 22, God made and confirmed His covenant with Abraham that promised him a great name, a nation of people who would come through his loins, a special Seed of promise, and a land where Abraham's people would dwell forever. Four hundred years later, Abraham's offspring through Isaac was indeed a great nation, and although they were enslaved in Egypt for a time, Moses led them out of Egypt and into the land God promised to Abraham—the land of Canaan. God promised that they would be secure in their land insofar as they continued to obey Him (cf. Deut. 28).

For his part, Moses led God's people faithfully, but he knew he was not the ultimate Seed that God had promised to Abraham

---

[264] Mehmet Caner, 1754.

who would be a prophet to God's people. Moses prophesied about this future Prophet in Deuteronomy 18:15, and the Jews awaited its fulfillment for over 1400 years. The fact that the Jews were inquiring of John the Baptist to see if he was the fulfillment of Moses' prophecy (cf. John 1:21) attests to the fact that over 1400 years after Moses prophesied about the coming Prophet, His arrival was still greatly anticipated. That is where John the Baptist is so important. As the forerunner to the Christ, the Prophet whom Moses told them about hundreds of year prior, it was John who announced to the Jews that Jesus was the Christ (Matt. 3:3; John 1:23, 29, 34).

Before Jesus came and fulfilled Moses' prophecy, God reconfirmed His covenant promises to King David, who lived 400 years after Moses. To David and his chosen line, God reconfirmed His promise regarding the Seed that He had previously promised to Abraham, promising David that his house, his kingdom, and his throne would endure forever (cf. 2 Sam. 7:12–16). This is why the New Testament traces Jesus' lineage through David, through Isaac, and through Abraham (cf. Matt. 1:1–7; Luke 3:31–34), calling Jesus the "Son of David" (Matt. 9:27; 15:22; Mark 10:47; 12:35; Luke 18:38). The Apostle Paul also attested to the fact that Jesus was the ultimate Seed fulfillment that God had originally promised to Abraham (cf. Gal. 3:16, 29).

From around the eighth century BC up to Jesus' birth, the Hebrew prophets made hundreds of prophecies about the coming Messiah and His eventual ministry. Therefore, the monotheistic religion of Judaism, defined in the Old Testament where all the prophecies about the coming Messiah originate, is an incomplete religion until such a time as the Messiah arrives and fulfills the prophecies. Dan Story commented:

> The Bible contains several hundred prophecies relating to the birth, life, ministry, death, resurrection, and future return of Jesus Christ. Almost thirty of them were literally fulfilled in one twenty-four-hour period just prior to His death (e.g., those relating to His betrayal, trial, crucifixion, and burial). Some of the most important prophecies about Christ accurately predicted His birthplace (Mic. 5:2), flight to Egypt (Hos. 11:1), the identity of His

forerunner (Mal. 3:1), His entering Jerusalem on a donkey (Zech. 9:9), betrayal for thirty pieces of silver (Zech. 11:12), humiliation and beating (Isa. 50:6), crucifixion with other prisoners (Isa. 53:12), hand and feet wounds (Ps. 22:16), side wound (Zech. 12:10), soldiers gambling for His clothing (Ps. 22:18), His burial in a rich man's tomb (Isa. 53:9), resurrection (Pss. 16:10; 49:15), and second coming (Ps. 50:3–6; Isa. 9:6–7; Dan. 7:13–14; Zech. 14:4–8)... Jesus could not have accidentally or deliberately fulfilled these prophecies. Obviously, events such as His birthplace and lineage, method of execution, soldiers casting lots for His garments, or being pierced in the side are events beyond Jesus' control. Peter Stoner and Robert Newman, in their book *Science Speaks*, demonstrate the statistical improbability of any one man, accidentally or deliberately, from the day of these prophecies down to the present time, fulfilling just eight of the hundreds of prophecies Jesus fulfilled. They demonstrate that the chance of this happening is 1 in 1,000,000,000,000,000,000.[265]

If we were to examine the Servant songs found in Isaiah's prophecies from chapters 42–53 (prophecies written over 700 years before Jesus' birth), we would see that Jesus is the *only* possible person who could have fulfilled these prophecies. In sum, Isaiah says the following about the Servant of the LORD:

1. He is sinless (Isa. 53:9).
2. He is selected by God, anointed by His Spirit, and promised success (42:1, 4).
3. Justice is a key feature of His ministry (42:1, 4).
4. His ministry goes beyond Israel, extending to the Gentiles (42:1, 6; 49:6).
5. God predestined Him to His calling (49:1).
6. He is a gifted teacher (49:2).
7. He experiences discouragement and opposition of a violent nature (49:4; 50:4–6).
8. He is determined to complete His task (50:7).

---

[265] Story, 79.

9. He has humble origins with nothing physical to attract others to Himself (53:1–2).
10. He experiences severe suffering and affliction (53:3).
11. He suffers on behalf of His people to atone for their sins (53:4–6, 12).
12. He is put to death after being condemned (53:7–9).
13. He returns to life and is exalted above all rulers (53:10–12; 52:13–15).

No thinking person can deny that Jesus is the fulfillment of the prophecies of the Old Testament, yet that is exactly what the Jews have done in order to avoid receiving Jesus as their Messiah and Lord. They conclude that the Servant of Isaiah 53 is actually Israel as a nation. The first Jew to make this claim was Shlomo Yitzchaki (ca. 1040–1105), and his view is the party line for modern Jews.[266]

The problem with Yizchaki's theology is that, first of all, Israel is not sinless, yet the Servant is (53:9). If Israel was sinless, why did God's prophets condemn her so absolutely for her sins? God instituted the sacrificial system of animal blood to atone for Israel's sin. Secondly, the lamb in Isaiah's prophecy submitted to His fate and was like a sheep led to the slaughter who does not open its mouth (53:7). Yet there is nothing in the history of Israel as a nation that depicts her as submitting to anyone in a willful way. Finally, the Servant in Isaiah's prophecy dies for the sins of others, willingly and as a substitute for them (53:4–6, 8, 10–12). Israel has never died for anyone's sins! She has redeemed no one and has suffered immensely for her own sins.

So, although Judaism is a wonderful monotheistic faith, it is an incomplete faith. Incompleteness is not a bad thing per se, but when the last piece of the puzzle has been revealed and the adherents refuse it because they do not like it, their religion cannot be called a legitimate faith that encompasses all truth. Jesus Christ of Nazareth, a Man attested in history, is the fulfillment of Judaism. Following are a few of the things written about Jesus in the Old Testament that were fulfilled in His birth, life, death, and resurrection:

---

[266] Geisler and Turek, 333.

1. "Those who hate me without a cause are more than the hairs of my head" (Psalm 69:4).

2. "The kings of the earth take their stand and the rulers take counsel together against the LORD and against His Anointed" (Psalm 2:2).

3. "Even my close friend in whom I trusted, who ate my bread, has lifted up his heel against me" (Psalm 41:9).

4. "Strike the Shepherd that the sheep may be scattered" (Zech. 13:7).

5. "I said to them, 'If it is good in your sight, give me my wages; but if not, never mind!' So they weighed out thirty shekels of silver as my wages. Then the LORD said to me, 'Throw it to the potter, that magnificent price at which I was valued by them.' So I took the thirty shekels of silver and threw it to the potter in the house of the LORD" (Zech. 11:12-13).

6. "With a rod they will smite the judge of Israel on the cheek" (Micah 5:1).

7. "I gave My back to those who strike Me, and My cheeks to those who pluck out the beard; I did not cover My face from humiliation and spitting" (Isa. 50:6).

8. "They pierced my hands and my feet" (Psalm 22:16).

9. "My God, my God, why have You forsaken me?" (Psalm 22:1).

10. "All who see me sneer at me; They separate with the lip, they wag the head, saying, 'Commit yourself to the LORD; let Him deliver him; let Him rescue him, because He delights in him'" (Psalm 22:7–8).

11. "They also gave me gall for my food, and for my thirst they gave me vinegar to drink" (Psalm 69:21).

12. "I am poured out like water, and all my bones are out of joint; my heart is like wax; it is melted within me" (Psalm 22:14).

13. "Surely our griefs He Himself bore, and our sorrows He carried; yet we ourselves esteemed Him stricken, smitten of God, and afflicted" (Isa. 53:4).

14. "He was oppressed and He was afflicted, yet He did not open His mouth; like a lamb that is led to

slaughter, and like a sheep that is silent before its shearers, so He did not open His mouth" (Isa. 53:7).

15. "They divide my garments among them, and for my clothing they cast lots" (Psalm 22:18).
16. "He poured out Himself to death" (Isa. 53:12).
17. "He Himself bore the sin of many, and interceded for the transgressors" (Isa. 53:12).
18. "You are not to...break any bone of it" (Exod. 12:46).
19. "He keeps all his bones, not one of them is broken" (Psalm 34:20).
20. "They will look on Me whom they have pierced" (Zech. 12:10).
21. "His grave was assigned with wicked men, yet He was with a rich man in His death, because He had done no violence, nor was there any deceit in His mouth" (Isa. 53:9).
22. "For You will not abandon my soul to Sheol; nor will You allow Your Holy One to undergo decay" (Psalm 16:10).
23. "You have ascended on high, You have led captive Your captives; You have received gifts among men, even among the rebellious also, that the LORD God may dwell there" (Psalm 68:18).
24. "The LORD says to my Lord: 'Sit at My right hand until I make Your enemies a footstool for your feet'" (Psalm 110:1).

If we were to read these passages to some random person on the street, it seems likely they would readily agree that Jesus is who the passages speak of. What is so amazing is that all these Old Testament passages were written hundreds of years before Jesus' incarnation! Clearly, Jesus is the only possible fulfillment of Israel's prophecies, and there is absolutely nothing about Him that mitigates against Him being their Messiah.

Modern Judaism should not be confused with the biblical Hebrew religion of the Israelites. The term *Judaism* did not appear until the first century BC (2 Maccabees 2:21; 8:1; 14:38). It describes the faith, norms, and rituals of Jews during the time they were influenced by the Greeks. Their religion changed greatly after their center of worship in Jerusalem was removed in AD 70. After that time, they adopted a religion in keeping with the Old Testament, but obviously not in a literal way. For example, without a temple, blood sacrifices had to be replaced with other kinds of sacrifices. Thus, observance of the mitzvoth (the commandments) replaced sacrifices, atoning for sin (Tobit 4:6–7, 9–11; 12:9–10). Larry Helyer said:

> The fundamental ideas of modern Judaism, in all its diversity, maintain continuity with the biblical revelation at Mount Sinai. These ideas include ethical monotheism (belief in one God), God's gift of Torah ("instruction") to Israel, and the choice of Israel as a light to the nations. A striving for peace, justice, and righteousness for all peoples derives from the Prophets, and a spirituality grounded in everyday life stems from the wisdom and hymnic literature of the OT.[267]

Therefore, along with Judaism's confusing view of prophetic fulfillment (cf. Isa. 53), the main difference between it and Christianity concerns the person of Jesus Christ. As Helyer also said:

> For Judaism, there is no human failing, whether collective or individual, that requires special divine intervention and that cannot be remedied with the guidance of Torah. Salvation consists of faithful, though not perfect, adherence to the mitzvoth. God in His mercy forgives those whose intentions are upright. The NT, however, unambiguously proclaims the finality of Jesus Christ. He is God's last word to sinners (Heb 1:1–3), the Word who became flesh, dwelt among us, and reveals the Father to sinners (Jn 1:1–18). By His atoning death on the cross, He draws all people unto Himself (Jn 3:16; 6:35–40; 12:32).[268]

---

[267] Larry R. Helyer, "How Does the Bible Relate to Judaism?" *The Apologetics Study Bible: Real Questions, Straight Answers, Stronger Faith,* ed. Ted Cabal, Chad Owen Brand, E. Ray Clendenen, et al. (Nashville, TN: Holman Bible Publishers, 2007), 1758-59.

[268] Helyer, 1759.

The Theism of Christianity

On the assumption that the Scriptures are true and without error, any Bible student can see that Jesus claimed to be God. And if Jesus is God, then His revelation of Himself in the Bible is the special revelation of God. Let us now evaluate what the Bible says about whether Jesus is God.

Though it is commonly taught that Constantine decided in AD 325 which books should be in the Bible, the truth is that the four Gospels, which contain eyewitness testimonies about Jesus of Nazareth being the Christ, were in circulation together at least as early as AD 150 since Clement of Alexandria listed them together at that time. Other lists of Bible books from other writers include most of the recognized New Testament writings as early as AD 150. The point is that the life of Jesus Christ is attested very early by both those who professed faith in Him and those who hated Him. In other words, the life of Jesus Christ was not invented by fourth century scribes. His ministry, life, death, and resurrection had transformed the lives of countless Jews and Gentiles by the time Constantine convened the first Church Council. At that Council in Nicea, all those present recognized the authority of the various books of the Bible. Their discussion centered on whether Jesus was God based upon the teachings of Scripture. Though at least one of their members, Arias, sought to relegate Jesus to something similar to God, the majority of the men who gathered in Nicea recognized from Scripture that Jesus is God—the same substance as God.

Of course the Bible does teach that Jesus is God (cf. John 1:1). He is called "God" as early as James' epistle written in the late 40s. Galatians, written by the Apostle Paul around AD 48, calls Jesus the "Son of God." He equates Himself with the Great I AM (YHWH) in John 8:58 (cf. 5:18), as the Messiah in Mark 14:61–64, accepts worship in Matthew 28:17 (cf. John 20:28), claims to have equal authority with God in Matthew 28:18, and tells His disciples to pray in His name in John 14:13–14. And these passages are just the tip of the iceberg, as it were. Jesus is indeed the Messiah, God in the flesh. He completes the religion of the Jews and thus makes Christianity superior to Judaism.

What the New Testament Writers Said About Jesus

In the Gospel of Matthew, Jesus is the fulfillment of the Isaiah 7:14 prophecy: "Behold, the virgin shall be with child and shall bear a Son, and they shall call his name Immanuel, which translated means, 'God with us'" (Matt. 1:23). Although Jesus was not named Immanuel, the word is actually a title depicting the nature and character of the virgin-born Son of Mary, whom she named *Jesus* in obedience to the angel's command to Joseph (cf. Matt. 1:21). The Gospel of John says that "the Word was God" and "the Word became flesh" (1:1, 14). John proceeds throughout his Gospel to call the Word "Jesus," saying in his first epistle that Jesus "is the true God and eternal life" (1 John 5:20).

The Apostle Paul claimed that Christ is "God over all" (Rom. 9:5, ESV), and "in Him all the fullness of Deity dwells in bodily form" (Col. 2:9). The writer of Hebrews said as much when he wrote, "The Son is the radiance of God's glory and the exact representation of his being, sustaining all things by his powerful word" (Heb. 1:3, NIV). He also quotes Psalm 45:6 in claiming that God says of the Son, *"Your"* throne, O God, is forever and ever" (Heb. 1:8). Peter, a three-year companion and close friend of Jesus, wrote that believers receive righteousness from "our God and Savior, Jesus Christ" (2 Pet. 1:1). Even the demons got in on the confession of Jesus as God, proclaiming Him to be the holy one of God (Matt. 8:29; Mark 1:23–24; Luke 4:34, 41).

What Jesus Said About Himself

When asked by the Jewish high priest, Caiaphas, as to whether He was the Son of the Blessed One, Jesus responded, "I am; and you shall see the Son of Man sitting at the right hand of Power, and coming with the clouds of heaven" (Mark 14:61–62). This response was so offensive and blasphemous to the high priest that he tore his clothes and cried out, "What further need do we have of witnesses? You have heard the blasphemy; How does it seem to you?" (Mark 14:63). They all condemned Him as worthy of death (14:64). The two offensive parts of Jesus' response was the statement "I am" and Jesus' reference to Himself as the "Son of Man." The former is the actual name of God—the I AM (Exod. 3:14), which comes from the Hebrew YHWH, the holy name of God (cf. John 8:58–59). The latter phrase was a reference to

Daniel's prophecy in 7:13–14 about the Son of Man who approaches the Ancient of Days and who comes on the clouds of heaven. Jesus' answer, therefore, was that He was indeed the Messiah, the Son of Man, God Almighty, and the entire world will bow to worship Him. Caiaphas would have none of it, so he sentenced Jesus to death and had the Romans crucify Him.

John's Gospel records a similar event when Jesus was asked a question about Abraham. He answered, "Truly, truly, I say to you, before Abraham was born, I am" (John 8:58). This was a clear affirmation of deity to the Jews, for they immediately picked up stones to kill Him for blasphemy (8:59). So the question to those who claim that Jesus never said He was God is, "Why would the Jews have condemned Jesus to death by crucifixion if He never claimed to be God?" Though it may not be obvious to modern skeptics that Jesus claimed to be God, it was certainly obvious to Jesus' first century enemies.

But Jesus' claims to deity do not end there. Note how Jesus prayed, saying, "Now, Father, glorify Me together with Yourself, with the glory which I had with You before the world was" (John 17:5). In light of the fact that the Old Testament teaches there is only one God (Deut. 6:4; Isa. 45:5ff.), and God says, "I will not give My glory to another" (Isa. 42:8), either Jesus is God or He was a deluded lunatic. Equally, Jesus declared, "I am the first and the last" (Rev. 1:17), the very words God used in reference to Himself in Isaiah 44:6.

Other examples are found in Jesus' claim to be the good shepherd (John 10:11) in light of the fact that the Old Testament says, "The LORD is my shepherd" (Psalm 23:1; cf. Ezek. 34:12). Jesus claimed to be the judge of all (Matt. 25:31ff.; John 5:27), yet the prophet Joel quotes God as saying that He alone will judge all the nations" (Joel 3:12). Jesus said, "I am the Light of the world; he who follows Me will not walk in the darkness, but will have the Light of life" (John 8:12). Yet the psalmist said, "The LORD is my light" (Psalm 27:1). Jesus said, "For just as the Father raises the dead and gives them life, even so the Son also gives life to whom He wishes" (John 5:21). Yet the Old Testament teaches that only God can give life (Deut. 32:39; 1 Sam. 2:6) and can raise the dead (Isa. 26:19; Dan. 12:2; Job 19:25). With these passages in mind, it is no wonder Jesus proclaimed that salvation could be found in no one excep0074 Himself (John 14:6).

What Jesus' Actions Said About Him

Jesus not only claimed to be God, His actions proved that He is. In the Gospel of Mark, Jesus commanded a paralyzed man to stand up and walk home, after telling him that his sins are forgiven, even though only God can forgive sins. The scribes correctly responded, "Who can forgive sins but God alone?" Then the man got up in the presence of all, proving that Jesus is God (Mark 2:5–12). It is no wonder Jesus declared that all authority in heaven and on earth had been given to Him (Matt. 28:18–19). He even taught His disciples to pray in His name, telling them, "If you ask Me for anything in My name, I will do it" (John 14:13–14; cf. 15:7).

Jesus accepted what is only to be given to God: *worship.* The entirety of Scripture teaches this, forbidding worship of anyone except God alone (Exod. 20:1–4; Deut. 5:6–9; Acts 14:15; Rev. 22:8–9). Jesus received worship, without ever forbidding it, from:

1. A leper He had healed (Matt. 8:2)
2. A ruler whose son Jesus had healed (Matt. 9:18)
3. The 12 disciples after a storm on the lake (Matt. 14:33)
4. A Canaanite woman whose daughter was exorcised (Matt. 15:25)
5. The mother of James and John (Matt. 20:20)
6. A demon-possessed man whom Jesus exorcised (Mark 5:6)
7. A blind man Jesus gave sight to (John 9:38)
8. The remaining 11 disciples (Matt. 28:17)
9. Thomas, who said, "My Lord and my God" (John 20:28)

Jesus not only claimed to be God, He lived a sinless life, which only the God Man could do. In John 8:46, Jesus asked, "Which one of you convicts Me of sin?" Those who followed Him and lived with Him, as Peter did, would never have depicted Him as sinless if He was not. Peter, using Old Testament imagery, compared Jesus to an "unblemished and spotless" lamb (1 Pet. 1:19) "who committed no sin, nor was any deceit found in His mouth" (1 Pet. 2:22). Likewise, the Apostle John said of Jesus, "in Him there is no sin" (1 John 3:5). And though Paul was not a companion of Jesus, he was an apostle, and he wrote that Jesus "knew no sin" (2 Cor. 5:21). Likewise, the writer of Hebrews claimed that Jesus was "without sin" (Heb. 4:15).

Although Jesus' enemies hated Him, even they could find nothing wrong with Him (cf. Mark 14:55). Not even Pontius Pilate could find a fault with Jesus, and he struggled to do so in order to justify sentencing Him to death (cf. Luke 23:22)!

Why was Jesus not more overt about who He is? Geisler and Turek offered four reasons why:

> First, Jesus didn't want interference from the Jews, who had the misconception that the Messiah would come and free them from Roman oppression. This actually became a problem despite Jesus' careful approach: at one point after performing miracles, Jesus had to escape from the Jews who wanted to make him king (John 6:15)! Second, Jesus could not be our supreme human example if he pulled rank every time he got into any earthly trouble. His conduct provides us with a perfect example of humility and servitude, and how we ought to glorify the Father rather than ourselves. Third, Jesus had to be very careful about when and where he revealed his deity so that he could accomplish his mission of sacrificial atonement. If he had been too overt with his claims and miraculous proof, they might not have killed him. But if he had been too reserved, there would have been little proof that he was really God, and he may not have attracted a large enough following to spread his message. Finally, we must understand the religious context in which Jesus lived and taught. He introduced the idea that he personally fulfilled the entire Old Testament law (Matt 5:17)—the law that had been revered and followed for centuries and was the foundation of all of the political and religious practices of the Jews... It's no wonder Jesus used parables to teach and made more indirect than direct references to his deity. He gave enough evidence to convince the open-minded, but not enough to overwhelm

the free will of those wishing to cling to their own traditions.[269]

Christianity Is the Only Legitimate Faith

Christian theism is the only worldview among all the rest that is actually undeniable. It offers an argument with undeniable premises that leads inescapably to the existence of an infinitely perfect and powerful Being beyond this world who is the current sustaining cause of all finite, changing, and contingent beings. Furthermore, as a worldview, Christian theism is consistent with itself, believing in one infinite, all-powerful, and transcendent God who created the universe and who works lovingly, providentially, and miraculously within it. Having spoken the universe into existence, God is intricately concerned with His creation, and although He rested after He created it in six days (Gen. 2:2), He continually works within it as He manifests Himself in the creation and through the Scriptures He inspired—the Bible.

J. I. Packer said:

> Christianity is like no other faith on earth, and those who try to assimilate it to the rest of the religions, speaking of them as if they reflect or foreshadow it or of it as reflecting or foreshadowing them, are flying in the face of the facts. Whether you compare Christianity to Judaism or Islam, its hostile half-brothers, or with Hinduism and its atheistic child Buddhism, or with Taoism or state Shintoism or any type of polytheism, or with any other religion that humanity has developed, the basic contrast is invariably the same. Non-Christian faiths have an inner structure different from Christianity, for they all bring changes on the theme of self-salvation. They offer ultimate happiness, however they conceive it, as a prize to be gained from God, or the gods, or the cosmic order, through knowledgeable and worthy action on our part. This is the universal formula of natural religion. But

---

[269] Geisler and Turek, 326-54.

Christianity, which sees ultimate happiness as rescue from sin and an unending love relationship with one's Creator, offers this salvation package as a gift, to be received here and now by admitting our helplessness and entering into a faith relationship with Jesus Christ, the divine-human Savior and Lord.[270]

Having quoted the Bible extensively, assuming its claims are true in in showing that Jesus is God, let us now turn our attention to the investigation of the Scriptures to determine whether they can be trusted as what they claim to be, namely, God's Word.

---

[270] James I. Packer, "Response to the Debate," in Gary R. Habermas and Anthony G. N. Flew, *Did Jesus Rise From the Dead? The Resurrection Debate,* ed. Terry L. Miethe (San Francisco: Harper & Row, 1987), 143.

Chapter 12

ARGUING FOR THE BIBLE AS GOD'S INERRANT WORD

God revealed Himself through His *general* revelation—transcendentally, cosmologically, ontologically, teleologically, morally, and through His miracles. So it is reasonable to assume that God would also reveal Himself *specifically* through a special revelation. This is what Christians believe God did when He spoke to His prophets and apostles and inspired them to record in the Bible what He said and did.

In this chapter, we will overview the Bible in order to determine if its claim of inerrancy and infallibility is at least partially warranted. I believe that our conclusions about what we believe about the Bible will dictate everything about our lives—from how we live to how we die. If we accept what the Bible teaches as coming from God, then we can know God the way He has revealed Himself. If we choose to reject any part of the Bible, however, we run the risk of rejecting what God has given to us and creating a god of our own making.

A Brief Introduction to the Bible

The English Bible is composed of 66 individual books. There are 39 Old Testament books and 27 New Testament books. Although the first five books of the Bible (Genesis, Exodus, Leviticus, and Deuteronomy—the Torah, or Pentateuch) are anonymous, having been written around 1400 BC, "it appears relatively certain that Jesus and the writers of the New Testament believed that Moses was the author of the Pentateuch (e.g., John 5:46)."[271] When read cover to cover, the Bible reveals the origins of the universe in Genesis and the culmination of all things in the book of Revelation. These two bookends, as it were, and all the books in between purport to contain within them the special revelation of God, specifically how God *has dealt* with mankind and how He *will deal* with us.

As to the *authors* of the Bible, more than 40 men wrote over a span of about 1500 years (ca. 1450 BC to AD 95). No one author dominates the holy writings, and each one had his own personality and occupation distinct from the other authors. For instance, Moses was a Hebrew who grew up as a wealthy son of the Egyptian pharaoh. His successor, Joshua, was a military general from an early age. Samuel and Ezekiel were priests, David was a shepherd who became king of Israel, and Daniel was a Jewish boy of royal stock who became a prime minister of sorts in Babylon. Nehemiah was a cupbearer to the king of Persia, Amos was a keeper of sycamore fig trees, Luke was a physician, Paul was a Pharisee, and Peter and John were fishermen. These men wrote in various cultures, on various continents (Africa, Asia, and Europe), and at various times—writing from captivity, jail cells, and out in the open fields. Yet we find amazing harmony in their words and doctrines with the rest of the biblical writers.

One of the unique features of the Bible's authors is that they do not gloss over the character of others when their actions are immoral or embarrassing. Instead, as McDowell noted, "The Bible deals very frankly with the sins of its characters, even when those sins reflect badly on God's chosen people, leaders, and the biblical writers themselves."[272] Noah, for example, is embarrassingly depicted as being drunk from too much wine while lying naked in his tent (Gen. 9:20–21). King David coveted another man's wife, committed adultery with her, murdered her husband, and brought shame on his God and his family (2 Sam. 11:3–15). Job incessantly

---

[271] John Sailhamer "Introduction to Genesis," in *The Expositor's Bible Commentary, Volume 2: Genesis, Exodus, Leviticus, Numbers,* ed. Frank E. Gaebelein, John H. Sailhamer, Walter C. Kaiser, et al. (Grand Rapids, MI: Zondervan Publishing House, 1990), 5.

[272] Josh McDowell, *The New Evidence that Demands a Verdict* (Nashville, TN: Thomas Nelson Publishers, 1999), 13.

complained about his misfortunes and even dared to confront God with his complaints (Job 13:15). Peter denied knowing Jesus on three separate occasions after swearing allegiance to Him just hours before (John 18:17, 25–27). Likewise, the Bible records that one of Jesus' closest friends, Judas Iscariot, betrayed Him for 30 pieces of silver (Matt. 26:15). The inclusion of embarrassing accounts like these (cf. Matt. 11:19; 19:12; Mark 10:18; 13:32) make a strong case for the authenticity of the Gospels.[273] If someone were inventing the stories of the Bible and trying to foist these legends on unsuspecting people, it makes little sense as to why they would invent stories that make the characters look so immoral. Certainly the words of Lewis Sperry Chafer, the founder and first president of Dallas Theological Seminary ring true. He said, "The Bible is not such a book a man would write if you could, or could write if he would."[274]

The *language* of the Bible is that of Hebrew, Aramaic, and Greek. The Old Testament was written primarily in Hebrew, although some wrote various portions in Aramaic (portions of both Daniel and Ezra). The New Testament, however, is written exclusively in the Greek language. In these languages, the authors spoke of the origin of the universe, God's nature, man's nature, and how God has provided reconciliation between Himself and man who sinned and brought evil into God's perfect world.

The *accuracy* of the Bible has always come under fire by those who would rather it be filled with errors. After all, if the Bible is the Word of God and is without error, a person might have to submit to the God who wrote it! With the record of so many events in so many locations in the Bible, it is wide open for investigation, and it even invites it. That is where the science of archaeology has been so helpful, for it has repeatedly confirmed the details of the Bible. Nelson Glueck, a famous Jewish archaeologist, observed, "It may be stated categorically that no archaeological discovery has ever controverted a biblical

---

[273] Robert H. Stein, "Criteria for Gospels' Authenticity," in *Contending With Christianity's Critics: Answering New Atheists and Other Objectors* (Nashville, TN: B&H, 2009), 93-94.

[274] Quoted in McDowell, 13.

reference."[275] Likewise, Sir Fredric Kenyon wrote the following concerning the New Testament documents:

> The interval then between the dates of original composition and the earliest extant evidence becomes so small as to be in fact negligible, and the last foundation for any doubt that the Scriptures have come down to us substantially as they were written has now been removed. Both the *authenticity* and the general *integrity* of the books of the New Testament may be regarded as finally established.[276]

The examples of archaeology proving the Bible are numerous. Let us consider just a few. First, "Sargon king of Assyria" (Isa. 20:1) was thought to be a figment of Isaiah's imagination because no excavation of Nineveh revealed such a king, although it had revealed many others. But in 1843, Paul Emile Botta began digging where no one else had and found that Sargon had built his own capital there in 717 BC. Because his son had moved the capital back to Nineveh, the site was lost as was Sargon's name.[277]

A second example concerns King Belshazzar whom Daniel claims was Babylon's final ruler (cf. Dan. 5:1, 30). Until 1929, however, it was believed beyond doubt that Nabonidus was Babylon's last king who fell to the Persians in 539 BC. It was in 1929 that Daniel was exonerated, for documents were discovered revealing that Nabonidus was an absentee king who lived in the oasis of Teima in northwestern Arabia, leaving his kingly duties to his son Belshazzar who reigned as his co-regent during the last eight years of Babylon's power.[278] Other biblical names have been confirmed by archaeological digs, including King Jehoiachin's presence in Babylon, Sanballat as governor of Samaria along with some of Nehemiah's adversaries such as Tobiah the Ammonite,

---

[275] Quoted in McDowell, 61.

[276] Quoted in Geisler, *Christian Apologetics*, 327.

[277] James M. Freeman and Harold J. Chadwick, *Manners & Customs of the Bible* (North Brunswick, NJ: Bridge-Logos Publishers, 1998), 274.

[278] Avraham Negev, "Nabonidus," *The Archaeological Encyclopedia of the Holy Land*, 3rd ed. (New York: Prentice Hall Press, 1990).

and Geshem the Arab (Neh. 2:19). Other discoveries confirm well-known biblical individuals such as Balaam, David, Ahab, Jehu, Hezekiah, Menahem, and others.[279]

A third example concerns the Hittite Empire, which, until 1906 when it was excavated by Hugo Winckler, was thought to be a myth concocted by Old Testament authors who wrote that it existed in the land of Canaan (cf. Gen. 10:15; Josh. 1:4). Now, however, the Hittites are so well documented that "a score of volumes has been necessary to build a Hittite dictionary based on the tablets left in their civilization."[280] Examples like this just scratch the surface of all that archaeology has done to show the Bible's accuracy. As Walter C. Kaiser said, "Archaeology, then, has illuminated and corroborated the Bible in numerous ways. The interpreter finds in archaeology a good friend for understanding and substantiating Scripture."[281]

The *survival* of the Bible through time and persecution is nothing short of remarkable. Although all original copies of the manuscripts have long since perished, the copies, believed to be true to the originals, continue to survive and thrive. McDowell gives one amazing example among hundreds to consider:

> In AD 303 the Roman emperor Diocletian wrote an imperial letter ordering the destruction of all churches, the burning of all Scriptures, and the loss of civil liberties by all professing Christians. That did not stop the spread of Christianity or the proclamation of God's revelation in the Bible. Constantine, the Roman emperor who succeeded Diocletian, converted to Christianity and eventually ordered Eusebius to make fifty copies of the Scriptures, to be produced by the best scribes at government expense.[282]

---

[279] Walter C. Kaiser Jr., "How Has Archaeology Corroborated the Bible?" in *The Apologetics Study Bible: Real Questions, Straight Answers, Stronger Faith,* ed. Ted Cabal, Chad Owen Brand, E. Ray Clendenen, et al., (Nashville, TN: Holman Bible Publishers, 2007), 1148-49.

[280] Kaiser Jr., 1149.

[281] Kaiser Jr., 1149.

[282] McDowell, 10.

As to the *content* of the Bible, it contains narrative, poetry, and prophecy. Some narratives are descriptive while others are prescriptive—some *describe* behaviors while others *prescribe* certain actions. The poetry of the Bible describes feelings of love, hate, revenge, and deep depression. Many of the prophecies predict the immediate future and at times the distant future, but all prophecy in the Bible begins with "Thus says the LORD," who declares, "Hear, O Israel! The LORD is our God, the LORD is one! You shall love the LORD your God with all your heart and with all your soul and with all your might." (Deut. 6:4–5) "You are my witnesses," declares the LORD, "and My servant whom I have chosen, so that you may know and believe Me and understand that I am He. Before Me there was no God formed, and there will be none after Me. I, even I, am the LORD, and there is no savior besides Me" (Isa. 43:10–11).

The New Testament apostles agree, for Paul said, "We know that there is no such thing as an idol in the world, and that there is no God but one. For even if there are so-called gods whether in heaven or on earth, as indeed there are many gods and many lords, yet for us there is but one God, the Father, from whom are all things and we exist for Him; and one Lord, Jesus Christ, through whom are all things, and we exist through Him" (1 Cor. 8:4–6).

What is evident in the Bible, contrary to all other religions, are the ideas of God's grace, mercy, and love. Whereas other religions teach that their god or gods must be appeased in order to receive rewards, the Bible teaches that God is love, and those who love Him obey Him out of love, not to be rewarded. This is what the Founder of Christianity said, telling His disciples, "If you love Me, you will keep My commandments" (John 14:15). He died the next day on the cross, and then He was resurrected bodily from His grave after three days—attested to by hundreds (cf. 1 Cor. 15). And while other religious traditions have ideas of spiritual or spirit resurrections (untestable hypotheses), only the Bible proclaims a bodily resurrection that passes all tests of historical reliability.[283]

The *wonder* of the Bible is that it still changes lives, from children with simple faith to academic skeptics who finally give in

---

[283] Josh McDowell, *Josh McDowell's Handbook on Apologetics*, electronic ed. (Nashville: Thomas Nelson, 1997).

and see the Light of the Gospel. Jesus said, "Come to Me, all who are weary and heavy-laden, and I will give you rest. Take My yoke upon you and learn from Me, for I am gentle and humble in heart, and you will find rest for your souls. For My yoke is easy and My burden is light (Matt. 11:28–30)… Whoever drinks of the water that I will give him shall never thirst; but the water that I will give him will become in him a well of water springing up to eternal life (John 4:14)… I came that they may have life, and have it abundantly. I am the good shepherd; the good shepherd lays down His life for the sheep" (John 10:10–11). The Bible has been changing lives for centuries, and given that no single passage has ever been refuted as inaccurate or wrong, the Bible will likely continue to change the lives of all who see it and submit to it for what it truly is, God's Word.

The historical *reliability* of the New Testament has been established through the *authenticity* of the manuscripts that still exist. Of the 5,686 Greek manuscripts, many date back very close to the time of Jesus. Gospel fragments such as a fragment of Mark found in the Dead Sea Scrolls date back to AD 50. The John Rylands fragment, dating to AD 117–138 has portions of John 18. The Bodmer papyri, dating circa AD 200, contains many portions of the Gospel of John, and the Chester Beatty papyri contain all the Gospels, dating circa AD 250, only 200 years after they were written.[284] Dating these manuscripts so early mitigates against the idea that the New Testament was written not by apostles and prophets in the first century but by charlatans who claimed they were Peter, Paul, or James sometime in the second or third century. The fact that the writings of the New Testament are quoted outside of the Bible as early as AD 100 also reveals that the writings of the Bible were widespread and well known by the end of the first century.

The *historicity* of the accounts of Christ's life, doctrine, death, and resurrection is also firmly established on sound historical evidence. The genuineness of the New Testament writers is established by the character of the witnesses as well as by the

---

[284] Doug Smith, "Dispelling Muslim Myths About the Bible," *Christian Apologetics Journal* Vol. 3:1 (Matthews, NC: Southern Evangelical Seminary, 2004), 53.

quantity and independent nature of their witness.[285] Throughout the New Testament, the writers claim that they were either eyewitnesses to the events they recorded or that they got their information via the eyewitnesses who saw Jesus and experienced His life, ministry, and miracles (cf. Luke 1:1–2; John 19:33–35; Acts 2:32; 3:15; 4:18–20; 26:24–28; 1 Cor. 15:3–8; Heb. 2:3–4; 1 Pet. 5:1; 2 Pet. 1:16; 1 John 1:1–2).

In the first three chapters of Luke's Gospel, Luke names 11 historically confirmed leaders: Herod the Great (1:5), Caesar Augustus (2:1), Quirinius (2:2), Tiberius Caesar (3:1), Pontius Pilate (3:1), Herod tetrarch of Galilee (3:1), his brother Philip tetrarch of Iturea and Traconitis (3:1), Lysanias tetrarch of Abilene (3:1), the former high priest of Israel Annas (3:2), the current high priest Caiaphas (3:2), and John son of Zacharias (3:2). In addition, the towns and districts Luke named where these men served are both historical and verifiable. If Luke was writing a historical novel, why did he use real names—the names of men who, if he misrepresented them for the world to read about, could destroy him?

Geisler and Turek quote classical scholar and historian Colin Hemer who chronicled Luke's accuracy in the book of Acts verse by verse. With painstaking detail, Hemer identified 84 facts in the last 16 chapters of Acts, written by Luke, that have been confirmed by historical and archaeological research.[286] So if the character of the biblical writers is established by their historical accuracy, then Luke passes with flying colors. And if Luke passes, then so do Matthew, Mark, and John, for each of them confirms Luke's historicity by their own Gospel accounts. Furthermore, since Luke was a traveling companion of the Apostle Paul, recording the places they went as Paul wrote letters to the churches he planted, then Paul's writings can be trusted. Likewise, not a single one of the other New Testament writers contradicts their fellow writers. Of course, this does not *prove* the Bible is God's Word, but it does give credence to its historicity.

In Jesus' day, there was no New Testament, for it was waiting to be written following the completion of His ministry on earth.

---

[285] Geisler, *Christian Apologetics*, 327.
[286] Geisler and Turek, 256.

But the Hebrew Scriptures, the Old Testament, were revered by the Jews and converts to the Jewish faith. Jesus' own belief in the writings of the Old Testament was that it was divinely inspired by God. He not only quoted it extensively, since as God He was the ultimate author of the Old Testament, He told others that the Scriptures pointed to Him (John 5:39). Jesus viewed the Old Testament Scriptures as:

- **Containing God's authority**—When He was tempted (Matt. 4; Luke 4), Jesus quoted from Deuteronomy; on 92 occasions Jesus pointed to the Old Testament, saying, "It is written…"
- **Indestructible**—Jesus claimed that not even the smallest little mark in the Scriptures would ever perish (Matt. 5:17).
- **Infallible**—"Scripture cannot be broken" (John 10:35); "Your word is truth" (17:17).
- **Without error**— "You are mistaken, not understanding the Scriptures" (Matt. 22:29).
- **Historical**—From Moses (Matt. 19:8) to Noah (Matt. 24:37–38) to Jonah (12:40) to Daniel (24:15), Jesus knew these people as historical characters.
- **Scientifically accurate**—Jesus spoke of the creation ex nihilo and marriage (Matt. 19:4–6).
- **Having ultimate and final authority**—"Why do you yourselves transgress the commandment of God for the sake of your tradition?" (Matt. 15:3–9).

So Is the Bible Inerrant?

When theologians speak of biblical inerrancy, they do not mean that the King James Version or the New American Standard Bible is without error. These two versions of the Bible, as good as they are, do not always agree with each other when put side by side, although they agree over 98% of the time. Paul D. Feinberg said:

> By *inerrancy*, we mean that when all the facts are known, the Bible—in its original manuscripts and

properly interpreted—will be shown to be true and never false in all that it affirms, whether related to doctrine, ethics, or the social, physical, or life sciences. Three matters in this definition are noteworthy. First, there is the recognition that we do not possess all the information to demonstrate the truth of the Bible. Much data has been lost due to the passing of time. It simply no longer exists. Other data await archaeological excavation. Second, inerrancy is defined in terms of truth that most philosophers today take to be a property of sentences, not words. This means that all the indicative sentences, or statements, of the Bible are true. Therefore, on this definition, an error in the Bible would require that it made a false statement. Finally, all information in the Bible, whatever the subject, is true. That is, it accurately records events and conversations, including the lies of men and Satan. It teaches truly about God, the human condition, and heaven and hell.[287]

The Bible is a document literally "breathed out" by God (2 Tim. 3:16). It is the result of prophets and apostles speaking for God while He speaks and writes through them (cf. 2 Pet. 1:21). Therefore, the Bible is both human and divine—just like Jesus!

The Bible says, through God's inspiration, that a prophet can only speak truth if in fact he is a prophet, for nothing short of truth will do (Deut. 13:1–5; 18:20–22). This means that God can use man and his personality to speak for Him while keeping man from speaking or writing errors about God's holy name and decree. Furthermore, the laws and prophecies given by God are said to be eternal (Matt. 5:17–20), and the tiniest details will be fulfilled and are hence not to be taken lightly. As Feinberg said, "At times arguments in Scripture rest on a single word (Psalm 82:6; John 10:34–35), the tense of a verb (Mat. 22:32), or the number of a noun (Gal. 3:16)."[288]

---

[287] Paul D. Feinberg, "Does the Bible Contain Errors?" *The Apologetics Study Bible: Real Questions, Straight Answers, Stronger Faith,* ed. Ted Cabal, Chad Owen Brand, E. Ray Clendenen, et al. (Nashville, TN: Holman Bible Publishers, 2007), 1412-13.

[288] Feinberg, 1412.

So, to answer the question of whether the Bible is inerrant, if there are no original autographs, how can we know? First, we must possess a sufficient number of discernable copies of the autographs in order to place them side by side to determine how much, if anything, has changed over time. Second, those who place these manuscripts side by side to determine what the original autographs would have said must adhere to a strict and sophisticated discipline of textual criticism. Not only does the New Testament contain literally thousands of manuscripts, textual critics abound as well.

The verdict? Once again, it goes back to your worldview, for there are brilliant scholars on both sides of the debate. Some naturally assume that God would want His words transmitted over time without error, and others believe that the Bible is the work of men who make errors and corrupt the once perfect text. In other words, what you believe about inerrancy depends on your view of God. All the evidence is there to conclude that the original autographs are contained within the copies and are reflected in the translations we read today. Feinberg said, "The fundamental issue is the Bible's teaching of its own inerrancy. And for those who are skeptical, evidence from science, archaeology, and history has supported this claim over and over again."[289]

History of the Bible Text and How it Came to Us in its Present Form

Historical knowledge of the Jewish Scriptures is vital to our appreciation of the Bible in its present form. Understanding the history provides a legitimate argument not only for God's existence, but also for the Scriptures themselves being God's special revelation to His people. As God's people, the Jews took strides to preserve what they believed was God's revelation to them. The priests, those who mediated God's Word to the people of Israel, were the first line of defense for the Scriptures. God instructed them to "Take this book of the law and place it beside the ark of the covenant of the LORD your God, that it may remain there as a witness against you" (Deut. 31:26).

---

[289] Feinberg, 1413.

Four hundred years later, when the monarchy was introduced in Israel under Saul and then David, the kings participated in this task, for they also were to read the Scriptures regularly so that they might follow the Lord faithfully as they led His people. Four hundred years before the monarchy, Moses wrote to the future kings in Deuteronomy 17:18–19: "Now it shall come about when he sits on the throne of his kingdom, he shall write for himself a copy of this law on a scroll in the presence of the Levitical priests. It shall be with him, and he shall read it all the days of his life, that he may learn to fear the LORD his God."

So it is clear that the Jews were tasked with preserving the Scriptures, but did they? Historical evidence points to the fact that not only did they preserve the Scriptures, what we have today in our Bibles is conclusively the exact same thing they had when God originally spoke it.

The Mishnah (ca. AD 200). The Mishnah is the basic authoritative document of rabbinic Judaism compiled by Rabbi Judah ha-Nasi. This compilation is a codification of traditions the Jews passed down orally, presenting the account of the people responsible for the preservation of the Hebrew Scriptures from the time of Moses until the Council of Jamnia (first century AD), which solidified the Jewish canon of inspired books into its present form.[290]

The Sopherim (400 BC to AD 200). Once the historical accounts of the Jewish people were complete (ca. 400 BC), the preservation of the Hebrew Scriptures came under the protection of a group of scribes called the *Sopherim* ("counters"). They were essentially proofreaders, but they also made copies of the Scriptures to replace the constantly perishing writing materials. As "checkers," they made a practice of counting the verses, words, and letters of each Bible book and appending this information in order to give future copyists some standard against which to check the accuracy of their copies.[291]

---

[290] Allen C. Myers, "The Mishnah," in *The Eerdmans Bible Dictionary* (Grand Rapids, MI: Eerdmans, 1987), 724.

[291] Walter A. Elwell and Barry J. Beitzel, *Baker Encyclopedia of the Bible* (Grand Rapids, MI: Baker Book House, 1988), 1414-15.

The *Zugoth* ("pairs" of textual scholars) and the *Tannaim* ("repeaters" or "teachers") were also working at this task up to AD 200.[292] The work of Tannaim can be found in the *Midrash* ("textual interpretation"), *Tosefta* ("addition"), and *Talmud* ("instruction"), the latter of which is divided into *Mishnah* ("repetitions") and *Gemara* ("the matter to be learned"). The Talmud gradually was written between AD 100 and 500.

The Masoretes (AD 500 to 900). Their name comes from *Masora*, which means "tradition." Between 500 and 950, the Masoretes added the vowel pointings and pronunciation marks to the consonantal Hebrew text received from the Sopherim on the basis of the *Masora* ("tradition") that had been handed down to them.[293] They did this to keep the Hebrew language alive since it had begun to pass away after the Jews were chased out of Israel in AD 135.

One of the practices of these scribes was to destroy old copies of the Scriptures once they completed the new copy. This is why, in contrast to the plethora of New Testament manuscripts in existence, the Old Testament is lacking in ancient manuscripts. The Jews believed that destroying old copies would protect readers from misreading God's Word because of worn spots in older manuscripts.[294] So, because of the meticulous way in which copies were made and the trust put into the new being a perfect representation of the old, scribes had no reason to cling to older manuscripts.

Targums. Targums are Aramaic renderings of Hebrew oral traditions that were part of regular worship in synagogues during the centuries when the Jews spoke Aramaic (cf. Ezra 8:7–8). Aramaic, similar to Hebrew, was the language spoken in Babylon, and when the Jews returned from their exile there in 539 BC, most of them spoke only Aramaic. Therefore, the older men who survived their time in exile and knew the Hebrew language began to read the Hebrew text aloud, then give an Aramaic paraphrase of their readings to the post-exile Jews (cf. Neh. 8:8). This practice continued until the entire Old Testament was in Aramaic. For

---

[292] Geisler, *Baker Encyclopedia of Christian Apologetics*, 548.
[293] Geisler, 548.
[294] McDowell, *The New Evidence that Demands a Verdict*, 75.

modern scholars, the Targums are vital given that they reflect the teachings of the Hebrew Scriptures.[295]

The Septuagint (LXX). In 250 BC, the Old Testament was translated into Greek for the Greek-speaking world. By this time, many Jews were living in or near the Egyptian city of Alexandria, and Ptolemy II Philadelphus wanted a copy of the Old Testament for his library in Alexandria. The first books completed were the Pentateuch around 250 BC, and sometime around 150 years later, the rest of the Old Testament was completed. Although it differs slightly in various places from the Masoretic text, it attests to the accuracy of the Hebrew Scriptures.

The Samaritan Pentateuch. The history of Israel includes a split of the Israelites and years of civil war between them. Sometime around 930 BC, Israel split between north (Israel) and south (Judah). Samaritans were half-breeds—the offspring of Gentiles and the Israelites of the north who were conquered by the Assyrians in 722 BC. After sacking Israel, the Assyrians transported the Jews to other conquered sites and repopulated their territories by breeding all their conquered peoples (2 Kings 17:5–6, 24). The offspring was a mixed breed who lost their former national identities (2 Kings 17:25–41). Jews who remained pure in the south (in Judah; also Judea) were able to keep their national identities even after they too were conquered and exiled to Babylon in 586 BC.

When about 50,000 of them returned to Judea around 537 BC, the Samaritans, who worshiped their God, offered to help them rebuild their temple. Ezra the priest, however, flatly rejected their offer (Ezra 4:1–2) and developed a segregation policy excluding them and all others of mixed races from fellowship with Israel (Ezra 9–10). Ezra's fear was that these pagan peoples would once again corrupt God's chosen people, and he did not want to risk that happening again. After all, it was Solomon who had begun the corruption of Israel 400 years prior by marrying foreign women and yoking Israel together with pagan peoples who ended up corrupting them (cf. 1 Kings 11:4–11).

After being rebuffed by Ezra and Nehemiah, the Samaritans departed and built their own temple on Mount Gerizim (ca. 400

---

[295] Myers, 984-85.

BC), although God had ordained Jerusalem as the place of worship (2 Chron. 6:6; cf. Psalm 48:1–2; 78:68–69; 132:13). Because they adopted the Pentateuch only as their holy book (rejecting the Writings and Prophets), they were partial to Mt. Gerizim (cf. Gen. 12:6–7; Deut. 11:29; 12:5; 16:2; 26:2). Hence, they wrote their own Bible with Mt. Gerizim as the epicenter of their worship[296] (cf. John 4:20–22) and rejected the rest of the Old Testament that the Jews held sacred. Then in 128 BC, the Jews destroyed their temple, further provoking them. So tensions in the days of Jesus were high between both groups. What is remarkable about the Samaritan Pentateuch is that although the oldest manuscript from this list of books dates only to the tenth century AD, there is very little difference between it and the Masoretic text.

The Dead Sea Scrolls. The remarkable discovery of the Dead Sea Scrolls has answered the questions of skeptics who, prior to 1948 when the scrolls were found, complained that the manuscripts scholars possessed were too far removed from the originals. If the Greek Septuagint contained the oldest writings of the Old Testament, then skeptics believed that errors surely had crept into the Hebrew texts since those were completed back in 400 BC.

The scrolls found near the Dead Sea in Israel contain portions of every book of the Old Testament except Esther.[297] According to Dead Sea Scroll scholar Harold P. Scanlin, although the exact dating of the scrolls is not possible, most dates can be considered accurate within 25 or 50 years, and Qumran manuscripts are no later than AD 70.[298] The majority of them were compiled between 100 BC and AD 68 by a community of pious Jews known as Essenes.

Regarding the dating of the Dead Sea Scrolls, Scanlin said:

> Any lingering doubts about the age of the Dead Sea Scrolls can now be dismissed because of the results of recent radiocarbon tests using the accelerator mass-spectrometry technique. Early Carbon 14 tests were done

---

[296] Borchert, 200.

[297] Harold P. Scanlin, *The Dead Sea Scrolls and Modern Translations of the Old Testament* (Wheaton, IL: Tyndale House Publishers, 1993).

[298] Scanlin, *The Dead Sea Scrolls and Modern Translations of the Old Testament.*

on associated material, rather than the scrolls themselves, because the amount of material that had been needed to run the tests would have destroyed too much of the manuscripts. Newer techniques now require far less material, so it was possible to test samples taken directly from fourteen manuscripts from four sites in the Dead Sea area. All but one of the manuscripts tested are within the range of dates given by paleographers.[299]

What stands out among the scrolls is a complete copy of the book of Isaiah that dates to 100 BC—1,000 years older than the oldest copy scholars possessed before the discovery of the scrolls. And when the two copies are put side by side, they say essentially the same thing. Scholars conclude that after more than 1,000 years of transcribing a text, the scribes involved kept the copies of God's Word accurately over the course of at least 1,000 years. Old Testament scholar Gleason Archer concluded that the Dead Sea Scrolls "proved to be word for word identical with our standard Hebrew Bible in more than 95 percent of the text. The 5 percent of variation consisted chiefly of obvious slips of the pen and variations in spelling."[300]

When all this is put in context, it certainly points to the fact that the Bible has been well preserved and kept intact down through the centuries. And why not? If the Bible is God's Word to man, His special revelation, then of course God would preserve the contents of it accurately for every generation to know Him and obey Him. Therefore, we can argue that the Bible we possess today is in fact infallible and completely authoritative in all matters— whether scientific, doctrinal, or simple matters of faith.

---

[299] Harold P. Scanlin, *The Dead Sea Scrolls and Modern Translations of the Old Testament* (Wheaton, IL: Tyndale House Publishers, 1993).

[300] Gleason L. Archer, *A Survey of Old Testament Introduction* (Chicago: Moody, 1964), 19.

A Brief History of the English Bible

From the Greek and Hebrew texts, the Bible was eventually translated into Latin, which was the language of the Roman Empire. It flourished in that language in the west, but the Greek text was preferred in the eastern part of the empire. Whereas John Wycliffe (d. 1384) translated the Latin into English in the fourteenth century, the Greek text was finally put into English in the sixteenth century beginning with William Tyndale. Although the King James Version was published in 1611 under the king's authority, it was certainly not the first English translation of the Bible.

Prior to 1881, the standard English Bible was the King James Version (KJV) of 1611 (aka the *Authorized Version*). In 1881, the English *Revised Version* was released by Westcott and Hort. They used older Greek manuscripts discovered in their day dating to the fourth century, whereas the KJV used later Greek manuscripts dating to the ninth century and beyond. As time passed, many other English versions were published based on manuscripts that date as early as the second century and possibly even the first century.[301] Many scholars believe that manuscripts closer to the original writing are more likely to be accurate since manuscripts are copied and recopied over time, resulting in slight changes that are reflected in the KJV.

Interestingly, comparing the Greek manuscripts from which the KJV was penned and the manuscripts from which all other English Bibles were penned reveals that they are 98.33% in agreement.[302] That means more than 98% of the time, the older Greek manuscripts agree in content with the earlier Greek manuscripts. In total, there are currently 5,686 Greek manuscripts

---

[301] Daniel Wallace, "Earliest Manuscript of the New Testament Discovered?" http://csntm.org/News/Archive/2012/2/10/EarliestManuscriptoftheNewTestamentDiscovered

[302] Norman L. Geisler and William E. Nix, *A General Introduction to the Bible*, Rev. and expanded. (Chicago: Moody Press, 1986), 474.

of the New Testament[303] (excluding the various ancient versions), so when they agree with each other that often, it is significant.

The differences in the earlier Greek manuscripts dating from the ninth century are the additions to the text. We might suppose that earlier manuscripts would reflect a loss of text through the centuries, but just the opposite is true. The oldest Greek manuscripts, for instance, do not contain Mark 16:9–20, but the more recent ones do. Why? Because Mark's Gospel ends abruptly at 16:8, and it seems evident that a scribe came along later and added an ending that was in keeping with Matthew's ending. Likewise, John's Gospel in the older manuscripts does not contain verse 5:4 (where the angel comes to annually stir the waters at Bethesda) and verses 7:53–8:11 (the woman caught in adultery). Clearly, these passages crept into the manuscripts over time by scribes who added material and/or were attempting to clarify the text. In the case of the woman caught in adultery in John 8, it is generally agreed that this event did occur, but it seems quite evident that John did not originally include it.[304]

---

[303] Norman Geisler and Peter Bocchino, *Unshakeable Foundations* (Minneapolis, MN: Bethany House Publishers, 2001), 256

[304] Most Bibles make some footnoted comment about John 7:53-8:11. Some bracket the section and footnote it with something along the lines of "Later manuscripts (mss) add the story of the adulterous woman" or "the oldest and most accurate mss do not include John 7:53-8:11." Others put the entire passage in the footnotes. Why? The simple answer is that the oldest Greek manuscripts of the NT, dating back to the second through the tenth centuries do not contain this passage. In short, the evidence is severely lacking for this passage being a part of John's original writing. So why is it in the Bible? Truth is, the story is likely true and was added by a later scribe and subsequently copied in later manuscripts. The story does not contradict any of Jesus' teachings in the NT, it does not mitigate against His character, and it does seem to complement all that is written about Jesus. Thus, scholars have included it as part of the life of Jesus.

It was God's Holy Spirit who prompted the teaching and the writing of the original New Testament manuscripts (2 Pet. 1:20–21). The originals would have made their way into the various churches all over the Roman Empire—from Rome to Egypt and everywhere in between. Over 25,000 copies of these manuscripts have been found in and around these areas through the centuries. The church in Ephesus, for instance, would have taken a letter written by the Apostle Paul and copied it while sending either the copy or the original onward to another church in the area. Making copies, however, was different then than now. There were no Xerox

Examples of changes in the Greek text are found in the more recent manuscripts. For instance, in 1 Timothy 3:16, the KJV says, "God was manifest in the flesh." But the older Greek manuscripts, which reflect the English NASB, NIV, and RSV, say, "*He* was manifest in the flesh" (emphasis mine). The older ones say "He" while the younger ones say "God." Examples like this (and there are several) point to a zealous scribe who replaced the pronoun "He" with the noun "God" simply because it was clearer. Other

---

machines, and ink and paper (animal skins and papyrus) were expensive given that literate scribes needed to be hired to make the copies. Some writers clearly copied portions of the original and kept what they could afford, for fragments written in short-hand have been discovered in abundance. The original writings, sadly, would have deteriorated and would have required more and more copies to keep them circulating.

So, with all the copying of those manuscripts, many various and minor errors crept into the text of those copies. Some words were added, others were dropped, and some letters were confused with other letters. Some of these small errors became bigger as the copies circulated more and more, for one small error would have been copied to multiple sources and distributed widely. There are clearly some instances where one scribe might try to correct an earlier mistake—or what he thought was a mistake—and create another variant in the text. The large majority of these errors are very minor, although some are a bit more complicated even though no doctrine is ever affected. But in cases where the meaning of the text might be affected, the sheer number of manuscripts available to scholars today—dating back to the early second century—make it relatively easy to correct the mistake the copyists made. And because most variants *added* to the text, like John 7:53-8:11, the original wording is usually quite simple to resolve.

As to John 7:53-8:11, some Greek manuscripts dating from the fifth and tenth centuries do include this passage. One particular manuscript places it after John 7:36 instead of 7:52 while a few others place it after 7:44. Some attach it to the end of John's Gospel. One manuscript even places it in Luke's Gospel after 21:38! No early church father comments on it prior to Irenaeus (early third century), and then only in the Latin version, which was translated possibly as late as the fourth century. Saint Augustine (354–430) believed it was expunged from the text by some over-zealous scribe who believed it might lead to a lax view of adultery since Jesus excused the woman's sin. But since Augustine commented on this passage, obviously it existed in his day and was being discussed as an event in Christ's life.

In conclusion, John 7:53-8:11 is likely *not* part of the body of inspired Scripture, for it was clearly not written by John the Apostle as can be determined by the very different vocabulary and style compared to the rest of his Gospel. It is thus not canonical. But, since it does seem to be historical and written without embellishment, it is accepted as biblical.

examples of differences in the KJV and other English versions are found in Revelation 22:19 and 1 John 5:7–8. In the Revelation passage, the KJV says "book of life" while the other English versions say "tree of life." On this particular issue, the NET Bible commentary says:

> When the Dutch humanist Desiderius Erasmus translated the NT he had access to no Greek MSS for the last six verses of Revelation. So he translated the Latin Vulgate back into Greek at this point. As a result he created seventeen textual variants which were not in any Greek MSS. The most notorious of these is this reading. It is thus decidedly inauthentic, while "the tree" of life, found in the best and virtually all Greek MSS, is clearly authentic. The confusion was most likely due to an intra-Latin switch: The form of the word for "tree" in Latin in this passage is *ligno*; the word for "book" is *libro*. The two-letter difference accounts for an accidental alteration in some Latin MSS; that "book of life" as well as "tree of life" is a common expression in the Apocalypse probably accounts for why this was not noticed by Erasmus or the KJV translators.[305]

Another example is 1 John 5:7–8, which in the KJV says, "These three testify: the Father, the Word, and the Holy Ghost." Unfortunately, that Trinitarian formula is not supported by the most ancient Greek manuscripts, which say, "These three testify: the Spirit, the water, and the blood." The former has no genuine manuscript support, but the latter has ample support in the ancient texts. Daniel Akin commented on this text:

> In versions following the (so-called) *Textus Receptus* or Received Text (KJV and NKJV) there is an additional section of v. 7 known as the *Comma Johanneum* or the Johannine Comma (Gk., comma = sentence or clause). Here vv. 7 and 8a read, "For there are three that testify in

---

[305] Biblical Studies Press, *The NET Bible First Edition* (Biblical Studies Press, 2006).

heaven: the Father, the Word and the Holy Spirit, and these three are one. And there are three that testify on earth: the ..." Why do most modern versions demote this additional section to a mere footnote? Are modern versions deliberately less Trinitarian than classic translations such as the KJV? The question involved in deciding whether this verse is authentic is not based on the truthfulness of the statement but on the external manuscript evidence. In other words, just because a statement is true does not make it Scripture. One must look at why and how the Johannine Comma came to be adapted into the Greek Edition of the New Testament known as the *Textus Receptus* (AD 1633). This is not a question of the *inspiration* of the text but of the *transmission* of the text. John's letter, whatever the original, is inerrant. What must be established is what the autographs actually said.

The oldest textual witnesses of this text occur in Latin manuscripts of the seventh century. With its eventual acceptance in the Latin Vulgate (Clementine edition, 1592), the Johannine Comma began to appear in many other translations and versions. It only appears in eight Greek manuscripts (minuscules), none of which can be dated before 1400. Furthermore, it is clear that the text has been translated from Latin back into Greek, and in four of the eight manuscripts the Johannine Comma appears only in the margin of the text. If the text is authentic, then its disappearance in the early manuscripts is an absolute mystery. Why would the church be so careless as to let such a valuable text be forgotten?

It should be noted that not only does the manuscript evidence strongly favor the omission of this passage, but the same is true concerning the testimony of the early church. Not one Greek or Latin Church Father ever quotes this passage in the first four and a half centuries. This is especially revealing in light of the many controversies revolving around the Trinity (especially Sabellianism and Arianism). If the Johannine Comma was a part of the original text, then what would be a better passage to quote in order to prove the Trinity? Nicea (AD 325) and Chalcedon (AD 451) almost certainly would have taken advantage of it. The absence of such usage causes one to doubt seriously the authenticity of this passage.

Erasmus, a prominent New Testament Greek scholar of the fifteenth century, rejected the Johannine Comma in the first two editions of his Greek New Testament (1516, 1519). Soon, however, he began to receive criticism for his omission of the Johannine Comma. The Englishman E. Lee was one of Erasmus's constant critics. After being criticized by Lee for several years, Erasmus wrote to Lee the following reply, "If a single manuscript had come into my hands, in which stood what we read (sc. In the Latin Vulgate) then I would certainly have used it to fill in what was missing in the other manuscripts I had. Because that did not happen; I have taken the only course which was permissible, that is, I have indicated (sc. In the Annotationes) what was missing from the Greek manuscripts."

Later, Lee suggests that Erasmus was negligent and that if he only had looked at other manuscripts he would have certainly found a copy that contained the Johannine Comma. Erasmus again explained to Lee that he had diligently consulted many manuscripts. He continues: "What sort of indolence is that, if I did not consult manuscripts which I could not manage to have? At least, I collected as many as I could. Let Lee produce a Greek manuscript in which is written the words lacking in my edition, and let him prove that I had access to this manuscript, and then let him accuse me of indolence." Shortly thereafter, a Greek manuscript containing the Johannine Comma was shown to Erasmus. It is almost certain that this manuscript was produced simply to induce Erasmus to include the Johannine Comma in his Greek New Testament. Even though Erasmus suspected this Greek manuscript to have been based on the Latin, there is doubt as to whether Erasmus knew that the manuscript had been created for the purpose of encouraging him to include the Johannine Comma. In the third edition of his Greek New Testament, Erasmus included the extra text (although he omitted the passage from later editions).

After Erasmus included the additional words of 1 John 5:7 in his Greek New Testament, others began to accept it without question. It was later included in Stephanus's edition (1550), which was a precursor to the *Textus Receptus*—the basis for the KJV.

Is the Johannine Comma Scripture? The evidence seems to say no. Is the Johannine Comma truthful? Is it sound theology? Yes. It is not necessary, however, to place the Johannine Comma in the text of Scripture. The Trinity can be adduced from many other texts of Scripture (e.g., Matt 28:18–20; 1 Cor 12:4–6; 2 Cor 13:14; Eph 1:3–14; 4:4–6). We are warned in the Bible neither to take away nor add to its words. On this basis it is best to leave out the disputed words.[306]

Although the Bible may seem to be a huge mess of contradictions, it is not. As stated before, manuscripts of the second century and manuscripts of the twelfth century agree with each other over 98% of the time. Even when they fail to agree, it is usually very minor, and never once is a biblical doctrine of the faith compromised. The differences have more to do with pronouns becoming nouns and additional information emended to the text. But even the additions to the text (like the longer ending of Mark and the woman caught in adultery in John 8) do not present doctrinal problems. The deity of Christ, His virgin birth, and salvation by God's grace through faith in Christ are fully represented in all the Greek manuscripts, whether old or young. All the major doctrines are fully represented in the Greek manuscripts without contradiction, and this is nothing short of amazing! The New Testament has at least eight different writers (Matthew, Mark, Luke, John, Paul, Peter, James, and Jude) who wrote at different times and in various locations. Each one, however, agrees with the

---

[306] Daniel L. Akin, "1, 2, 3 John," vol. 38, in *The New American Commentary* (Nashville: Broadman & Holman Publishers, 2001), 198-200.

other on *all* the issues, as reflected in both the manuscripts and the translations.

As to whether the Bible is inerrant, God-breathed, and without contradiction, the answer is yes, *but only in the original autographs*. God handed His words to His chosen writers, and inerrancy is found only in those original documents. Therefore, the Bible is inerrant insofar as it reflects the original writings as given by God. Somewhere in the 5,600+ manuscripts used today, God's original words can be found—words without error or contradiction.

The examples provided (concerning Erasmus' biblical texts and the older ones found over 200 years later) reveal how textual critics determine which text reflects the original writing. And though some texts are markedly different than others, there was no conspiracy to change the text by these ancient scribes. The scribes were only attempting to clarify and maintain the text by making sure they did not subtract accounts they believed might have occurred (such as the woman caught in adultery in John 8). English translations, and any other translations for that matter, are not inerrant but are infallible. They may seemingly disagree with each another, but no contradictions are in the original texts. The infallibility of translations means that they are foolproof and reliable. Where there are problems, there are always solutions. Where solutions do not exist today, we trust that they will be provided in the future.

Prior to 1895 when a man named Adolph Deissman found Greek manuscripts in an ancient Egyptian garbage dump, Christians were taught that the Greek text behind the New Testament was a special and unique form of Greek.[307] The reason being was that the Greek of the New Testament was very different from classical Greek. It was believed that God used His own language for the New Testament. But Deissman found ancient ledgers in a 2,000 year old garbage dump that used the same Greek as the Bible. It was called *Koine* Greek—"common." It was simply the language of the people. God, therefore, did not invent His own

---

[307] George Thomas Kurian, *Nelson's New Christian Dictionary: The Authoritative Resource on the Christian World* (Nashville, TN: Thomas Nelson Publishers, 2001).

Greek; rather, He inspired the common language of the people so that all would understand His message to mankind.

Deissman found that the term "propitiation" meant "satisfied" and "it is finished" meant "paid in full."[308] Both of these terms were used for financial purposes in common ledgers and conversations. Also, "only begotten son" in John 3:16 means "unique son." Whereas the former might imply that Jesus had a beginning (even though He is eternal), the *unique son* clarifies that Jesus was God's one and only Son, not one who had a beginning. Modern translations, based on older manuscripts, remedy these issues and make the text more understandable.

So the New Testament, though written in Greek originally, was written to be understood by all, as evidenced by the common language God inspired. Pastors and teachers would do well to teach it in such a way that is understandable and promote Bible versions that do the same. Ideas such as "the KJV was good enough for Paul so it's good enough for me!" are ludicrous. The English Bible has evolved for the better, and it is still based on the most reliable inspired Greek texts.

What Does the Bible Say About Itself?

When the Apostle Paul talked about the Old Testament, he said, "...the sacred writings which are able to give you the wisdom that leads to salvation through faith which is in Christ Jesus. All Scripture is inspired by God and profitable for teaching, for reproof, for correction, for training in righteousness; so that the man of God may be adequate, equipped for every good work" (2 Tim. 3:15–17).

Paul wrote to his young protégé Timothy back in the first century, and in verse 15, he affirmed Timothy's strong knowledge of the Scriptures that led him to salvation. Timothy had known this salvation since childhood as a result of having been taught the truth of Jesus Christ by his mother and grandmother (cf. 2 Tim. 1:5). The "sacred writings" is a reference to the Old Testament

---

[308] Daniel B. Wallace, "Why So Many Versions," http://bible.org/seriespage/part-iv-why-so-many-versions (accessed June 2012).

teachings that give wisdom to those who read them, and they lead one to salvation in Jesus Christ, which comes from faith. Clearly, Timothy knew Christ through the Old Testament Scriptures.

In verse 16, Paul speaks of the "inspiration" of Scripture. Once again, "Scripture" is a reference to the Old Testament writings since some of the New Testament writings had not been completed at that time. Passages such as 1 Timothy 5:18 and 2 Peter 3:15–16 clearly show that some New Testament writings had been accepted as Scripture, but Paul's main reference is to the Old Testament. These writings are said to be "inspired"—literally "God-breathed." In other words, God Himself participated in the writing of the Scriptures and guided the writers to say exactly what He wanted them to say. As such, Christians can firmly believe in the accuracy of God's Word, for because it is inerrant in the original autographs, it is infallible in its present form.

Because Scripture is without error as a result of being "breathed-out" by God, it is "profitable for teaching, for reproof, for correction, for training in righteousness" (v. 16). First, it is "profitable" but *not* in the sense of financial profitability. The Greek word means "beneficial" for teaching. This is logical in that if God inspired the sacred writings, He did so for the benefit of those who would read them. Therefore, reading His words are profitable because they are *beneficial* to the reader. Second, the inspired Scriptures are profitable for "reproof." This word has to do with conviction of sin. The reading of God's infallible Word is beneficial to anyone needing to be convicted of their sins. Nothing else works as well.

The third purpose of God's Word, and the reason He inspired it, is for the benefit it grants for "correction." This means "to set right; to restore to an upright state of being." So, following the word order in verse 16, a person is first taught, then convicted of sins, then instructed on how to make their life right with God. The Scriptures are profitable for correction. Finally, the Scriptures are beneficial for "training in righteousness." The Greek word for "training" is a verb form for "child," and it is often translated as "discipline" as you would train a child. In short, God's inspired Word is about instruction that has as its aim the increase of virtue.

Verse 17 is a purpose clause. It reveals that the purpose of God's inspired Word is so that "the man of God may be adequate, equipped for every good work." In other words, God protected and guided His Word, the Bible, so that all who read it will be fully enlightened—in need of no other instruction to do His good and perfect will. The Bible alone is given for that very purpose.

The *plenary* inspiration of the Bible simply means that the *entire* Bible is inspired, not just a few or the majority of its parts (cf. Jer. 15:19; 26:2; 36:2; Matt. 5:17–18; Luke 24:44; Rom. 15:4; Rev. 22:18–19). Let us be cautious, however, for although every word in the Bible is recorded accurately, not every word in the Bible is true. After all, Satan is quoted on a few occasions in the Bible, yet as the father of lies (John 8:44), he was known to twist the truth a time or two (cf. Luke 4:9–13).

The *verbal* inspiration of the Bible means that every single word is inspired as opposed to just phrases and ideas (cf. Exod. 34:27; Jer. 1:7, 9; Matt. 4:4; John 6:63). In passages such as Galatians 3:16, Paul's entire message hinges on just one word: "Now the promises were spoken to Abraham and to his seed. He does not say, 'And to seeds,' as referring to many, but rather to one, 'And to your seed,' that is, Christ" (Gal. 3:16).

Is it possible that the writers of Scripture made errors? Yes it is. But is it also possible that they did not make errors? Indeed it is. Therefore, with God's guidance to keep men from saying something wrong, can the Lord of all creation influence the writers of His words to keep them error free? Of course He can! It comes down to our view of God, whether He *could* keep the Bible free of error and whether He *would*. The Bible itself does not point to any errors, so given that God could keep it free from errors, it stands to reason that He did.

Is the New Testament Trustworthy?

Darrell Bock, New Testament scholar from Dallas Theological Seminary, offers six statements of fact that affirm the accuracy of the New Testament manuscripts as they are represented in various English translations.[309]

---

[309] Darrell L. Bock, "Is the New Testament Trustworthy? *The Apologetics Study Bible: Real Questions, Straight Answers, Stronger Faith,* ed. Ted Cabal,

First, *the books of the New Testament were recognized through a careful sifting process.* From the end of the first century up through the fourth century, the books of the New Testament were the foundation for the early Church's worship and the criteria for identifying false teachers. These books were hated by the enemies of Christ to the point where they were burned in a futile effort to rid the world of Christianity. Therefore, if certain books were banned and burned, it stands to reason that the early Church and the enemies of Christianity knew exactly which books were so offensive! Specifically, they were the books that claimed to have divine authority, books associated with an apostle, books in keeping with other accepted New Testament writings, and books that were widely read and received by the early Church.

Second, *the New Testament is based on reliable sources carefully used and faithfully transmitted.* The Gospel writer Luke explained that he researched the life of Christ by using available sources (cf. Luke 1:1–4). It does not hurt that Luke's account fits right in with the Gospels that preceded his (i.e., Matthew and Mark), and it makes perfect sense as to why. After all, Jesus told His disciples on the night before His crucifixion that He was going away and the Holy Spirit would bring to their minds all that He had taught them (cf. John 14:25–26). This means that the inspiration of the Scriptures entails God using human personalities while making certain that no detail in their writings was inaccurate. Of course, the eyewitnesses would not have needed sources, but those like Luke who were not eyewitnesses used the text and testimony of eyewitnesses. This ensured the credibility of their writings, and they were hence accepted into the canon of Scripture by the early Church. Bock said:

> The distance between event and recording is not great—less than a lifetime, a small distance of time by ancient standards. For example, the first-century Roman historians Livy and Dionysius of Halicarnassus were centuries removed from many of the events they chronicled. Judaism depended on the ability to pass things

---

Chad Owen Brand, E. Ray Clendenen, et al. (Nashville, TN: Holman Bible Publishers, 2007), 1452-53.

on with care from one generation to the next, recounting events with care. This does not exclude some variation, as is obvious by comparing the Gospel accounts or parallel accounts in 1 and 2 Samuel, 1 and 2 Kings, and 1 and 2 Chronicles. Judaism, and the Christianity that grew out of it, was a culture of memory. People memorized long liturgical prayers and more often than not worked from memory rather than from a written page. Anyone who has read a children's book again and again to his child knows that the mind is capable of absorbing vast amounts of wording and retaining it.[310]

In fact, the Bible we read today can be trusted as essentially mirroring the words God inspired when He originally gave it to the apostles and prophets of the first century. The manuscript evidence supports this, for the New Testament far exceeds the manuscript evidence of any other document of antiquity. Bock said:

> Where most classical works, such as those of Plato, Herodotus, and Aristophanes, have from one to 20 manuscripts, the NT has over 5,600 Greek manuscripts that we can compare to determine the original wording, not to mention more than 8,000 ancient Latin manuscripts.[311]

Third, *the various accounts given are not verbatim accounts.* Whereas some have claimed that the Gospel accounts differ to the point of contradiction, differences in details do not equate to contradiction, nor does subsequent reflection mean a denial of history. As with anything else, people view the same events from different angles and offer various details that simply add to the account. This does not necessarily corrupt the historical nature of the account. Anyone who has read the four Gospels with this truth in mind appreciate the way Jesus has given us four perspectives on Himself. Since the Gospels are historical narratives, and since history involves both past events and their results, the Gospels are

---

[310] Bock, 1452.
[311] Bock, 1452.

clearly noncontradictory given that they record the same events with the same results while recording those events from various angles.

Fourth, *trustworthiness demands not exhaustive but adequate knowledge of the topic.* In other words, the accounts that are written in the New Testament, though not exhaustive, are indeed sufficient and accurate. John the Apostle said as much when he wrote, "And there are also many other things that Jesus did, which if they were written in detail, I suppose that even the world itself would not contain the books that would be written" (John 21:25). Therefore, believing in the trustworthiness of Scripture means that the accounts given are not contrary to what actually happened and what we have is sufficient to comprehend what God would have us know (cf. 2 Tim. 3:16–17). In short, what we have is sufficiently accurate without being insufficiently exhaustive.

Fifth, *archaeology teaches us to respect the content of Scripture.* As we previously saw, archaeology has helped put many former mysteries to rest by showing that the biblical writers knew exactly what they were saying. It cannot prove than an event took place per se, but has shown that the details of an event fit the time, context, and culture of the event being described. Archaeology has also shown those who are less eager to believe the Bible that alleged errors sometimes just need time before an archaeologist digs in the soil and exonerates the biblical account. Bock said:

> For example, there was once a debate about the description in John 5:2 of a pool with five porticoes in Jerusalem, called Bethesda or Bethsaida. Many questioned its existence despite its wide attestation in ancient tradition. Different spellings of the locale in the NT manuscript tradition added to the tendency by many to reject the claim. In 1871 a French architect, C. Mauss, was restoring an old church and found a cistern 30 meters away. Later excavations in 1957–1962 clarified that it consisted of two pools large enough to hold a sizable

amount of water and people. Today virtually no one doubts the existence of John's pool.[312]

Sixth, *the Bible's claim for miracles is plausible considering the response to resurrection claims.* Since the accounts written in the Gospels were actually written by eyewitnesses, they obviously were written in their lifetime. In other words, the Gospel accounts are not legends written long after the fact. Compare the disciples before the resurrection of Christ and after. They acted cowardly when Jesus was arrested (cf. Matt. 26:56; Mark 14:50), and they were frightened before they knew He had risen (cf. John 20:19). Yet later, these same men valiantly preached the risen Christ to His enemies (cf. Acts 3:17–26; 4:8–12). Only eyewitnesses could undergo such a transformation.

The disciples never boasted of being trained or pious men; in fact, they were anything but. They were cowardly and slow to understand all that Jesus had told them. Yet they became fearless leaders who took the Gospel to the world. Even Paul, a former Christ-hater and persecutor of the Church, was transformed after Jesus appeared to him (cf. Acts 9). Paul, James, and Jude came to trust in Jesus as their Lord and God after having seen the risen Christ. Their subsequent transformation and writings are enough for anyone who wants to believe in miracles to believe in the miracle of the transformation of the human heart after encountering the one holy God.

---

[312] Bock, 1453.

Chapter 13

THE RESURRECTION OF JESUS CHRIST FROM THE DEAD

We have seen that if God exists, then miracles are possible. From the creation of the world out of nothing to the resurrection of Jesus Christ from the dead—all things are possible for God. John the Apostle was one of the eyewitnesses to the resurrected Lord. He had watched Jesus die on Friday, consoled Jesus' mother in her agony, and saw Jesus alive from the dead, after which his life was never the same. Let us look at the Gospel of John and his depiction of Christ's resurrection.

John 20:1 says, "Now on the first day of the week Mary Magdalene came early to the tomb, while it was still dark, and saw the stone already taken away from the tomb." It is noteworthy that all the Gospels refer to the day Christ rose from the dead as "the first day of the week" instead of "the third day after His death." To be sure, Christ's death on Friday is central to the Christian faith, but it is His resurrection on Sunday that sets Jesus above all other religious leaders. They are all dead—Jesus is alive! Not one of them ever claimed to be God, and none of them prophesied their own death and resurrection. Jesus is unique in this regard.

A certain theology is behind Christian worship on the first day of the week (John 20:19, 26; cf. Rev. 1:10). No Jew would ever have concocted such a story, foisted it on the world, and attempted to convince other Jews to forego their Saturday Sabbath for Sunday worship. New Testament scholar Walter Liefeld said, "The change from the traditional and biblical Sabbath is in itself a strong evidence of the Resurrection because it shows the strength of the disciples' conviction about what happened on that day."[313]

Since the Jews rested on the Sabbath, the women waited until the next day to come anoint Jesus' body. It was "early" when they arrived at the place where they had witnessed the burial of Jesus (cf. Matt. 27:61; Mark 15:47; Luke 23:55). Although John's Gospel mentions only Mary Magdalene coming to the tomb early, the Synoptics (Matthew, Mark, and Luke) include other women who were also present: the "other Mary" (Matt. 28:1; cf. Mark 16:1) who was the mother of James and Joses, the wife of Clopas (Matt. 27:56; John 19:25); Salome, the mother of James and John, the wife of Zebedee (Mark 16:1; cf. Matt. 27:56); and Joanna and "other women" (Luke 24:10). Therefore, it seems evident that there were many witnesses present on that fateful day.

Though each Gospel says these women arrived "early," John says it was still dark and Mark says the sun had already risen (16:2). But since "dark" and "early" are relative terms, both could be correct depending on your viewpoint. It could also be that the women rose while it was still dark but arrived at the tomb after the sun had risen.

John 20:2 says, "So [Mary Magdalene] ran and came to Simon Peter and to the other disciple whom Jesus loved, and said to them, 'They have taken away the Lord out of the tomb, and we do not know where they have laid Him.'"

John's account, written much later than the Synoptics, focuses on Mary Magdalene who, upon seeing the empty tomb, immediately ran to tell Peter and John while the other women peered into the tomb and saw the angels. Later, when Mary arrived at the place where Peter and "the other disciple whom Jesus loved" (likely John) were staying, she informed them that Jesus had been taken from the tomb. Mary's actions in this account imply that she had no preconceived notion of Jesus being resurrected. She was simply frightened and confused over the only possibility she could conceive to account for Jesus' body being gone, namely, who had

---

[313] Walter Liefeld, "Commentary on John," *The Expositor's Bible Commentary,* Volume 8: *Matthew, Mark, Luke,* ed. Frank E. Gaebelein, D. A. Carson, Walter W. Wessel, and Walter L. Liefeld, (Grand Rapids, MI: Zondervan Publishing House, 1984), 1047.

taken Him and why, for stealing a dead body violated all forms of human dignity.

John 20:3–9, says, "So Peter and the other disciple went forth, and they were going to the tomb. The two were running together; and the other disciple ran ahead faster than Peter and came to the tomb first; and stooping and looking in, he saw the linen wrappings lying there; but he did not go in. And so Simon Peter also came, following him, and entered the tomb; and he saw the linen wrappings lying there, and the face-cloth which had been on His head, not lying with the linen wrappings, but rolled up in a place by itself. So the other disciple who had first come to the tomb then also entered, and he saw and believed. For as yet they did not understand the Scripture, that He must rise again from the dead."

If Peter and John had stolen the body of Jesus like the Jews accused them of doing (cf. Matt. 28:13–15), they would not have run to Jesus' tomb so quickly after Mary told them He had been taken. Had they been guilty of stealing the body or been aware of a theft, they would not have acted so concerned about it by racing to the tomb as they did. John got there first, but being hesitant to enter, he simply stooped down to peer in. Peter, however, in his impetuous style, arrived and entered the tomb immediately and observed the "linen wrappings lying there, and the face-cloth which had been on His head, not lying with the linen wrappings, but rolled up in a place by itself" (John 20:6–7).

The men noted an *orderly* scene, atypical of a grave robbery, for if Jesus' body had been stolen, why did the robbers unwrap His body? Transporting Him would have been much easier with the body wrapped. Furthermore, if someone stole the body, would not the scene have appeared more chaotic with the linen wrappings scattered? John clearly portrays an orderly scene. Andreas Kostenberger said, "In contrast to Lazarus, who came out of the tomb still wearing his grave-clothes (11:44), Jesus' resurrection body apparently passed through the linen wrappings very much in the same way as He later was able to appear to His disciples in a locked room (20:19, 26)."[314]

---

[314] Andreas J. Kostenberger, "John," in *Baker Exegetical Commentary on the New Testament* (Grand Rapids, MI: Baker Academic, 2004), 563.

Note three different words to describe the perceptions of the two men when they arrived at the tomb. First, in verse 5, John "looking in...saw" (Gr. *blepeis*) the linen wrappings. This means he had a clear picture of the scene and did not believe based on rumors. Second, in verse 6, Peter "saw" (Gr. *theōrei*) or "considered" the linen wrappings. This means that Peter thought about what he saw, though he was confused by it. Third, in verse 8, John "saw" (Gr. *eiden*) in that he *understood* the impact of the evidence his eyes perceived. Clearly, John's observations of the scene reveal a thinking man, using the forensic evidence of the scene to determine the meaning of what he saw. And although he says that he "believed," he also explains in verse 9 that he still did not understand the teaching of Scripture, namely that Jesus had to rise from the dead. He may have believed Jesus had risen from the dead based on what he saw, but he did not believe based on the teachings of Scripture—*at least not yet.* In other words, John did not fabricate a story in his Gospel or invent a Messiah to fit the teachings of the Scriptures.

John 20:10–15 says, "So the disciples went away again to their own homes. But Mary was standing outside the tomb weeping; and so, as she wept, she stooped and looked into the tomb; and she saw two angels in white sitting, one at the head and one at the feet, where the body of Jesus had been lying. And they said to her, 'Woman, why are you weeping?' She said to them, 'Because they have taken away my Lord, and I do not know where they have laid Him.' When she had said this, she turned around and saw Jesus standing there, and did not know that it was Jesus. Jesus said to her, 'Woman, why are you weeping? Whom are you seeking?' Supposing Him to be the gardener, she said to Him, 'Sir, if you have carried Him away, tell me where you have laid Him, and I will take Him away.'"

When the four Gospels are read as a single narrative, the perspectives of the different writers paint the following story.

Early on Sunday morning, the angel of the Lord descended from heaven, and a violent earthquake shook the land. Though Jesus had already risen, the angel rolled the stone away from the tomb and sat on it. The Roman soldiers became so afraid that they fainted and became like dead men (Matt. 28:1-4). Meanwhile, the women who had followed Jesus so faithfully throughout His ministry departed for Jesus' tomb while it was still dark to anoint His body, ignorant of the events that had transpired. They arrived just as the sun appeared over the horizon and discovered the empty tomb. While the other women stayed to investigate, Mary Magdalene ran immediately to tell Peter and John that Jesus had been taken away.

During the time Mary was gone, two angels told the other women that Jesus had risen from the dead (Luke 24:4–5), and they invited the women to look into the tomb (Matt. 28:6). The women saw a young man dressed in a white robe sitting to the right of where Jesus once lay, and he too told the women that Jesus had risen (Mark 16:5). With fear and great joy, they ran to tell the disciples what they had seen, knowing that Mary Magdalene had already gone to do so. As they departed, Jesus appeared to the women, and they fell at His feet and worshiped Him (Matt. 28:8–9).

Peter and John arrived to survey the scene without seeing the other women, oblivious to the previous events. Once they investigated and left, Mary Magdalene returned and stood outside Jesus' tomb weeping. She looked into the tomb and saw two angels sitting on either side of where Jesus once lay. The angels— confused as to why anyone would be crying on the single greatest day the world has ever known—asked Mary why she was weeping. Her answer reveals a woman who was so distraught that even heavenly beings were of no comfort to her, and she probably did not initially recognize them as such. She thought they, along with the man outside the tomb whom she perceived was a gardener, were the culprits who had taken away her Lord (John 20:11–13). Turning away from the tomb, Mary saw Jesus, still believing He was a gardener. After He too asked why she was weeping and whom she was seeking, Mary pleaded with Him to tell her where Jesus was (John 20:14–15).

The climax of the scene is in John 20:16–18: "Jesus said to her, 'Mary!' She turned and said to Him in Hebrew, 'Rabboni!' (which means, Teacher). Jesus said to her, 'Stop clinging to Me, for I have not yet ascended to the Father; but go to My brethren and say to them, "I ascend to My Father and your Father, and My God and your God."' Mary Magdalene came, announcing to the disciples, 'I have seen the Lord,' and that He had said these things to her."

As Mary wept outside the tomb of Jesus, the man she thought was a gardener was Jesus, alive from the dead! All Jesus needed to do to reveal Himself to her was to say one word, her *name*. Although a common gardener may have known Mary by name, it was the *way* Jesus spoke her name that identified Him as her "Rabboni" (Aramaic for "my Teacher"). Like the raging sea that Jesus stilled with a word (Mark 4:39), Mary's troubled soul was calmed by *one word* from Jesus. Consider also the disciples on the Sea of Galilee after Jesus instructed them to cast their nets on the other side of the boat (John 21:6–7) and the two disciples on the road to Emmaus (Luke 24:31). All these examples reveal that recognition of Jesus does not follow a single pattern—and that He changes people's lives in an instant.

Mary's joyful response to Jesus was to call out to Him in reverential awe as to who He was to her, namely her Teacher, her Lord. But given Jesus' response to her, she must have also embraced Him physically as the other women had done when Jesus revealed Himself to them (cf. Matt. 28:9). He told her, "Stop clinging to Me." Though the NASB sounds quite harsh, Jesus was not pushing Mary away. His words were not meant to keep her from actually touching Him, for that would conflict with the invitation He gave the disciples to touch Him in Luke 24:39 and the challenge to Thomas to touch His hands and His side in John 20:27 (cf. Matt. 28:9).

What Jesus was telling Mary, given the present imperative verb tense, was to refrain from fastening herself to the idea that Jesus was there to stay. The fact that He told her to "stop" means she had already begun to think that Jesus being back from the dead meant He would be with Mary and the others in a physical sense from then on. The truth of the matter was that Mary's relationship to Jesus, as with all others, would no longer be through her physical senses. Once Jesus ascended to the Father (John 20:17), a forthcoming event, her relationship with Him would be through the presence of the Holy Spirit (cf. John 14:16, 26).

Jesus made many physical appearances after His death, prior to His ascension (cf. Acts 1:3, 9). This was so that writers like John could claim to have been eyewitnesses who had heard, seen, and touched Jesus—the "the Word of life" who grants eternal life (1 John 1:1–3). Even in his Gospel, John asserted that seeing and touching Jesus had ceased to be the means by which people would come to faith. From that point onward, after Mary, Thomas, and the disciples came to faith, God's blessing came upon those who believed without seeing (John 20:29).

It is interesting to note that in all the Gospel accounts, the women were the first witnesses to the resurrection. In Jewish society the witness of women was unaccepted.[315] So if the accounts of Jesus' resurrection are myths concocted by liars (as skeptics have suggested), then why would they have said that women were the first to witness it? The early Church suffered for this testimony because women were considered ineligible witnesses. But the fact that women were the first to witness the resurrection attests to its authenticity, because anyone making up such a story would have certainly used men to witness the account, thus making it seem more valid.

From the earliest of days after Jesus was raised to life, theories have abounded in an attempt to explain away His resurrection. The first lie to be spread was that Jesus' disciples stole His body from the tomb (cf. Matt. 28:11–15). Although this is possible, it is highly unlikely. First of all, the character of the disciples in the Gospels before the resurrection is downright cowardly. It would be difficult to comprehend how these men who had been frightened away a couple of nights prior had now gained the courage to confront the Roman guards, break the Roman seal from the tomb, and steal Jesus' body. In addition, because the disciples were dispersed all over the world after the resurrection, spreading the news that Jesus was alive, it makes no sense that they would have done that knowing it was all a lie. Furthermore, most of them died horrific deaths as martyrs, and although we might surmise that one or two might have died for a lie, we cannot conclude that all of them did so. The evidence against the disciples stealing the body is overwhelming, so that theory must be discarded.

A second theory to explain away the resurrection is that the disciples did not really see the risen Lord; rather, they were hallucinating when they saw Jesus. This seems quite unlikely given that Jesus appeared to hundreds of people over a *40-day* period (cf.

---

[315] Liefeld, 1049.

1 Cor. 15:1–6). If those who saw the empty tomb were hallucinating, then why did the Jews not go to the tomb and produce Jesus' corpse? That would have ended the deception. David J. MacLeod offered the following eight reasons why the hallucination theory is untenable:

> First, the theory cannot explain why the eyewitnesses to the gospel events had no control over these fictions or why the apostles allowed them to replace the true accounts of Jesus' death. Second, while hallucinations do play a major role in religious cultures, they are induced by drugs or by the extreme deprivation of food, drink, or sleep, and there is no evidence of any of these in the New Testament. Third, the details of the various appearances of Christ, which in several instances were to more than one person at a time, make hallucinations an improbably explanation. A visual hallucination is a private event and not one that takes place in the minds of, for example, more than 500 people at once. Fourth, the appearances to Mary Magdalene, to Cleopas, to the disciples on the shore, and to Paul on the Damascus road all differ in their circumstances. Fifth, as C. S. Lewis suggests, the theory of hallucination breaks down on the fact "that on three separate occasions this hallucination was not immediately recognized as Jesus (Luke 24:13–31; John 20:15; 21:4)." Sixth, hallucinations would never have led to the conclusion that Jesus had been raised from the dead. As Craig notes, in a hallucination a person experiences nothing new, because hallucinations cannot exceed the content of a person's mind. Seventh, this thesis fails to account for the other evidence, viz., the displaced stone, the empty tomb, and the grave clothes. It (like all alternative theories) fails "to provide a comprehensive, overarching explanation of all the data." Finally, the theory is ruled out by the fact that the disciples were thoroughly dejected at the death of Christ. They were utterly crushed and in no frame of mind to hallucinate. As Turner remarked, "The disciples to whom [the women] finally report do not believe for joy.

There is no avid clutching at any straw. Something quite unexpected had happened, rather than something longed for having failed to occur."[316]

A third theory is that the women who visited Jesus' tomb went to the wrong tomb. It was early, they were sad, and they just did not know where Jesus was buried. Aside from the fact that the women were present at the tomb two days before when Joseph buried Jesus (Luke 23:55), even if they did go to the wrong tomb on Sunday morning, why did the disciples go the wrong tomb also? And why did the Romans go to the wrong tomb as well? Even if it could be explained away like that, why did the Sanhedrin, who knew the precise location of the authentic burial place, publicly concede that the tomb was empty? Why did they not exhibit the corpse of the crucified Jesus and thus silence forever the resurrection message of the early Church?[317] This theory, though once espoused by Kirsopp Lake, a prominent professor at Harvard, shows just how hard skeptics must work to search for alternative theories to Jesus not being God.

A fourth theory is that Jesus did not really die, but was still alive when He was placed in the tomb. Not only does this view ignore the fact that both the Roman centurion and Pontius Pilate signed Jesus' death certificate (Mark 15:44–45), this theory overlooks the brutality of Roman crucifixion. Jesus was beaten severely after a night of no rest, then nailed to a cross for six hours, and before the Romans removed His body, they thrust a sword into His side (John 19:34).[318] Ironically, it was a skeptic, David Strauss, who put this theory to rest. Strauss wrote:

> It is impossible that a being who had stolen half-dead out of the sepulcher, who crept about weak and ill, wanting medical treatment, who required bandaging, strengthening and indulgence, and who still at last yielded to his sufferings, could have given to His disciples the

---

[316] David J. MacLeod, "The Resurrection: Myth, Hoax, or History?" *Emmaus Journal* 7, no. 2 (Winter 1998), 188.

[317] Carl Ferdinand Howard Henry, *God, Revelation, and Authority,* Volume 3 (Wheaton, IL: Crossway Books, 1999), 149.

[318] MacLeod, 178.

impression that he was a Conqueror over death and the grave, the Prince of Life, an impression which lay at the bottom of their future ministry. Such a resuscitation could only have weakened the impression which he had made upon them in life and in death…but could by no possibility have changed their sorrow into enthusiasm, have elevated their reverence into worship.[319]

A fifth theory offered by skeptics is that the man who died on the cross was not Jesus! This is the Muslim explanation, for the Koran says, "They killed him not, nor crucified him, but so it was made to appear to them, and those who differ therein are full of doubts, with no (certain) knowledge, but only conjecture to follow, for of a surety they killed him not: Nay, Allah raised him up unto Himself; and Allah is Exalted in Power, Wise" (Sura 4:157–158). But why would the disciples give their lives for a Savior they neither saw die on the cross nor alive again from the dead?

The Apostle Paul later wrote to the Corinthian Church, "For I delivered to you as of first importance what I also received, that Christ died for our sins according to the Scriptures, and that he was buried, and that he was raised on the third day according to the Scriptures, and that he appeared to Cephas, then to the twelve. After that He appeared to more than five hundred brethren at one time, most of whom remain until now, but some have fallen asleep" (1 Cor. 15:3–6).

In these verses, Paul passes on the historical event of greater importance than any other in history and provides possibly the first Christian creed given in Scripture. Jesus died for sins just like the Hebrew Scriptures said He would. He was buried in a tomb and raised to life three days later. This was not some fanciful story, for He appeared to many people following His resurrection. Paul's audience knew Peter, to whom Christ appeared, and they knew the other apostles.

The grand finale came 40 days after Christ's resurrection, when, after appearing to His disciples *and more than 500 other people at one time* (1 Cor. 15:5–6), He ascended into heaven. As

---

[319] David Friedrich Strauss, *A New Life of Jesus*, 2 vols. (London: Williams & Norgate, 1879), 1:412. Quoted in MacLeod, 178.

His disciples observed Him being taken up into the clouds, two messengers of God told them, "This Jesus, who has been taken up from you into heaven, will come in just the same way as you have watched Him go into heaven" (Acts 1:11). Of course, that day still awaits us, but his return will look somewhat like his departure.

Paul's point in writing was to say what he does in 1 Corinthians 15:17: "And if Christ has not been raised, your faith is worthless; you are still in your sins." Jesus spoke the truth about God, and He clearly predicted His own death and resurrection (Matt. 16:21; 17:23; 20:17–19; 26:12, 28–29, 31–32; Mark 9:30–32; 14:28; Luke 9:22; 18:31–34; John 2:19–22; 10:17–18).

The New Testament includes at least 17 appearances of Jesus after He rose from the dead. Consider Jesus' appearance to:

1. Mary Magdalene (John 20:11–17; cf. Mark 16:9–11)
2. The women (Matt. 28:9–10)
3. Peter (Luke 24:34; 1 Cor. 15:5)
4. The disciples on the road to Emmaus (Mark 16:12–13; Luke 24:13–35)
5. The 10 disciples (Mark 16:14; Luke 24:36–43; John 20:19–24
6. The 11 disciples a week after His resurrection (John 20:2629)
7. Seven disciples by the Sea of Galilee (John 21:1–23)
8. Five hundred at one time (1 Cor. 15:6)
9. James, the Lord's brother (1 Cor. 15:7)
10. Eleven disciples in Galilee (Matt. 28:16–20; 1 Cor. 15:7)
11. His disciples on the Mt. of Olives (Luke 24:44–53; Acts 1:3–9)
12. Stephen before his martyrdom (Acts 7:55–56)
13. Paul on the road to Damascus (Acts 9:3–6)
14. Paul in Arabia (Acts 20:24; 26:17; Gal. 1:12,17)
15. Paul in the temple (Acts 22:17–21; d. 9:26–30; Gal. 1:18)
16. Paul in prison in Caesarea (Acts 23:11)
17. The Apostle John (Rev. 1:12–20)

There are actually 456 identifying traits of the coming Christ fulfilled in Jesus of Nazareth. In light of this, statisticians have noted that the odds of one man fulfilling just *eight* prophecies are 1 in 10^{17} (1 in 1,000,000,000,000,000,000), and the odds of one man fulfilling just 48 prophecies are 1 in 10^{157}. This latter one can be illustrated with electrons. It would take 2.5×10^{15} of electrons, laid side by side, to comprise just one inch of electrons. If someone attempted to count them, counting 250 per minute all day and night, it would take 19 million years![320] If you marked one electron and gave a blindfolded man just one chance to choose it, he has the same odds of choosing the marked electron than one man has in fulfilling just 48 prophecies. Yet Jesus fulfilled hundreds of them!

The truth from the eyewitness perspective is that Jesus' tomb was empty three days after He was buried (Matt. 28:6; Mark 16:6; Luke 24:3,6,12; John 20:2, 5–8). The witnesses were not gullible, but were slow to comprehend the evidence (John 20:9, 11–15, 25). After they were convinced, they boldly proclaimed the truth, and they died painful deaths as a result of their faith. Their sorrow over Christ's death was replaced by the joy of seeing Him alive, and according to the book of Acts, their lives were completely transformed. They not only opposed the very priests who killed Jesus and rebuked them for their actions, they changed their day of corporate worship from Saturday (the Sabbath) to Sunday—the day Christ rose from the dead (cf. Acts 20:7; 1 Cor. 16:2). If Christ did not rise from the dead, then none of the early Church practices nor the early Church itself are explainable.

It is clear that without the resurrection of Jesus Christ, Christians would be just like all other religions who worship or pay homage to some dead leader. The significance of the resurrection, therefore, cannot be overstated. First, the resurrection is necessary for salvation (Rom. 4:25; 10:9), for "If Christ has not been raised, your faith is worthless; you are still in your sins" (1 Cor. 15:17). Second, because of Christ's resurrection, all men will be resurrected, though not all will be saved (1 Cor. 15:22; cf. John 5:29).

Third, Christ's resurrection proves His divinity. Romans 1:4 says that Christ was "declared the Son of God with power by the resurrection from the dead." Fourth, the resurrection shows that

---

[320] McDowell, *The New Evidence that Demands a Verdict*, 194.

Christ is Lord over death. The fact that He rose from the dead never to die again proves it (cf. Rom. 6:9). Finally, the resurrection defeated the enemy of God and man, namely, Satan (cf. 1 John 3:8). Those who place their faith in Jesus Christ are assured of eternal life, which begins at the moment they believe (cf. John 5:24).

Chapter 14

WHAT SHALL WE CONCLUDE ABOUT JESUS?

Was Jesus a Legend? Was He a fictional character foisted on the world as the Jewish Messiah? Agnostic Bertrand Russell believed so, for in his essay *Why I Am Not a Christian,* he wrote, "Historically, it is quite doubtful whether Christ ever existed at all, and if He did we do not know anything about Him."[321] Most historians today, however, even the staunchest anti-Christians, know that Jesus of Nazareth was a historical figure, not a legend. F. F. Bruce said:

> Some writers may toy with the fancy of a "Christ-myth," but they do not do so on the ground of historical evidence. The historicity of Christ is as axiomatic for an unbiased historian as the historicity of Julius Caesar. It is not historians who propagate the "Christ-myth" theories.[322]

Jesus Christ of Nazareth could not have been a legend, for even secular sources speak of Him as historical. First, the famed Roman historian Cornelius Tacitus wrote about the six-day fire during Emperor Nero's reign. Calling Jesus "Christus," Tacitus wrote:

> Consequently, to get rid of the report, Nero fastened the guilt and inflicted the most exquisite tortures on a class hated for their abominations, called Christians by the populace. Christus, from whom the name had its origin, suffered the extreme penalty during the reign of

---

[321] Quoted in Josh McDowell, *The New Evidence That Demands a Verdict,* 119.
[322] McDowell, 120.

Tiberius at the hands of one of our procurators, Pontius Pilatus, and a most mischievous superstition, thus checked for the moment, again broke out not only in Judea, the first source of the evil, but even in Rome, where all things hideous and shameful from every part of the world find their centre and become popular. Accordingly, an arrest was first made of all who pleaded guilty; then, upon their information, an immense multitude was convicted, not so much of the crime of firing the city, as of hatred against mankind.[323]

A second quote comes from Lucian of Samasota, a Greek satirist who lived in the latter part of the second century, who, although he spoke condescendingly of Jesus, nevertheless spoke of Him as a historical figure. He wrote:

He was second only to that one whom they still worship today, the man in Palestine who was crucified because he brought this new form of initiation into the world... [the Christians] Having convinced themselves that they are immortal and will live forever, the poor wretches despise death and most willingly give themselves to it. Moreover, that first lawgiver of theirs persuaded them that they are all brothers the moment they transgress and deny the Greek gods and begin worshiping that crucified sophist and living by his laws.[324]

A third quote comes from another Roman historian, Suetonius, a court official under Emperor Hadrian. In his *Life of Claudius* 25.4, he wrote, "As the Jews were making constant disturbances at the instigation of Chrestus, he (Claudius) expelled them from Rome."[325]

A fourth quote comes from the Jewish historian Josephus, himself not a Christian. In his *Antiquities of the Jews* he wrote:

---

[323] Wikipedia, "Tacitus on Christ," http://en.wikipedia.org/wiki/Tacitus_on_Christ (accessed on August 5, 2012).

[324] Wikipedia, "Lucian on Christ," http://en.wikipedia.org/wiki/Lucian_on_Jesus (accessed on August 5, 2012).

[325] Quoted in McDowell, 121.

Now, there was about this time Jesus, a wise man, if it be lawful to call him a man, for he was a doer of wonderful works—a teacher of such men as receive the truth with pleasure. He drew over to him both many of the Jews, and many of the Gentiles. He was [the] Christ; (64) and when Pilate, at the suggestion of the principal men amongst us, had condemned him to the cross, those that loved him at the first did not forsake him, for he appeared to them alive again the third day, as the divine prophets had foretold these and ten thousand other wonderful things concerning him; and the tribe of Christians, so named from him, are not extinct at this day.[326]

Speaking indirectly about Jesus in *Antiquities* 18.3, Josephus later wrote, "Festus was now dead, and Albinus was but upon the road; so he assembled the sanhedrin of judges, and brought before them the brother of Jesus, who was called Christ, whose name was James, and some others, [or, some of his companions]."[327]

Other quotes about Jesus come from Pliny the Younger, Thallus, Phlegon, and Mara Bar-Serapion. Each quote attests that Jesus was no legend but a true historical figure. Of course, this does not mean that Jesus was the Messiah or God in the flesh. It merely means that Jesus was a historical figure whose many followers were considered by the Roman government, and other Greek writers, to be annoying yet faithful to their Master.

Was Jesus a liar or possibly a lunatic? Jesus made many spectacular claims about Himself. He called Himself "I AM" (the holy name of God) in John 8:58 and in Mark 14:61–64. In the Mark account, Jesus also equated Himself with the prophesied Son of Man that Daniel spoke about 600 years prior (Dan. 7:13–14). Furthermore, He spoke of Himself as giving water that wells up into a fountain of eternal life (John 4:13–14), as being the Bread of Life (John 6:35), the Light of the World (John 8:12), and equal with God the Father (John 14:9). C. S. Lewis said:

---

[326] Flavius Josephus and William Whiston, *The Works of Josephus: Complete and Unabridged* (Peabody: Hendrickson, 1996), 18.63.

[327] Josephus, 18.3.

Among these Jews there suddenly turns up a man who goes about talking as if He was God. He claims to forgive sins. He says He has always existed. He says He is coming to judge the world at the end of time. Now let us get this clear. Among Pantheists, like the Indians, anyone might say that he was a part of God, or one with God; there would be nothing very odd about it. But this man, since He was a Jew, could not mean that kind of God. God, in their language, meant the Being outside the world Who had made it and was infinitely different from anything else. And when you have grasped that, you will see that what this man said was, quite simply, the most shocking thing that has ever been uttered by human lips.[328]

When Jesus said these things about Himself, He was either a deluded madman who truly believed He was these things, or He knew He was not God and was just lying about who He was. If He was lying, then He was also a hypocrite, for the corpus of Jesus' teaching held that honesty, integrity, love, and compassion were the hallmarks of godliness. Furthermore, if Jesus was lying, then He was no casual hypocrite; rather, He was evil! For only an immensely evil person would deliberately lie to others by telling them to put their eternal future on the line by believing in him, all the while knowing that he was lying.

But Jesus could not be called a liar, for as McDowell asked, "How can we explain the fact that He left us with the most profound moral instruction and powerful moral example that anyone ever has left? Could a deceiver—an imposter of monstrous proportions—teach such unselfish ethical truths and live such a morally and exemplary life as Jesus did? The very notion is incredulous."[329]

Equally, using the same moral criteria to evaluate Jesus, He could not have been a lunatic. For the sake of argument, only a lunatic would go to the staunch monotheistic Jews, as opposed to the polytheistic Greeks or Egyptians, and tell them He was the Son

---

[328] C. S. Lewis, *Mere Christianity,* 54-55.
[329] McDowell, 159.

of God, the Great I AM. On top of that, being from the despised town of Nazareth would have made Jesus look all the more insane given that He was a simple carpenter. But the argument does not hold water, for no abnormalities can be observed in Jesus' words or actions that are in keeping with a madman. Psychiatrist J. T. Fisher said:

> If you were to take the sum total of all authoritative articles ever written by the most qualified of psychologists and psychiatrists on the subject of mental hygiene — if you were to combine them and refine them, and cleave out the excess verbiage — if you were to take the whole of the meat and none of the parsley, and if you were to have these unadulterated bits of pure scientific knowledge concisely expressed by the most capable of living poets, you would have an awkward and incomplete summation of the Sermon on the Mount. And it would suffer immeasurably through comparison. For nearly 2,000 years the Christian world has been holding in its hands the complete answer to its restless and fruitless yearnings. Here...rests the blueprint for successful human life with optimism, mental health, and contentment.[330]

So if we agree that Jesus was not a legend, not a liar, and not a lunatic, we are only left with one alternative—*Jesus is the Lord God*. We cannot chalk Him up to just being a good person, a good prophet, or a good preacher. Good teachers, prophets, and men do not mislead people intentionally or unintentionally. Lewis debunked the absurdity of Jesus being a good man thinking when he wrote:

> I am trying here to prevent anyone saying the really foolish things that people often say about Him: "I'm ready to accept Jesus as a great moral teacher, but I don't accept His claim to be God." That is the one thing we must not say. A man who was merely a man and said the sort of things Jesus said would not be a great moral

---

[330] Quoted in McDowell, 162.

teacher. He would rather be a lunatic—on a level with the man who says he is a poached egg—or else he would be the Devil of Hell. You must make your choice. Either this man was, and is, the Son of God: or else a madman or something worse. You can shut Him up for a fool, you can spit at Him and kill Him as a demon; or you can fall at His feet and call Him Lord and God. But let us not come with any patronizing nonsense about His being a great human teacher. He has not left that open to us. He did not intend to.[331]

Jesus claimed to be God. He gave no other option for how we should view Him. Furthermore, He claimed that salvation is in no one else but Him (John 14:6). The question He asked His disciples, "Who do you say that I am?" (Matt. 16:15) is the same question He asks those we speak to when we present the Gospel. Whatever answer they give, whether good, bad, or ugly, we can know that wherever Jesus has been preached, lives have always been changed—for almost 2,000 years now. Drunkards cease from drinking, murderers repent of their crimes, people filled with hate are filled with love and compassion, and legalists are won over by grace. We may not be able to convince everyone we talk to that Jesus is the Christ, the Son of God, but it is important that we know it, that we are able to explain it, and that we can find comfort in it. Atheists, whether they admit it or not, desperately want to see a true Christian who not only knows all about their faith, but who lives it.

---

[331] Lewis, 55-56.

Chapter 15

WHICH VERSION OF CHRISTIANITY DO I CHOOSE?

Sadly, although Christianity is one faith, many false versions of it have evolved throughout the centuries. One early version of it, called Arianism, claimed that Jesus was just a man and not really God in the flesh as the Bible teaches. Arias (ca. AD 280–336) believed that although God is one, unbegotten, eternal, and without beginning or change, Christ is distinct from God, created out of nothing by the will of God, not eternal, yet created before all time or the world. In spite of being just a man, however, He is the world's mediator and redeemer.[332] This idea was considered heretical in the early Church, and it was spurned at the Council of Nicea in AD 325. But Arianism continued and many were led astray by it.

The heresy was dangerous in its subtlety, for it gave glory to Jesus as God's Son, and Jesus was so well respected by the Arians that it was difficult to distinguish them from real Christians. What was true then is still true today, for Arianism has morphed into various so-called "Christian" religions. What is common to all these heresies is that although they hail Jesus as a good man and a good prophet, they do not believe He is God. This is the most glaring difference between biblical Christianity and the cults.

---

[332] Fahlbusch and Bromiley, *The Encyclopedia of Christianity,* vol. 1, 121.

The Heresy of the Watchtower Society
(Jehovah's Witnesses)

The Jehovah's Witnesses (JWs) believe in Jesus, but their version of Jesus is different than orthodox, biblical Christianity. The JWs believe that Jesus was a *created* being—that Jesus has not always existed, but came into being as all humans do. Oddly enough, JWs believe that prior to becoming man, Jesus was actually Michael the archangel, a created spirit being mentioned in the Bible (cf. Dan. 10:13, 21; 12:1; Jude 9; Rev. 12:7). However, JW literature has changed in this belief over the years. First, Jesus was said to be distinct from Michael, then He was equated with the pope, and then He was Michael! It is believed that Jesus moved from being Michael to the Messiah at His baptism. In the JW publication *Let God Be True* (p. 33), Jesus is "a mighty one, although not almighty as Jehovah God is." This is why in John 1:1of the JW Bible—the *New World Translation* (NWT)—Christ is *a* god but not *the* God. JWs teach that Jesus "was and is and always will be beneath Jehovah" and that "Christ and God are not co-equal" (*The Watchtower,* April 15, 1957).

The Bible reveals many discrepancies with JW theology, such as the following three examples. First, Matthew 1:23 says that Jesus is called "Immanuel." This is two words combined as one in Hebrew that comprises a preposition ("with us") along with a common Hebrew designation for God ("El"), so the name means "God with us." Thus, *Jesus is God,* and He came to be with mankind in the flesh at His birth, although as God He has existed from eternity past. Second, in John 20:28, Jesus received worship—something limited only for God Himself. When Thomas touched the wounds of the risen Jesus, he exclaimed, "My Lord and my God," yet Jesus did not rebuke him or tell Thomas not to worship Him. In Matthew 28:9, the NWT omits "worship" and inserts "did obeisance" to Jesus. Third, Colossians 2:9 says of Jesus that in Him "all the fullness of the deity dwells in bodily form." The NWT, however, says that "all the fullness of divine quality dwells bodily."

The first Christian martyr, Stephen in Acts 7, called Jesus *Lord* as he was dying (Acts 7:59–60). The Apostle Paul referred to Jesus as Lord throughout his writings and said that true Christians are to confess Jesus as Lord (Rom. 10:9; 1 Cor. 12:3). "Lord" in these texts comes from the Greek word *Kurios*, the same word for *Jehovah* in the Greek version of the Old Testament (the Septuagint, or LXX). It seems evident from this that Jesus is the Lord—He is Jehovah God.

Although Jesus is not named in the Old Testament, it actually affirms that Jesus is Jehovah (aka *Yahweh* or YHWH). First, Isaiah the prophet wrote about Jehovah (Isa. 6:1–10). Later in the New Testament, the Apostle John wrote that Isaiah saw Jesus' glory and spoke of Him (John 12:31–42). Thus, *Jesus is Jehovah.* Second, in Exodus 34:14, it is clear that man is to worship only Jehovah. Yet the Jewish writer of the Epistle of Hebrews says that the angels worship Jesus Christ (1:6)—the same angels who surrounded Jehovah in Isaiah 6 and worshiped Him, calling Him "holy, holy, holy." Finally, in Isaiah 44:6, Jehovah is called the *first and the last* and in Revelation 22:13, Christ is the first and the last.

In lovingly refuting the JWs, we must read Revelation 1:8, which reveals God as the Alpha and the Omega. The Greek word used is "Lord," not Jehovah as it is written in the NWT. Next, we must turn to Revelation 22:12–16 and read the entire passage. The speaker is Jesus, and He calls Himself the Alpha and the Omega! There is a change of speaker in verse 17, and this is noted only because JWs typically say that there are many speakers in these verses. But for the sake of argument, if verse 12 is a different speaker than verse 13, the Alpha and the Omega in verse 13 calls Himself the *first and the last.* So, He is equating the first and the last with the Alpha and the Omega. It is clear that Revelation 1:17–18 is Jesus speaking, and He calls Himself the *first and the last*! Clearly, Jesus is Jehovah. He was dead, and He is alive forevermore according to verse 18.

Since there cannot be two firsts nor two lasts, it seems evident that Jehovah and Jesus comprise one God, although they exist eternally as two separate persons within the Godhead. They are one in nature and essence, but they are distinct in their person and roles. This reveals that "Jehovah" is used not only of God the Father, but also of God the Son. Though they are distinct persons, they are each called "Jehovah" because they are both divine, yet one.

Although some, if not most, JWs are simply confused as to who Jesus truly is, many through the years have blatantly twisted the Bible so as to exclude any reference of Jesus being God. In orthodox English Bibles, Hebrews 1:8 says that the throne of Jesus (called "God" in v. 8) will endure forever. Yet the NWT says that God *is* a throne forever. Thus, Jesus in the NWT is a piece of furniture! Certainly Jesus is God throughout the New Testament (cf. 1 Tim. 1:16–17; 1 John 5:20), for He knows all things (John 1:48; 2:25; 6:64; 16:21:17), is eternal (Micah 5:2), is omnipotent (Matt. 28:18; Heb. 1:3), is sinless (John 8:46), and is unchanging (Heb. 13:8). Thus, since only God possesses these attributes, this indicates that Jesus possesses deity.

Furthermore, the works of Christ in the New Testament reveal that He has the power to forgive sins (Mark 2:5–7; Eph. 1:7), He has control over nature (Matt. 8:26), He gives eternal life (John 10:28; 17:2), and He will judge the world (John 5:22, 27)—things that only God can do. And as previously noted, Jesus received worship, something also exclusive to God. He was worshiped by angels (Heb. 1:6) and by man (Matt. 14:33), yet only Jehovah is to be worshiped (Exod. 34:14)! Even Jesus Himself said that worship is due to God alone (Matt. 4:10), yet He accepted it. Thus, if Jesus in His preexistent state were the archangel Michael, how could He have received worship since angels are not allowed to receive worship (Rev. 19:10; 22:8–9)? We must therefore conclude that if Jesus were not God, then worship of Him would be idolatrous and sinful.

Bad Exegesis in JW Theology

JWs have an exegetical issue with a foundational passage in the New Testament. John 1:1 says, "In the beginning was the Word, and the Word was with God, and the Word was God." JWs translate the passage in such a way that reads, "Christ the Word is 'a god'" (NWT). They reason that the small "g" is required because the Greek word for God *(theos)* is not preceded by the definite article, "the" *(ho)*. Those who study Greek, however, know that this interpretation is not in keeping with the rules of Greek grammar. The definite article (the) is omitted according to the basic technical rules of Greek grammar.

A definite predicate nominative (the predicate noun in a sentence written in the nominative case when used with a "be" verb) that precedes a verb does not normally have the definite article as the rules of Greek grammar demand. The order of the Greek words in the last clause of John 1:1 is "God was the Word" *(theos en ho logos)*. The subject of the sentence is "the Word," the verb is "was," and the predicate nominative is "God." Usually the predicate nominative follows the verb, but in this case it precedes it, so an article is unnecessary. When a Greek writer wanted to stress the quality of the person or thing that was in the predicate nominative case, he would put it before the verb rather than after it. This is what John did to stress the fact that the Word (Christ) possesses the qualities of Godhood. This fundamental principle of Greek grammar supports the deity of Christ and gives no support whatsoever to the translation, "The Word was a god." The intent of John was clearly, "The Word (Jesus) was fully God."

Even the NWT does not always follow its "no article–small 'g'" rule. For example, in John 1:6, 12, 13, "God" does not have the article in the Greek text, but it does have a capital "G" in the NWT. It is correct to use the capital in those passages, but it is inconsistent with the NWT of John 1:1 where they omit it. Note also that in John 13:3, the word "God" occurs twice, each time with a capital "G." But in the Greek text, the first occurrence of the word does not have the definite article and the second occurrence does. Since both obviously refer to the same person, namely God the Father, it would again be wrong to assume that the alleged "no article–small 'g'" rule has any validity in Greek grammar.

Another observation is that without the article, *theos* (God) signifies divine essence, and with the article, *theos* suggests divine personality.[333] Since *theos* is a definite noun, it cannot have the indefinite article "a." So when John 1:1 states that "the Word was God," it simply cannot mean that Jesus is God the Father nor that Jesus is the Trinity. The JW booklet, *"The Word": Who Is He?*

---

[333] Dana and Mantey, *A Manual Grammar of the Greek New Testament* (England: MacMillan, 1957). 139.

According to John (p. 6), incorrectly suggests that this is what all non-JWs mean by their translation, "The Word was God." Obviously, it is inaccurate on their part to suggest such. What the Apostle John wrote is that in the beginning the Word existed, and He was with God the Father, for He is divine. Many passages in the Bible clearly refer to Christ being "God," and they *do* have the definite article (the). This shows that Jesus *is* God; *Jesus is Jehovah.*

JWs say that Jesus Christ is "a god" according to their interpretation of John 1:1. But how could Jesus be "a god" when passages like Isaiah 43:10 have Jehovah saying that there is no God before Him or after Him? And since the JWs believe that Jesus is a created being, why would Jehovah create Jesus to be a god when He clearly stated, "Before me there was no God formed, and after me there continued to be none" (NWT)? Furthermore, John 1:1 states that the Word (Christ) was with God. Yet in Deuteronomy 32:39, Jehovah says, "There is no god with Me." If Christ is not God but "a god," then Deuteronomy 32:39 reveals a contradiction either in the text or in Jehovah Himself.

To be sure, other gods *are* mentioned in the Bible, but they are most often spoken of as the wicked and false gods created in the minds of wicked man to do obeisance to them rather than Jehovah God. At times, they are spoken of in sarcastic terms as the imagery of the pagan pantheon of gods who are God's subjects and who must render an account to the God of Israel for all their evil and unjust acts of evil and the darkness of the world.[334] Also, the term "gods" (Heb. *Elohim*) is used of earthly kings, rulers, and judges (cf. Exod. 21:6; 22:8–9), so although the Bible speaks of them as existing, they are either in existence as phantoms of the mind or of men who govern.

Most Christians know that Isaiah 9:6 is a prophecy about the Christ, spoken of Him over 700 years before Jesus was born, where He is called "the mighty God." JWs, however, distinguish Christ as "the mighty god" from Jehovah who is "the *Al*mighty

---

[334] Willem VanGemeren, "Introduction to Psalms," in *The Expositor's Bible Commentary,* Volume 5*: Psalms, Proverbs, Ecclesiastes, Song of Songs,* ed. Frank E. Gaebelein, Willem VanGemeren, Allen P. Ross, et al. (Grand Rapids: Zondervan Publishing House, 1991), 534.

God." Yet Jeremiah 32:18 reveals that Jehovah is the "Mighty One." Since both Jesus and Jehovah are the *mighty God* (Isa. 9:6; Jer. 32:18), they are both God because they both possess full might and deity.

In Colossians 1:15, the Apostle Paul wrote that Jesus is the "firstborn over all creation." JWs use this passage, however, to support their belief that Jesus was Jehovah's creation (e.g., *Let God Be True,* p. 35). But the term has a much deeper meaning than simply being the firstborn of a father or mother. Truly, if this verse were teaching that Jesus Christ is the first created being made by Jehovah, Paul would have used the Greek term that means "first-created" (*protoktistos*) rather than "firstborn" (*prototokos*). What is the difference? *Protoktistos* (first-created) speaks of just that, while *prototokos*, the term used by Paul, speaks of an heir, a begotten one, the first in rank. So, what Paul is saying about Jesus Christ in Colossians 1:15 is that He is first in *rank* above all creation; thus, He is the Heir of all things.

The JWs did an interesting thing with Colossians 1:15–17 in their NWT. They added the word "other" four times throughout the passage so it states that Christ created "all *other* things," that is, everything except Himself. But there is no foundation for doing this. "Other" does not occur in the Greek text in Colossians 1:15–17, which is why the NWT translators put brackets around "other." Obviously, the JWs are mistaken in their understanding of *firstborn*, so they are wrong to add "other." Jesus being created by Jehovah is foreign to the Scriptures.

Another pertinent example of Scripture twisting by the JWs is how they render Revelation 3:14. Although the NWT says of Jesus "the beginning of the creation of God" (also in the NASB), it is their *interpretation* of what it means that is to be critiqued. Obviously, the JWs use this passage to point to Jesus as a created being who was the first of Jehovah's many creations. But the Greek word for "beginning" speaks of the source or origin of something within God's creation. Thus, the more orthodox and proper interpretation of Jesus being the "beginning" is to say that Jesus is the "source" or "origin" of all that has been created. This is in keeping with the statements in Colossians 1:16 and John 1:3 that all things were created by Jesus, or they had their origin in Jesus. And since all things were made by Christ (John 1:1) and all things were made by Jehovah (Heb. 3:4), both persons are God and possess this omnipotent creative power.

Scripture Twisting by the Jehovah's Witnesses

Throughout the Bible, in passages like 1 Timothy 1:17, Jesus is spoken of as God—the eternal and only God. In the case of Micah 5:2, it is Jesus who is being prophesied about 700 years before His birth, yet He is called "eternal." But Jehovah is also called "eternal" in Psalm 90:2. JWs use Proverbs 8:22, 30 as one of their passages supposedly pointing to Jesus' origin. Yet Jesus is not even the subject of the passage! Wisdom personified is the subject.

Likewise, in Philippians 2:6, the NWT suggests that Christ was not equal with God and did not even desire to be: "Although he was existing in God's form, gave no consideration to a seizure, namely, that he should be equal to God." This interpretation of the passage, however, only reveals the ignorance of the translators in dealing with the Greek text. The passage is discussing the incarnation of Christ, His temporary departure from heaven's glory, and His coming to earth. J. B. Phillips' *The New Testament in Modern English* says, "He, who had always been God by nature, did not cling to His prerogatives as God's equal." The *New American Standard Bible* says, "Who, although He existed in the form of God, did not regard equality with God a thing to be grasped." And *The Living Bible* says, "Who, though He was God, did not demand and cling to his rights as God." By stating that Jesus did not cling to His prerogatives and rights as God, Philippians 2:6 is saying that He willingly came to the earth. But in coming to earth from heaven, Jesus had to have "existed in the form of God." The term for "form" means *essential attributes.* Therefore, since Jesus was in the *form* of God—possessing all the attributes of deity—it is incorrect to suggest that He did not want to be equal with God. He already was, and is, God! Those who interpret Jesus being equal to God as something that He had to grasp for is excluded by the fact that He already existed in the form of God!

A final example to cite in how the JWs twist Scripture is John 10:30, where Jesus said, "I and the Father are one." JWs use this passage to promote that Jesus was one with God the Father in *purpose* but not in *nature* or *essence*. The problem with this interpretation is that if this was all Jesus was saying, why did the Jews want to stone Him for blasphemy? Certainly they would not stand against someone who simply had the same purpose as God. The truth is, the Jews knew that Jesus was equating Himself with God, and that was blasphemy. As is also true in John 5:18, the fact that Jesus called God His Father meant to the Jews that He was making Himself "equal with God."

Was Not Jesus Also a Man?

Although the Bible teaches that Jesus is Jehovah God and is fully divine, it also teaches that Jesus was a man. The JWs agree with Jesus being a man, but they believe that He was only a man, albeit a very good man. But Jesus, who existed from eternity in John 1:1–5, *became flesh* according to John 1:14. Hebrews 2:9 teaches that His humanity was only temporary, stating that He was made lower than the angels "for a little while." Philippians 2:5–8 teaches that Jesus existed in the form of God, meaning that He never ceased to be God. Yet He voluntarily gave up His right of divinity in favor of humility to die on man's behalf. Man could only be redeemed if Jesus became a man. The lex talionis of an eye for an eye was the law of God. Thus, Jesus, a perfect man, had to redeem man (Rom. 5:12, 15) by offering His life for the life of mankind.

JWs believe only in the humanity of Jesus and that He was inferior to Jehovah. They make this assertion based on John 14:28, where Jesus said the "Father is greater than I." But only in Jesus' humanity and during His time on earth was the Father "greater" (Gr. *megas*, "higher in position") than Jesus. They also like to ask, "Who was Jesus praying to when He prayed to God?" This is a pertinent question, but Isaiah 55:9 and Luke 1:37 reveal that man cannot limit God, who can do anything He pleases. He does not have human limitations, so His ability to pray to Himself should not create a foundation to believe that Jesus was inferior to Jehovah.

After all, Jesus' contemporaries either believed He was Jehovah, or they believed He at least equated Himself with Jehovah. In John 5, 8, and 10:30–33, Jesus claimed equality with God. If Jesus was claiming only to be "a" god, the Jews would not have taken up stones to throw at Him for equating Himself with God. In fact, Jesus called Himself "I AM"—the very name YHWH in Hebrew (John 8:58; cf. Exod. 3:13–15). And unless a person believes that Jesus is I AM, they will die in their sins (John 8:24).

The Apostle Paul warned about people coming to preach a false Jesus in 2 Corinthians 11:4. Christians should therefore heed the admonition of 1 Peter 3:15 and defend the true faith of the true Jesus. What the JWs do is present a false message about Jesus, and they go door to door all over the world preaching that He is not God and that He is not eternal but had a beginning. Christians must first understand what true Christian theology is according to the Bible, and then they must engage the battle for truth, yet with love and compassion for these lost JWs. The message of hope in Christ alone must be shared.

JWs must turn to Christ as Jehovah God for salvation. To receive forgiveness of sin, a person must first recognize their sin and their need for God's grace apart from works (Rom. 3:10, 23; Jer. 17:9; Eccl. 7:20; Eph. 2:1–2; 1 John 1:8). Second, they must realize that Jesus came to earth for the purpose of dying as a substitute for each sinner (Isa. 53:6; 1 Pet. 2:24; 3:18), bearing the penalty of man's sins on Himself. Third, they must trust in Christ as Lord and Savior (Acts 16:30, 31; John 1:12: 3:16, 36; 5:24: 6:47; Acts 4:12; Rom. 10:13).

The truth is, Jesus came to do more than simply atone for Adam's sin and to restore "perfect human life with its rights and earthly prospects" *(Let God Be True,* p. 96). He came to forgive sins (Eph. 1:7), to give eternal life (John 10:28; 17:2), to declare believers righteous by His grace (Rom. 3:24), to die for man's sins (1 Pet. 2:24; 3:18; Rom. 5:6, 8), to remove the enmity between man and God (Rom. 5:10), to redeem us from the penalty and power of sin (Gal. 4:4, 5; Eph. 1:7), and to make believers children of God (John 1:12). Forgiveness of sins does not come by trying to pass the test Adam failed or by maintaining "integrity" (as the August 15, 1956 issue of *The Watchtower* suggests). By attempting to keep integrity or by works of the law, "no flesh will be declared righteous before him" (Rom. 3:20, NWT).

Salvation "is as a free gift that they are being declared righteous by his undeserved kindness through the release of the ransom paid by Christ Jesus. God set him forth as an offering for propitiation through faith in his blood" (Rom. 3:24–25, NWT). And on the basis of Christ's atonement, man can be pardoned from his sins and declared righteous in Christ. "By means of him (Christ) we have the release by ransom through the blood of that one, yes, the forgiveness of our trespasses, according to the riches of undeserved kindness" (Eph. 1:7, NWT).

False Prophets and Changed Doctrines

Charles Taze Russell (1852–1916) was the first prophet of the Watchtower Society. He grew up in a Presbyterian family, but he did not like the teachings of the Bible regarding God's grace (predestination) and the doctrine of hell.[335] So, like most people who are dissatisfied with God's revelation, he left the church, became interested in end-times theology, and was eventually named "pastor" of a Bible class he started in Pittsburgh in defiance of organized religion.[336] Eventually Russell established Zion's Watchtower Tract Society in Pittsburgh, and after recruiting hundreds of followers, they went door-to-door passing out the literature that Russell published. Later, he published the six-volume *Studies in the Scriptures*, which he believed were more important than the Bible itself. After prophesying that Christ would return in 1874, then adjusting the date to 1914 after Jesus did not return, Russell proclaimed that Jesus returned spiritually and had set up His kingdom on earth through the faithful Watchtower Society. He died in 1916, exposed as the false prophet he was.

After Russell died, Joseph Franklin Rutherford (1869–1942) took the leadership of the Watchtower Society. It was under his leadership that the Watchtower Society became known as Jehovah's Witnesses.[337] Rutherford also proved to be a false prophet, for he prophesied that Abraham, Isaac, and Jacob would return visibly to earth to help promote the kingdom of the JWs. He was so sure of his prediction that he built a large palatial mansion in San Diego, California for them to live in when they returned sometime between 1925 and 1929.[338] When they failed to show up,

---

[335] Rhodes, *Find it Quick Handbook on Cults and New Religions*, 98.
[336] Martin, *The Kingdom of the Cults*, 38.
[337] Rhodes, 99.
[338] Carlson and Decker, *Fast Facts on False Teachings,* 119-120.

Rutherford moved into the mansion himself and lived there until his death in 1942. He too died as a false prophet.

After Rutherford died, Nathan Knorr (1905–1977) took the reins of leadership. It was under his guidance that the JWs authorized their own translation of the Bible. Though they claimed to use Greek scholars to put the NWT together, anyone who knows basic Greek grammar sees right away that the only people consulted were those who knew enough about the Bible to be able to remove almost every reference to Jesus' deity in the New Testament. Notwithstanding, Knorr also proved himself to be a false prophet when he prophesied Armageddon would be in the year 1975.[339] Of course, 1975 has come and gone, Christ has not returned, and the world is still here. Hence, Knorr was another false prophet.

Though JWs are mostly quite zealous for their faith and are to be admired for going door to door promoting their beliefs, Christians must beware. JW theology contains more false and changed prophecies and doctrines than space will allow here. But consulting former JWs and doing a little homework will go a long way to helping a Christian see the blatant errors of the JW theology.

The Heresy of the Mormon Church, the Church of Latter-Day Saints

The story of Mormonism begins with the Jaredites who are said to have left Babylonia during the building of the Tower of Babel around 2250 BC. These people later came to Central America and established a civilization that lasted 2,000 years. They eventually became corrupt and were subsequently destroyed by God for their apostasy.

A second group that Mormonism highlights is a group of Jews who supposedly traveled across the Pacific and landed on the western coast of South America to escape the Babylonian exile that occurred in 586 BC. This group was led by Lehi and his son Nephi, a group that was later divided into two warring camps, the

---

[339] Carlson and Decker, 120.

Nephites and the Lamanites. The Lamanites were later cursed by God with dark skin because of their evil deeds and were the forefathers of the American Indians.[340] These Lamanites eventually annihilated the Nephites in a battle near the hill of Cumorah in Palmyra, New York, approximately AD 385.[341] The Lamenite civilizations continued to degenerate and eventually forgot their Jewish history.

Mormons believe that a man named Mormon and his son Moroni, sometime before the end of the fourth century before the Lamanites destroyed the Nephites, compiled the records of these two civilizations using the Reformed Egyptian language (a language that has never been observed) and recorded all of their history on golden plates that they buried in the ground near the hills of Cumorah in New York. The Mormon record claims that Jesus Christ visited the American continent, preached the Gospel, and instituted baptism and communion after He had ascended to heaven from the Mount of Olives (Acts 1:9).

The Mormon religion began to take root when Moroni, the son of Mormon, appeared to Joseph Smith in 1827 as a glorified resurrected being. He then gave Smith the golden plates from their hiding place in the Cumorah hills, and Smith, using an occult seer stone, was able to translate the history of the Lamanites and Nephites into the *Book of Mormon*.[342] Smith claimed that after he translated the plates, he returned them to the angel Moroni, so the veracity of the plates or Smith's translation cannot be verified.

Archaeology and the Book of Mormon

The *Book of Mormon* states that large cities were built so that by AD 322, "The whole face of the land had become covered with buildings and the people were as numerous almost as it were the sand of the sea" (Mormon 1:7). Thirty-eight cities are specifically mentioned in the *Book of Mormon*. Also, in the final battle between the Nephites and Lamanites, 230,000 Nephites were killed near the hills of Cumorah in New York. However, not a single piece of archaeological evidence substantiates such large

---

[340] Martin, 178.

[341] Martin, 178.

[342] Martin, 179.

civilizations. Because of this, archaeologists concluded that the *Book of Mormon* is nothing more than a fictional work.[343] B. H. Roberts, a former Mormon apologist, concluded at the end of his life after years of research that the *Book of Mormon* was a fictional work created by Joseph Smith. He wrote, "The evidence I sorrowfully submit, points to Joseph Smith as their creator. It is difficult to believe that they are the product of history, that they come upon the scene separated by long periods of time, and among a race which was the ancestral race of the red man of America."[344]

Contrary to the *Book of Mormon*, the historical accuracy of the Bible has been proven by the discovery of hundreds of ancient civilizations, artifacts, historical records, and inscriptions. Dr. William Albright wrote, "Discovery after discovery has established the accuracy of innumerable details, and has brought increased recognition to the value of the Bible as a source of history."[345]

Although the introduction page of the *Book of Mormon* claims it is the most perfect book ever written, it contains numerous historical, geographical, and scientific errors along with many false (and silly) teachings. For instance, Alma 24:16 teaches that burying swords deep in the earth will keep them bright, yet basic science proves that burying steel objects causes decay and rust. Other absurdities are that baldness is caused by sin (2 Nephi 13:24), that Indians have dark skin because they are cursed (2 Nephi 5:21; Jacob 3:3–9; Mormon 5:15–17; Alma 3:6–10), and when Indians accept the Mormon teaching, they will become white and delightsome (2 Nephi 30:5–7).

Was Joseph Smith a True Prophet?

The test for a prophet is found in Deuteronomy 18:20–22. If the prophet prophesies anything that does not come to pass, he is a false prophet and is to be stoned to death to keep his satanic prophecies away from God's people so as not to corrupt them. Jesus said, "Beware of the false prophets, who come to you in sheep's clothing, but inwardly are ravenous wolves" (Matt. 7:15).

---

[343] Martin, 183.

[344] B.H. Roberts, *Studies in the Book of Mormon* (Urbana, IL: University of Illinois Press, 1985), 243.

[345] William Albright, *The Archaeology of Palestine* (Pelican Books, 1960), 127. Quoted in McDowell, 65.

Often, however, false prophets are nice people with a life full of good works. But Jesus was warning against their doctrines, not their works. No matter how sincere a teacher or his followers are, if his doctrine is not biblical, he is a false prophet.

Joseph Smith does not pass the test of a true prophet. Although he should not be judged on his open-dated prophecies, self-fulfilling prophecies, and conditional prophecies, Smith is to be judged as a false prophet based on his specific-dated prophecies.

One such false prophecy is preserved in *Doctrine and Covenants*, Section 84. In this revelation given on September 22 and 23, 1832, Joseph Smith foretold of a Latter-Day Saints (LDS) temple to be built in Independence, Missouri. The prophecy specifies that the city of "New Jerusalem" including the temple was to be constructed "beginning at the temple lot which is appointed by the finger of the Lord, in the western boundaries of the State of Missouri" (v. 3). Smith placed a time limit on the new temple saying, "which temple shall be reared in this generation. For verily this generation shall not all pass away" (vv. 4–5). However, the generation of 1832 did pass away, and no such temple was ever built there. In fact, no LDS temple exists in the entire state of Missouri. Although a splinter group from the LDS later took possession of the lot, they never built on it, either. The Reformed LDS attempted to build a temple across the street from the temple lot within sight of the spot where the cornerstone was laid, but even if they did, that would hardly be a fulfilled prophecy. After all, Smith not only pointed to the specific lot (which still lies empty), he said the temple would be built in his generation.

Aside from the facts that Smith was a polygamist, a heretic who added to and subtracted from the Bible, and a known treasure hunter affiliated with the occult and the Masonic lodge, he was a proven false prophet. Smith made other prophecies in addition to the LDS temple, but given the test of a prophet in Deuteronomy 18:20–22, he failed the test with this one false prophecy. Smith died in 1832 as a false prophet.

Is Mormonism Christian? No. It fails both the doctrinal test and the experiential test. In reality, Mormonism is neither monotheistic nor Trinitarian but polytheistic. In Smith's *The Pearl of Great Price*, he wrote that the world was fashioned "by the gods." Smith said as much in a sermon where he stated that God was once as we are and that we may become as He is—a god. Mormonism's view of the Father, Son, and Spirit is that all are gods, but that does not mean that they are tritheistic. In fact, they believe in billions of gods. One of their gods, Jesus, is simply an incarnation of *Elohim*, conceived as the literal son of God. He is therefore not Almighty God incarnate, but simply a man who is a good example for all to follow. This means that in Mormon theology, Jesus did not save anyone by dying on the cross. Mormonism is not Christian, for they reject Jesus and add to His words by calling other texts holy, like the *Book of Mormon, Doctrine and Covenants*, and *The Pearl of Great Price*. As Chad Owen Brand concluded, "Because of these departures from standard Christian teachings, Mormonism falls outside orthodox Christianity.[346]

Other False Versions of Christianity

The genius of Satan is that he does not specialize in converting people to Satanism, sacrificing animals, drinking blood, or holding séances. His genius is found in his ability to twist the true faith of Jesus Christ by twisting the words of the Bible. This has produced a plethora of groups who are moral and likeable people (as the Jehovah's Witnesses and Mormons most certainly are!). There are the Christadelphians who deny Jesus' divinity and the Trinity,[347] the Christian Identity movement who believe that they are God's chosen race and that the Jews are a mongrel race,[348] Christian Science who are pantheists,[349] and Oneness Pentecostals who deny Jesus' divinity and promote salvation by works.[350] There are numerous other false versions of Christianity, and each one begins

---

[346] Chad Owen Brand, "Is Mormonism Compatible with the Bible?" *The Apologetics Study Bible: Real Questions, Straight Answers, Stronger Faith,* ed. Ted Cabal, Chad Owen Brand, E. Ray Clendenen, et al. (Nashville, TN: Holman Bible Publishers, 2007), 39.

[347] Rhodes, 47-56.

[348] Rhodes, 52-56.

[349] Rhodes, 57-60.

[350] Rhodes, 150-153.

by denying the words of the Bible in favor of man-made teachings and the denial of Jesus' divinity.

Christ's Church Trumps the Confused Gospel of the Emerging Church

One final false version of Christianity that is becoming more and more common today is the Emerging Church. This church is *tailored* for the postmodern culture since it stands against all dogmatic doctrinal teachings of systematic theology and any systematic method of sharing the Gospel of Jesus Christ in order to convert a lost person. Furthermore, its adherents stand against denominational affiliations and churches that preach social change. In short, the Emerging Church stands against all traditional church methodologies, believing that they are *coercive*. Leaders of this recent movement (e.g., Brian McLaren) believe that Christians need to contextualize the Gospel of Christ to reach the new postmodern culture.[351] Although this might sound valid at face value, what the Emerging Church promotes is a watered down and unbiblical gospel to share with the lost world—a gospel that the culture will respond to in light of their new way of thinking.

The Gospel of Christ can never fit that mold. After all, it is Christ's Gospel that calls mankind to repent of his sinful ways and depraved thinking and trust only in Him for salvation (cf. John 14:6). It actually *is* that simple.

---

[351] R. Scott Smith, "Reflections on McLaren and the Emerging Church," in *Passionate Conviction: Contemporary Discourses on Christian Apologetics,* ed. Paul Copan and William Lane Craig (Nashville: B&H Publishers, 2007), 227-241.

Chapter 16
CONCLUSION

If Christianity is the one true faith as it purports to be (cf. John 14:6), then everything about it should stand head and shoulders above all other faiths. It must be the most defensible, the most logical, and the most outstanding faith simply because it is the one true faith. Arguments for the truth of the one true faith cannot be mundane or equal with arguments for any other faith. Either Christianity is true, thus it stands out above all others, or it is just another option that people can take or leave. In forming a conclusion to the arguments for God's existence, specifically for the Christian God, it seems that the only logical choice is that God not only exists, but that Jesus Christ of Nazareth is God. Hence, *Christianity* is the one true faith.

If a person chooses to shun logic, Jesus will not be the conclusion they draw from the plethora of evidence that points to Him as the one true God. But is that not the crux of the matter? Our starting point is to make logical arguments drawn from premises that are rational, cogent, and coherent. If we choose anything less, we might as well speak gibberish to make an argument. Logic is the necessary beginning point unless we decide that gibberish is an option. And although the naturalist will agree with this starting point, he cannot defend *why* he must be logical since his worldview cannot account for the existence of the laws of logic. So why would he insist we begin there? After all, there is nothing logical about the naturalist's position that nothing became everything without a first cause who has always existed, namely God. Therefore, from the outset of any argument concerning God's existence, the Christian worldview stands head and shoulders above all others. It is the only one that can account for the laws of logic, and is thus the only option that is consistent with itself since Christianity alone believes that God and logic are inseparable. This is the transcendental argument for the existence of God—that we must begin with the fact of God's existence in order to make sense of anything.

Our ability to reason could have only come from one of two places: either it arose from preexisting intelligence, or it arose from mindless matter. Naturalists (i.e., atheists, Darwinists, materialists) believe, *by faith,* that the complexity of the human mind arose by chance and from mindless matter devoid of any intelligent intrusion. This takes great faith to believe given that it contradicts all scientific observation. It is an established fact that no effect cannot be greater than its cause. In truth, non-intelligent mindlessness cannot produce what it does not contain, yet naturalists continue to espouse that dead, obtuse matter produced intelligent life. They might as well believe that the works of Shakespeare were created after his print shop exploded!

It takes faith to reject the one true faith, belief in Jesus Christ. In fact, it takes far more faith to reject the existence of God and of Jesus Christ His Son than it does to simply receive Jesus as God and Savior. In other words, it does not take an illogical leap of faith to be a Christian theist. Once we look at the evidence for a Creator and read the words He left behind for us to know Him in the Bible, it makes perfect sense to believe that human beings are made in the image of God and from the eternal mind of God. And since we are made in God's image (Genesis 1:26-27), the mind He gave us is able to understand Him along with every truth He has revealed. Though many reject this logic, no other worldview is able to demonstrate how we can know anything at all. Therefore, since it is logical to assume we can begin with logic, given to us by the God who embodies logic, we can defend not only theism but Christian theism.

In the cosmological argument for God's existence is the argument from the cause of creation—the *cause*mological argument, as it were. The premise of this argument is that the universe had a beginning. All things that have a beginning must have a cause because of the law of cause and effect. Therefore, the universe had a cause. And He is God! God Himself needs no cause because He is eternal and hence has no beginning or end.

In the ontological argument for the existence of God, we assume that if God does exist, He must be conceived of as a necessary Being, for in order for anything to exist that does exist, we must trace backwards to a necessary Being who must exist for anything to exist. By definition, a necessary Being must exist and cannot not exist. Therefore, if something exists, then God must exist, and if God exists, then He is necessary and cannot not exist. His necessary existence is why anything exists at all.

In the teleological argument for God's existence, the argument stems from the design of the universe and the earth's unique ability to allow for and sustain life. All designs imply that someone or something designed them. The universe, and specifically the earth, reveal intricate design—from the tweaking of the earth to the intricacies of the human cell and the DNA contained within it. Therefore, the universe had a Designer. He is the necessary Being to whom the ontological argument points to and the cause the cosmological argument deduces.

In the moral argument for God's existence, the logical first premise stems from an observation that all of mankind is aware of an objective moral law. From the strict legalist who denounces what he considers to be morally wrong to the staunch defender of tolerance who is tolerant because he believes some things are wrong but must be tolerated—everyone believes in objective moral laws. Those who say they do not believe in moral absolutes curiously believe in their right to reject moral laws. In doing so, they prove by their rejection of moral laws that they believe in moral laws, for they must believe in a moral law in order to reject it. So, since moral laws exist and every law requires a lawgiver, there must be an ultimate Lawgiver. After all, how could universal moral laws stem from a naturalistic universe that exploded out of nothing, by chance, and without any direction from the chaos of exploding matter (which itself cannot be accounted for without a Creator)?

In the argument for the existence of evil, and how a perfect God can exist alongside the existence of evil, in actuality, the affirmation of the existence of evil points toward the existence of God. For how we define evil unless we first know good? We must first affirm that there is a moral law, hence a moral Lawgiver, before we can affirm that something is wrong or evil. Is it logical that God and evil can exist alongside each other? It is, for if God created freewill beings, and if those beings can use their freewill without God's intervention, then it is logical that they might rebel against God. It is certainly logical that God created the best possible world where His created beings could enjoy their freewill. It is also probable that God and evil can exist alongside one another given that God can use that which plagues His created beings to mold and make them into better people. We see this every day, all the time! Suffering, hard work, pain, and toil mold us into mature people far better than a life without such. God uses the hardships man brings upon himself from his rebellious freewill to reveal His love, mercy, and grace. God even subjected Himself to the consequences of man's sin by suffering pain, rejection, and heartache—even a torturous death on the cross—in order to reveal His love, mercy, and grace for His created beings. So, since it is both logical and probable that God and evil exist alongside one another, the argument for the existence of evil against God's existence is actually an argument for God's existence.

As to the existence of miracles, if there is a God, then He is certainly capable of miracles. After all, His eternal nature and creation of all things proves that His capabilities are beyond human understanding. So, there should be nothing to keep us from believing in the miraculous, especially as it relates to Jesus' virgin birth and resurrection from the dead. A God who created all things out of nothing is certainly capable of performing miracles. And if we accept any historical account written by an eyewitness, we cannot overlook the plethora of accounts in the Bible where miracles were attested to by eyewitnesses. In order to be consistent, if we were to reject their eyewitness accounts of miracles, we would also have to reject all historical accounts of everything ever recorded by eyewitnesses.

As to whether truth can be known, it can. First, through reason and logic, sifting through empirical evidence, using scientific methods, and drawing conclusions, we can know certain things. Second, we know that the opposite of truth is non-truth. Third, the logical arguments for God's existence provide more evidence for His existence than for His nonexistence. And to say that God does not exist is to use logical principles and language that cannot be accounted for by God's nonexistence. Therefore, if

God exists, He must be eternal, uncreated, omnipotent, omniscient, omnipresent, omnibenevolent, and immutable. And if these qualities are indeed His, then there can be only one of Him, for by definition, this all-everything God can be only one. There cannot be more of Him than one because they would either be non-distinguishable since they would have no limits to define one over the other, or one would have to lack what the other has. Therefore, there can be only one necessary Supreme Being and hence only theism can be true. All other forms of faith are false.

Now since God exists, and truth can be known, we would expect that God would reveal Himself not only in His created order but also in personhood. This He did in His Son, Jesus Christ, who is God (John 1:1), who became flesh (John 1:14), and who explains God (cf. John 1:18). Such a God would not only display His godly characteristics of love, mercy, and grace, He would ensure that everything He wanted His created beings to know would be accurately recorded for all generations. This He did in the Bible, the holy Scriptures from Genesis to the Revelation. He would furthermore ensure that His special revelation to man, since it offers eternal salvation to those who receive Jesus Christ as Lord and Savior, would remain pure and without error. Why would a perfect God allow His perfect Word to be corrupted and mislead those He offers salvation to? He would not, and therefore the Bible is God's Word, without error, and containing the words of eternal life.

EPILOGUE

Jude, a half-brother of the Lord Jesus Christ, wrote, "Beloved, while I was making every effort to write you about our common salvation, I felt the necessity to write to you appealing that you contend earnestly for the faith which was once for all handed down to the saints. For certain persons have crept in unnoticed, those who were long beforehand marked out for this condemnation, ungodly persons who turn the grace of our God into licentiousness and deny our only Master and Lord, Jesus Christ" (Jude 3–4).

Though originally wanting to write about "our common salvation," Jude was compelled to appeal to his audience to deal with the false teachers who had infiltrated their ranks, those who had "crept in unnoticed." Clearly, the enemy the Church saw as *outside* their doors was actually *inside* their ranks posing a grave danger for Christians. Therefore, Jude's purpose was to exhort the Church not to tolerate all peoples for the sake of unity, but to "contend earnestly for the faith which was once for all handed down to the saints."

The Greek term for "contend" is an intense form of a word from where "agony" derives. It is a military term (cf. John 18:36; Eph. 6:12) and portrays a man in a passionate effort as in a wrestling match (cf. 1 Cor. 9:25; 2 Tim. 4:7; Heb. 12:1). Jude's form of the verb is a present infinitive, showing that the Christian's struggle against false teaching and false teachers is *ongoing*. The word itself sets the tone for the Christian Church worldwide in its never-ending pursuit of pure doctrine and orthodox Christian behavior. To *contend earnestly*, therefore, is to perpetually engage in the spiritual battle for the truth as a faithful slave of Jesus Christ.

Jude is very clear about what the battle is for, namely, *the faith*. Now although "faith" in many contexts of the New Testament concerns the action someone takes when they are awakened spiritually for salvation, in this context "faith" is a noun, referring to the message of the gospel (Gal. 1:23; Eph. 4:5; Col. 1:23; 1 Tim. 3:9; 4:1; 6:10, 21; cf. Acts 6:7; 13:8). This faith was "once for all handed down to the saints." This modifying phrase to "faith" plainly states that the Christian faith is unchangeable. Its foundational truths are nonnegotiable in that no matter how many folks might want to water down the difficult sayings of Christ, Christ's words can never change. Now this does not in any way imply that Christians cannot be tolerant of relatively minor theological issues (modes of baptism, eschatology beliefs, etc.). What it does plainly say is that allowing or tolerating unbiblical teaching, anti-God beliefs, or simply disregarding Bible teaching is destructive. It must be contended with, and it must be done with intense fervor.

In describing the charlatans who had crept into the Church, Jude says they "were long beforehand marked out for this condemnation." This means that the presence of these pseudo-Christians and their actions had not taken God by surprise, for God knew when they would appear (cf. vv. 14, 17). The Greek term for "marked" simply means to "write before," referring to previously written predictions regarding the eventual presence and doom of apostates—those who fall away from the faith. We must not conclude that God ordained certain people to be ungodly, for God is never responsible for man's rebellion. It was simply prophesied in the Old Testament that apostates of this nature would dwell among God's people and attempt to corrupt them.

Jude calls apostates "ungodly," a term used for infamous sinners whose behavior betrays their true selves. First, they "change the grace of our God into licentiousness." That term indicates "license," and it is most often used for sexual sins (Rom. 13:13; 2 Cor. 12:21; Gal. 5:19; Eph. 4:19) or some form of vulgar behavior (Mark 7:22; 1 Pet. 4:3; 2 Pet. 2:2, 7, 18). It seems evident that these false teachers promoted God's grace as a license to indulge in all kinds of sexual depravity, all the while teaching others that God's grace would cover over all their wicked behaviors. The entire context of Jude's epistle suggests the presence of sexual sins, for Jude goes on in verses 6–7 to reference the judgment of the angels and Sodom and Gomorrah and then the sin of Balaam who caused Israel to sin sexually with the Baal of Peor (v. 11).

Second, the ungodly are characterized by their denial of "our only Master and Lord, Jesus Christ." Though Jude does not specify how this was done, clearly Christ is denied by those who profess Him when they live immorally and contrary to His commands. As Paul told Titus, these people "claim to know God, but by their actions they deny him" (Titus 1:16). These sinful actions almost always occur in people who deny the deity and sovereignty of Jesus Christ. These can never be trusted as Christians but only as those needing to be led to Christ for salvation.

The third group who "deny our only Master and Lord, Jesus Christ," are the atheists and naturalists who permeate our society today. Many of them are employed as professors in the universities where our young people attend after leaving home for the first time. These ungodly people prey on them, bully them, and far too often convince them that everything they learned in church was myth. Therefore, we must train our young people to face these ungodly people in order to contend for the faith. These young people should be seen as soldiers in training, and their training must be a thorough knowledge of the holy Scriptures and general revelation of God, which speaks loudly for His existence (cf. Psalm 19).

Therefore, may God's children equip themselves for the preaching of the Gospel, train future apologists to make cogent arguments for God's existence, and contend earnestly for the faith once for all delivered to the saints. The battle has come to our doorstep; it has entered the Church. May we faithfully defend that which God has given to us to defend faithfully.

Bibliography

Akin, Daniel L. *1, 2, 3 John*. In *The New American Commentary*, Volume 38, edited by E. Ray Clendenen, et al., 198-200. Nashville, TN: Broadman and Holman Publishers, 2001.

Alberts, B. "The Cell as a Collection of Protein Machines." *Cell 92* (Winter 1998): 291-294.

Albright, W .F. *The Archaeology of Palestine and the Bible*. Old Tappan, NJ: Fleming H. Revell Publishing Company, 1933.

Archer, G. L. *A Survey of Old Testament Introduction*. Chicago, IL: Moody, 1964. Aristotle, *Physics*, Book VIII, chapter 9.

Bahnsen, G. "The Crucial Concept of Self-Deception in Presuppositional Apologetics." *Westminster Theological Journal*, Volume 57 (Spring 1995): 2-33.

Bock, D. L. "Is the New Testament Trustworthy?" In *The Apologetics Study Bible: Real Questions, Straight Answers, Stronger Faith*, edited by Ted Cabal, Chad Owen Brand, E. Ray Clendenen et al., 1452-53. Nashville, TN: Holman Bible Publishers, 2007.

Borchert, G. L. *John 1-11*. In *The New American Commentary*, Volume 25A, Nashville, TN: Broadman and Holman Publishers, 2001.

Bradley, W. L. "Does Science Support the Bible?" In *The Apologetics Study Bible: Real Questions, Straight Answers, Stronger Faith*, edited by Ted Cabal, Chad Owen Brand, E.

Ray Clendenen, et al., 831-32. Nashville, TN: Holman Bible Publishers, 2007.

Brand, C. "Is Mormonism Compatible with the Bible?" In *The Apologetics Study Bible: Real Questions, Straight Answers, Stronger Faith,* edited by Ted Cabal, Chad Owen Brand, E. Ray Clendenen, et al., 39. Nashville, TN: Holman Bible Publishers, 2007.

Brown, F., S. R. Driver, and C. A. Briggs. *A Hebrew and English Lexicon of the Old Testament.* Peabody, MA: Hendrickson Publishers, 1906; reprint, 2000.

Budziszewski, J. *How to Stay Christian in College.* Colorado Springs, CO: NavPress, 2004.

Bush, L. R. "Christ in the New Age." In *Passionate Conviction: Contemporary Discourses on Christian Apologetics,* edited by Paul Copan and William Lane Craig, 170-186. Nashville, TN: B&H Publishers, 2007.

Cabal, T. "Notable Christian Apologist: Anselm." In *The Apologetics Study Bible: Real Questions, Straight Answers, Stronger Faith,* edited by Ted Cabal, Chad Owen Brand, E. Ray Clendenen, et al., 801. Nashville, TN: Holman Bible Publishers, 2007.

Calvin, J. *Institutes of the Christian Religion,* vol. 7, Logos Research Systems, Inc., 1997.

Caner, E. F. "Islam and Christianity." In *Passionate Conviction: Contemporary Discourses on Christian Apologetics,* edited by Paul Copan and William Lane Craig, 187-204. Nashville, TN: B&H Publishers, 2007.

Caner, E. M. "Is Allah Identical to the God and Father of Our Lord Jesus Christ?" In *The Apologetics Study Bible: Real Questions, Straight Answers, Stronger Faith*, edited by Ted Cabal, Chad Owen Brand, E. Ray Clendenen, et al., 1754. Nashville, TN: Holman Bible Publishers, 2007.

Carson, D. A. *New Bible Commentary: 21st Century Edition,* 4th ed. Leicester, England; Downers Grove, IL: Inter-Varsity Press, 1994.

Carter, B. M. "Communication As General Revelation: The Anti-evolutionary and Pro-Trinitarian Implications of Communication Phenomena." *Journal of Christian Apologetics,* Volume 2 (Summer 1998): 78-91.

Center for Naturalism, "Worldview Naturalism in a Nutshell," Narturalsim.Org. www.naturalism.org (accessed June 12, 2012).

Clark, D. K. "Is Logic Arbitrary?" In *The Apologetics Study Bible: Real Questions, Straight Answers, Stronger Faith,* edited by Ted Cabal, Chad Owen Brand, E. Ray Clendenen, et al., 930-31. Nashville, TN: Holman Bible Publishers, 2007.

Cline, Austin. "Cosmological Argument: Does the Universe Require a First Cause?" About.Com. http://atheism.about.com/od/argumentsforgod/a/cosmological.htm (accessed June 5, 2012).

Copan, P. "A Moral Argument." In *Passionate Conviction: Contemporary Discourses on Christian Apologetics*, edited by Paul Copan and William Lane Craig, 79-92. Nashville, TN: B&H Publishers, 2007.

Craig, W. L. *Reasonable Faith*. Wheaton, IL: Crossway, 2008.

——. *Hard Questions, Real Answers*. Wheaton, IL: Crossway Books, 2003.

Cross, F. L., and E. A. Livingstone. *The Oxford Dictionary of the Christian Church*, 3rd ed. rev. Oxford, New York: Oxford University Press, 2005.

Crossan, J. D., *The Historical Jesus: The Life of a Mediterranean Jewish Peasant*. San Francisco, CA: HarperCollins, 1991.

——. *Jesus: A Revolutionary Biography*. San Francisco, CA: HarperCollins, 1994.

Dana, H. E., and J. R. Mantey. *A Manual Grammar of the Greek New Testament*. England: MacMillan, 1957.

Darling, D. "On Creating Something Out of Nothing." *New Scientist*, Volume 151, September 14, 1996.

Darwin, C. *The Origin of Species*. New York: New York University Press, 6th ed., 1998.

Davies, P. *The Anthropic Principle,* DVD. England: BBC LTD Productions, 1988.

Davies, P. C. W. *Other Worlds.* London: Dent, 1980.

——. "The Anthropic Principle." *Particle and Nuclear Physics* 10, 1983.

Dawkins, R. *The Blind Watchmaker*. New York: Norton, 1987.

——. "Entropy Alone Can Create Complex Crystals from Simple Shapes; Tetrahedra Packing Record Broken." News. http://richarddawkins.net/articles/4746-entropy-alone-can-create-complex-crystals-from-simple-shapes-tetrahedra-packing-record-broken (accessed June 5, 2012).

Dembski, W. A. "Does the Design Argument Show There Is A God?" In *The Apologetics Study Bible: Real Questions, Straight Answers, Stronger Faith*, edited by Ted Cabal, Chad Owen Brand, E. Ray Clendenen, et al., 1327. Nashville, TN: Holman Bible Publishers, 2007.

DeWeese, G. "How Can We Know Anything At All?" In *The Apologetics Study Bible: Real Questions, Straight Answers, Stronger Faith*, edited by Ted Cabal, Chad Owen Brand, E. Ray Clendenen, et al., 1766-67. Nashville, TN: Holman Bible Publishers, 2007.

Douglas, J. D., P. W. Comfort, and D. Mitchell. *Who's Who in Christian History*. Wheaton, IL: Tyndale House, 1992.

Duffield, G. P., and N. M. Van Cleave. *Foundations of Pentecostal Theology*. Los Angeles, CA: L.I.F.E. Bible College, 1983.

Edgar, William, and K. S. Oliphint. *Christian Apologetics, Past and Present*: *A Primary Source Reader,* Volume 2. Wheaton, IL: Crossway, 2011.

Enns, P. *The Moody Handbook of Theology*. Chicago, IL: Moody Press, 1997.

Evans, W., and S. M. Coder. *The Great Doctrines of the Bible*, Enl. ed. Chicago, IL: Moody Press, 1998.

Fahlbusch, E., and G. W. Bromily. *The Encyclopedia of Christianity,* Volume 4. Grand Rapids, MI: Leiden, Netherlands: Eerdmans; Brill, 2005.

Feinberg, P. D. "Does the Bible Contain Errors?" In *The Apologetics Study Bible: Real Questions, Straight Answers, Stronger Faith,* edited by Ted Cabal, Chad Owen Brand, E. Ray Clendenen, et al., 1412-13. Nashville, TN: Holman Bible Publishers, 2007.

Ferré, F. "Design Argument," *Dictionary of the History of Ideas*, Volume 1. New York: Charles Scribner's Sons, 1973.

Freeman, J. M., and H. J. Chadwick. *Manners & Customs of the Bible*. North Brunswick, NJ: Bridge-Logos Publishers, 1998.

Geisler, N. L. *Christian Apologetics*. Grand Rapids, MI: Baker Academic, 1976.

——. and P. D. Feinberg. *Introduction to Philosophy: A Christian Perspective*. Grand Rapids, MI: Baker Book House, 1980.

——. *Baker Encyclopedia of Christian Apologetics.* Grand Rapids, MI: Baker Books, 1999.

——. and A. Saleeb. *Answering Islam: The Crescent in Light of the Cross,* 2nd ed. Grand Rapids, MI: Baker Books, 2002.

——. and W. E. Nix. *A General Introduction to the Bible.* Chicago, IL: Moody Press, 1986.

——. and P. Bocchino. *Unshakeable Foundations.* Minneapolis, MN: Bethany House Publishers, 2001.

——. and F. Turek. *I Don't Have Enough Faith to Be an Atheist.* Wheaton, IL: Crossway Books, 2004.

——. and W. D. Watkins. *Worlds Apart: A Handbook on World Views.* Grand Rapids, MI: Baker Book House, 1989.

——. and Paul K. Hoffman. *Why I Am a Christian: Leading Thinkers Explain Why They Believe.* Grand Rapids, MI: Baker Books, 2001.

——. and R. M. Brooks. *When Skeptics Ask.* Wheaton, IL: Victor Books, 1990.

Glueck, N. *Rivers in the Desert: History of Negev.* Philadelphia, PA: Jewish Publication Society, 1969.

Hawking, S. W. *A Brief History of Time.* New York: Bantam Books, 1988.

Hazen, C. J. "Christianity in a World of Religions." In *Passionate Conviction: Contemporary Discourses on Christian Apologetics,* edited by Paul Copan and William Lane Craig, 140-53. Nashville, TN: B&H Publishers, 2007.

Helyer, L. R. "How Does the Bible Relate to Judaism?" In *The Apologetics Study Bible: Real Questions, Straight Answers, Stronger Faith,* edited by Ted Cabal, Chad Owen Brand, E.

Ray Clendenen, et al., 1758-59. Nashville, TN: Holman Bible Publishers, 2007.

Henry, C. F. H. *God, Revelation, and Authority*, Volume 3. Wheaton, IL: Crossway Books, 1999.

Hooper, William. "Richard Dawkins on Intelligent Alien Design," TheOligarch.Com. http://www.theoligarch.com/richard-dawkins-aliens.htm (accessed July 20, 2012).

Hume, D. *Dialogues Concerning Natural Religion.* Indianapolis, IN: Bobbs-Merrill, 1980.

———. *An Enquiry Concerning Human Understanding.* LaSalle, IL, 1955.

Internet Encyclopedia of Philosophy, "Ontological Argument," IEP. http://www.iep.utm.edu/ont-arg/ (accessed August 5, 2012).

Jastrow, R. *God and the Astronomers.* New York: W. W. Norton & Co., 1978.

Kaiser Jr., W. C. "How Has Archaeology Corroborated the Bible?" In *The Apologetics Study Bible: Real Questions, Straight Answers, Stronger Faith,* edited by Ted Cabal, Chad Owen Brand, E. Ray Clendenen, et al., 1148-49. Nashville, TN: Holman Bible Publishers, 2007.

Kennedy, D. J. *Skeptics Answered.* Sisters: Multnomah, 1997.

Kenyon, F. G. *The Bible and Archaeology.* New York: Harper, 1940.

Kostenberger, A. J. *Baker Exegetical Commentary on the New Testament: John.* Grand Rapids: Baker Academic, 2004.

Kreeft, P., and R. Tacelli. *Handbook of Christian Apologetics.* Downers Grove, IL: Inter-Varsity Press, 1994.

Kurian, G. T. *Nelson's New Christian Dictionary: The Authoritative Resource on the Christian World*. Nashville, TN: Thomas Nelson Publishers, 2001.

Levine, Michael. "Pantheism," *The Stanford Encyclopedia of Philosophy*. http://plato.stanford.edu/entries/pantheism/ (accessed August 5, 2012).

Lewis, C. S. *A Grief Observed*. London: Faber & Faber, 1985.

———. *Mere Christianity*. New York: Collier Books, 1943.

Liefeld, W. "Commentary on John," *The Expositor's Bible Commentary, Volume 8: Matthew, Mark, Luke,* edited by Frank E. Gaebelein, D. A. Carson, Walter W. Wessel, and Walter L. Liefeld, 1047-48. Grand Rapids: Zondervan, 1984.

Linville, M. D. "The Moral Poverty of Evolutionary Naturalism," *Contending with Christianity's Critics: Answering the New Atheists and Other Objectors*, ed. Paul Copan and William Lane Craig. Nashville, TN: B&H Publishers, 2009.

Lisle, J. *The Ultimate Proof of Creation*. Green Forest, AR: Master Books, 2009.

Louw, J. P., and E. A. Nida. *Greek-English Lexicon of the New Testament: Based on Semantic Domains,* Volume 2. New York: United Bible Societies, 1996.

MacLeod, D. J. "The Resurrection: Myth, Hoax, or History?" *Emmaus Journal,* Volume 7:2 (Winter 1998): 157-200.

McDowell, Josh. *Josh McDowell's Handbook on Apologetics*, electronic ed. Nashville, TN: Thomas Nelson, 1997.

———. *The New Evidence That Demands a Verdict.* Nashville, TN: Thomas Nelson Publishers, 1999.

McGrath, A. *Mere Apologetics: How to Help Seekers & Skeptics Find Faith.* Grand Rapids: Baker Books, 2012.

Meta Research, "The Top 30 Problems with the Big Bang," Meta Research.   http://metaresearch.org/cosmology/BB-top-30.asp (accessed June 15, 2012).

Mohler, A. *Atheism Remix.* Wheaton, IL: Crossway, 2008.

Montgomery, J. W. "Is Man His Own God?" *JETS*, Volume 12:2 (Spring 1969): 73-85.

Moreland, J. P. "What Are Self-Defeating Statements?" In *The Apologetics Study Bible:*

Real Questions, Straight Answers, Stronger Faith, edited by Ted Cabal, Chad Owen Brand, E. Ray Clendenen, et al., 1741-42. Nashville, TN: Holman Bible Publishers, 2007.

——. "Does the Cosmological Argument Show There Is A God?" In *The Apologetics Study Bible: Real Questions, Straight Answers, Stronger Faith,* edited by Ted Cabal, Chad Owen Brand, E. Ray Clendenen, et al., 806-07. Nashville, TN: Holman Bible Publishers, 2007.

Morris, Henry M. *The Bible and Modern Science.* Chicago: Moody, 1968.

——. *Their Words Against Them.* San Diego: Institute for Creation Research, 1997.

Mounce, R. H. "Romans" in *The New American Commentary*, Volume 27. Nashville: Broadman & Holman Publishers, 1995.

Myers, A. C. "Mishnah." In *The Eerdmans Bible Dictionary*, edited by Allen C. Myers, 724. Grand Rapids: Eerdmans, 1987.

Nash, R. "Are Miracles Believable?" In *The Apologetics Study Bible: Real Questions, Straight Answers, Stronger Faith,* edited by Ted Cabal, Chad Owen Brand, E. Ray Clendenen, et al., 96. Nashville, TN: Holman Bible Publishers, 2007.

National Aeronautics and Space Administration, "How Old is the Universe?" Universe 101. http://map.gsfc.nasa.gov/universe/uni_age.html (accessed June 15, 2012).

Negev, A. *The Archaeological Encyclopedia of the Holy Land,* 3rd ed. New York: Prentice Hall Press, 1990.

Netland, H. "The East Comes West (or Why Jesus Instead of Buddha?)." In *Passionate Conviction: Contemporary Discourses on Christian Apologetics,* edited by Paul Copan and William Lane Craig, 154-69. Nashville, TN: B&H Publishers, 2007.

Newton, I. *Principia,* edited by F. Cajori, 544-46. Berkeley: University of California, 1934.

Nietzsche, F. *The Will to Power*, trans. Walter Kaufmann and R.J. Hollingdale, edited by Walter Kaufman. New York: Random House, 1967.

——. "The Gay Science." In *The Nietzsche Reader*, edited by Keith Ansell Pearson and Duncan Large, 219, 224. Oxford: Blackwell Publishing, 2006.

——. "On Truth and Lies in a Nonmoral Sense." In *The Nietzsche Reader*, edited by Keith Ansell Pearson and Duncan Large, 267. Oxford: Blackwell Publishing, 2006.

O'Neill, Ian. "The 'Astronomical Unit' May Need An Upgrade As the Sun Loses Mass," Universe Today. http://www.universetoday.com/12743/the-astronomical-unit-may-need-an-upgrade-as-the-sun-loses-mass/ (accessed June 13, 2012).

Packer, J. I. "Response to the Debate." In *Did Jesus Rise From the Dead? The Resurrection Debate,* edited by Terry L. Miethe, 143. San Francisco: Harper & Row, 1987.

Pearcey, N., and C. B. Thaxton. *The Soul of Science: Christian Faith and Natural Philosophy, Turning point Christian Worldview Series.* Wheaton, IL: Crossway Books, 1994.

Pemberton, B. B. "How Does the Bible Relate to Islam?" In *The Apologetics Study Bible: Real Questions, Straight Answers, Stronger Faith,* edited by Ted Cabal, Chad Owen Brand, E. Ray Clendenen, et al., 1602. Nashville, TN: Holman Bible Publishers, 2007.

Philosophy of Religion, "Anselm's Ontological Argument," Philosophy of Religion. http://www.philosophyofreligion.info/theistic-proofs/the-ontological-argument/st-anselms-ontological-argument/ (accessed June 5, 2012).

Pinnock, C. "The Moral Argument for Christian Theism" *Bibliotheca Sacra,* Volume 131:522 (Spring 1974): 114-119.

Plantinga, A. "Necessary Being." In *The Analytic Theist: An Alvin Plantinga Reader.* Grand Rapids: Eerdmans, 1998.

Purcell, E. M. "The Efficiency of Propulsion by the Rotating Flagellum." http://w3.impa.br/~jair/pnas.pdf (accessed August 25, 2012).

Quotes Archive, http://www.quotesarchive.com/authors/w/frank-wedekind/quotes, Quotes Archive (accessed August 6, 2012)

Rhodes, R. *Find it Quick: Handbook on Cults and New Religions.* Eugene, OR: Harvest House, 2005.

Richards, J. W. "The Contemporary Argument for Design: An Overview." In *Passionate Conviction,* edited by Paul

Copan and William Lane Craig, 69-78. Nashville, TN: B&H Publishing, 2007.

Roberts, B. H. *Studies in the Book of Mormon.* Urbana, IL: University of Illinois Press, 1985.

Robertson, A. T. *Word Pictures in the New Testament.* Oak Harbor: Logos Research Systems, 1997.

Roth, A. *Origins.* Hagerstown, MD: Herald, 1998.

Rowe, W. L. *William L. Rowe on Philosophy of Religion: Selected Writings.* UK: Ashgate Publishing, 2007.

Ryrie, C. C. *A Survey of Bible Doctrine.* Chicago: Moody Press, 1995.

Sagan, Carl. *Cosmos.* New York: Random House, 1980.

Scanlin, H. P. *The Dead Sea Scrolls and Modern Translations of the Old Testament.* Wheaton: Tyndale House Publishers, 1993.

Smith, D. "Dispelling Muslim Myths About the Bible" *Christian Apologetics Journal* Volume 3:1 (Spring 2004): 39-61.

Smith, R. S. "Reflections on McLaren and the Emerging Church." In *Passionate Conviction: Contemporary Discourses on Christian Apologetics,* edited by Paul Copan and William Lane Craig, 227-41. Nashville, TN: B&H Publishers, 2007.

Spitzer, Robert J. *New Proofs for the Existence of God: Contributions of Contemporary Physics and Philosophy.* Grand Rapids: Eerdmans, 2010.

Sproul, R. C. *Defending Your Faith: An Introduction to Apologetics.* Wheaton, IL: Crossway, 2003.

Stein, R. H. "Criteria for Gospels' Authenticity." In *Contending With Christianity's Critics: Answering New Atheists and*

Other Objectors, edited by Paul Copan and William Lane Craig, 88-103. Nashville, TN: B&H, 2009.

Story, Dan. *Defending Your Faith*. Grand Rapids, MI: Kregel Publications, 1997.

Strauss, D. F. *A New Life of Jesus*, 2 vols. London: Williams & Norgate, 1879.

Strobel, L. *The Case for a Creator*. Grand Rapids: Zondervan, 2004.

———. *The Case for Faith*. Grand Rapids: Zondervan, 2004.

Theopedia: An Encyclopedia of Christianity, "The God of the Gaps."   http://www.theopedia.com/God_of_the_Gaps (accessed August 5, 2012).

Tiessen, T. *Providence and Prayer: How Does God Work in the World?* Downers Grove, IL: InterVarsity Press, 2000.

Van der Breggen, H. "Awakening from the Nightmare: A Critical Overview of Friedrich Nietzsche's Philosophy." *Christian Research Journal*, Volume 34:1 (January 2010), 34-41.

VanGemeren, W. "Introduction to Psalms." In *The Expositor's Bible Commentary, Volume 5: Psalms, Proverbs, Ecclesiastes, Song of Songs,* edited by Frank E. Gaebelein, Willem VanGemeren, Allen P. Ross, et al., 3-51. Grand Rapids: Zondervan, 1991.

Van Til, C. *A Survey of Christian Epistemology*. Philadelphia: P & R Publishing, 1969.

———. *The Defense of the Faith*. Philadelphia: P & R Publishing, 4th edition 2008.

Wallace, Daniel, "Earliest Manuscript of the New Testament Discovered?" The Center for the Study of New Testament Manuscripts.

http://csntm.org/News/Archive/2012/2/10/EarliestManuscri
ptoftheNewTestamentDiscovered (accessed July 1, 2012).

——. "Note on Revelation 22:19" in *The NET Bible.* Biblical
Studies Press, 2006.

——. "Why So Many Versions," http://bible.org/seriespage/part-
iv-why-so-many-versions (accessed June 2012).

Wells, D. F. *No Place for Truth.* Grand Rapids: Eerdmans, 1993.

Wikipedia,   "Tacitus   on   Christ,"   Wikipedia.
http://en.wikipedia.org/wiki/Tacitus_on_Christ   (accessed
on August 5, 2012).

Wikipedia, "Lucian on Christ," Wikipedia.
http://en.wikipedia.org/wiki/Lucian_on_Jesus (accessed on
August 5, 2012).

Wikipedia, "Flagellum," Wikipedia.
http://en.wikipedia.org/wiki/Bacterial_flagellum#cite_note-0
(accessed June 15, 2012).

Zacharias, R. *The End of Reason: A Response to the New Atheists.*
Grand Rapids, MI: Zondervan, 2008.